FROM

ABUSE

TO

GOD'S BLESSINGS

a memoir

of his grace

and glory

JIM KISSOCK

Produced by Inksnatcher.com.

Printed in the United States of America.

LCCN record available at https://lccn.loc.gov/Library of Congress Cataloging-in-Publication Data

Names: Kissock, James, author

Title: From Abuse to God's Blessings: A Memoir of His Grace and Glory / Jim Kissock

Subjects: | BISAC: BIOGRAPHY & AUTOBIOGRAPHY/Religious. RELIGION/Christian Living/Personal Memoirs. RELIGION/Christian Living/Family & Relationships.

Description: First edition. | Joshua 24:15 Publishing, Holts Summit, MO, 2025. | Summary: "A faith-filled memoir of survival, healing, and redemption, tracing Jim Kissock's journey from a violent childhood to a life transformed by God's grace." —Provided by publisher.

Identifiers: LCCN 2025912028 | 979-8-9990692-1-4 (paperback) | 979-8-9990692-0-7 (hardback) | 979-8-9990692-2-1 (e-book) | 979-8-9990692-3-8 (audiobook)

Unless otherwise stated, all Scripture quotations are from the King James Version of the Bible, public domain.

For information about special discounts for bulk purchases, please contact the author at jimkissockauthor@gmail.com.

A special thanks to my wife, Dee, and to all of our children, grandchildren, and future generations.
Thanks as well as other friends and family who have helped with this memoir and, of course, to God, who made my story.

Contents

Acknowledgments

Before sharing my story, I would like to thank my lovely wife, Dee. She has played a vital role in my writing of this story by encouraging and joining with me in the learning process of our lives. Special thanks also to my sister, Glenda, for her contributions to this book (and to my life).

My greatest thanks go to God. Whatever is good in my life, I owe to him. I cannot take any personal credit for his guidance in my life. He has been incredible, providential, and inordinately kind.

My first complete manuscript for this book left a significant need for a good developmental editor. Enter Jessica Snell (https://jessicasnell.com/). Jessica sliced, diced and rearranged my manuscript, making significant improvements to this book's flow. Jessica is extremely professional but also very personable and easy to work with. If you need a developmental editor, I strongly recommend Jessica Snell and I thank her for her arduous labors to make this book better.

I was blessed to find Joyce Parker (https://parkerchristianediting.com) for my copyediting. Joyce has an editor's eye for finding those pesky (sometimes little and sometimes not so little) mistakes that can be challenging to eliminate. Thankfully, she was not grading my writing. Joyce was very good to work with and made my manuscript much better from her labors. I strongly recommend Joyce Parker for copyediting, and I thank her for making this book a better read.

A completed manuscript was a major milestone in my journey to self-publishing this book. However, the hurdles in my path to complete this journey were still numerous and formidable. Once again, I was blessed with professional expertise to get this book across the finish line. Inksnatcher.com provided me with the checklist and know-how to complete this writing journey. They were very easy and knowledgeable to work with and provided detailed assistance to complete my goal of having this book finished. For anyone who might need some assistance to go from a manuscript to having a book available for purchase, I wholeheartedly recommend Inksnatcher.

Finally, I want to acknowledge a good friend and coworker, Keith. One Friday near the end of January 2018, Keith and I completed what seemed like a regular workweek. We expected to see each other the next Monday. However, Keith never made it back to work: he unexpectedly passed away in a few short days. My story could have wound up on a mountain heap of good intentions that never materialized. Instead, Keith's untimely and sudden loss motivated me to commence writing this story. His passing was a reminder that life is short. We have no promise of tomorrow, as God's Word declares:

> Whereas ye know not what shall be on the morrow. For what is your life? It is even a vapour, that appeareth for a little time, and then vanisheth away. (James 4:14)

Note, all scripture references in this book are from the King James Version of the Bible.

Introduction

God and His Glory
God's glory I'll try to bare – In this my story I share
There is some good you will see – And some bad and some ugly
For my school of life has been – So blessed with God's instruction
Whether you agree or not – I hope this is food for thought
Not of me or my story – But of God and his Glory

As a child, I was traumatized by the cruel foe of domestic abuse. As an adult, I'm experiencing the proverbial "living the dream" life.

How does a person build such a good life on such a terrible foundation? The answer is: this human being could have never done such on his own, but God's blessings are more than sufficient.

My name is James (Jim, Jimmy) Kissock, and this is my story. Over the course of seventy-plus years, *God* has been constructing my life and has delivered me from domestic abuse as a child to divine blessings as an adult.

In this book, I will endeavor to encapsulate some of my more pertinent recollections. Hopefully, some of the lessons I've learned will be useful to you, the reader. Even though this book isn't the sort of thriller Tom Clancy would write, I hope you will still be entertained by my life escapades, such as the time that I was a key player in a potentially catastrophic military mishap which could have precipitated WWIII!

As a child, I grew up in a dysfunctional home. I was a child of divorce before divorce became cool. And by *cool*, I am not implying *good*, but rather *common*. Alcohol was another constant antagonist in my childhood. As a child, my life was threatened many times by the uncomely behavior of a drunken man.

By God's grace, I survived those life-threatening events in my childhood. Thus, one of my goals in writing this book is to share about God's provision in my life—and his protection. I grew up in rural southern Missouri. I claim no great fame or fortune. I can claim God has been good to a kid born into a dysfunctional family and has blessed me beyond my wildest dreams.

Growing up, I was basically fatherless. Nevertheless, God promises to be a Father to the fatherless, and such has been the reality in my life. Despite being raised in a house where I was forbidden to sing or play a musical instrument, God granted a love of music to me, and now I'm a musician and a songwriter, albeit an amateur. One of the songs I've written is from the perspective of an unborn child, simply petitioning his or her mama to "let me grow." That chorus could have applied to me, an already-born child just hoping to survive numerous madman drunken rages:

Let me grow
Only God knows
How my life will unfold

Indeed, only God knew how my life would unfold. God deserves all the glory for any good in my life. I take personal blame for my shortcomings, which are multitudinous enough that I could not record them all. Hopefully, I will not cast myself as anything great. Rather, I credit God for any success in my life, as all the good in my life has come from his grace.

My life story is the sum of my good times and my bad times. The bad times seem to have been the most important learning times. In the 1950s, rural southern Missouri was transitioning to a modern, electrified world. I consider myself fortunate to have tasted life in a more primitive time, having had experiences such as using an outhouse. Many of the old-timers I grew up with lived most of their life before electricity, phones, TV, tractors, etc. I will share a few memories from some of those old-timers who made a significant impact in my life.

Today, I can look back on a long career of being a computer professional. But I got my start out on the farm, milking cows by hand. Computers and electronics have enabled me to be somewhat prosperous, but my heart will always favor the more natural aspects of country living.

I want to share some valuable life lessons I have learned, which I hope will be a blessing in your life. I make no claim of being a wise old sage, but I can share what has worked in my life and some things I've tried which have not worked. While I have learned much from instruction, and I'm sure you have too, I think we both know that sometimes we can learn even more from our own mistakes—and from hearing about the mistakes of others.

I have also made some unconventional decisions in life. My upbringing made me more open than many for some deviation from some social norms. My approach to family size is an unusual one these days, and so is my position on alcohol. Even if you don't agree with me, I think you'll be intrigued by my life experiences regarding these and other sometimes-contentious issues. You, the reader, will have to conclude how effective I am in presenting my case.

I will conclude this introduction with a song God gave me about God being a Father to the fatherless.

A father of the fatherless ... is God in his holy habitation. (Psalms 68:5)

Father of the Fatherless

Verse 1:

It's like he had no daddy at all – Because his daddy was livin' for the bottle
He never knew from day to day – You see that bottle makes a man crazy
Such a young life so many heartaches – That bottle never gives it only takes
Now it's taken his daddy away – Tomorrow's still an uncertain day
What's a little boy to do – Who can he turn to

Chorus:

Just in case you've never heard – God left this promise in his Word
I am a Father of the fatherless – Child to me you are so precious
You are no stranger to me – For in the womb I fashioned thee
From every hair to every toe – Everything about you I know
In you my handiwork is found – My love for you has no bound
Call upon me as the years go by – I will always hear your cry
Just let me be – A Father to thee

Verse 2:

She can still remember the day – Her daddy would leave to go far away
She was so young and very small – In uniform to her he looked so tall
He gave her lots of hugs and kisses – and said I'll miss you, my little princess
But for our freedom and liberty – He laid his life down for his country
What's a little girl to do – Who can she turn to

(Chorus Repeats)

Part I

The Springtime of My Life

Spring is the season of new life. I was born in the spring. There is not much better than a mild, sunny springtime day, with birds chirping and flowers blooming. Typically, at least a few storms accompany the otherwise beautiful spring weather.

Unfortunately, the spring season of my life was brief and mostly dominated by turbulent weather. Now, for the storm report.

1

Un-Precious Memories

A photographer will sometimes leave the background of a picture blurry in order to bring the subject into sharp focus. Such is the case with my earliest childhood memories. Unfortunately, the subjects in sharp focus are all in less-than-desirable situations. I am sure amidst the blurry background in my early childhood, there were many good times. However, I can't remember any good times before my mom and dad separated and then divorced when I was about four years of age.

My earliest memory occurred on the main street in Houston, Missouri. I was with my dad, and he stopped at what I am guessing was the only tavern in town. Apparently, his parental standards were too high to take a young child into a bar—so he left me alone in the car, for what seemed like forever. The weather was cool and a light rain fell. I stood in the front seat on the passenger side of the car with my face pressed against the somewhat steamy door window while watching shoppers pass by.

Life has been a learning process, and that was the day I began learning one of many valuable life lessons to come my way.

Finally, my dad came out of the bar and staggered to my side of the car. I was excited that my long wait was over. I continued to lean on the door window, because I didn't yet know enough to predict the kinds of bad decisions a drunk man might make. I kept leaning on the window, and my dad suddenly yanked the door wide open. Of course, I went tumbling out headfirst to test the durability of my head versus the concrete sidewalk. The concrete won as I busted my head, leaving me bleeding and crying in the light rain. I do not remember what happened after that, and I guess the injury must not have been too severe, as I am still here to record the event.

Of course, I might have become a rocket scientist without that head injury.

Later, my mom told me I would not sit close to a car door for a long time after that fall. I had begun the learning process.

My mom, Oneta, was on her second marriage, which was to my dad, James Kissock, who went by the nickname of Junior. Mom had one daughter, Glenda, from her first marriage. That marriage only lasted about a year because of Glenda's dad's drinking problems and issues with marital fidelity. I will not go into detail about that story, but alcohol did no favor for my mom's first marriage. All of my sisters are genetically half sisters to me, but we have always thought of each other as full siblings. So, I will not use the term half sister going forward. After Mom's first divorce, Glenda stayed primarily with Mom's parents, Luther and Tennie, in southern Missouri, near Tyrone.

During Mom's pregnancy with me, my parents were living in Bolivar, Missouri, where they were both attending college. I hope my dad was excited about having a child, but unfortunately, he was absent during my delivery. He was on a drinking binge, and he didn't show up until several days after my arrival. If I could have reasoned as a newborn, I would have known the late arrival of my dad on the scene of my grand entrance was not a good sign.

Dysfunctional families can encounter some rather bizarre twists, and one of ours is that Glenda had the same experience when she was born: her dad was also not present because of alcohol—and also because of infidelity. When Glenda's dad finally showed up to meet his new daughter, he brought with him supposed friends, a husband-and-wife couple. It turns out Glenda's dad was having an affair with the wife, unbeknownst to the husband and our mom.

However, strangely enough, Glenda's dad came to the hospital to see Mom and me after my delivery, and he was even sober. So Glenda's dad missed her delivery because of drunkenness but saw me before my dad saw me because of drunkenness. I have joked that as a child I lived my life in 3D: Drinking, Dueling, and Divorcing.

Life in 3D can be complicated.

My second-earliest childhood memory took place at the house of my dad's parents, my grandma and grandpa Kissock, between Licking and Salem, Missouri. My mom and dad were living there, and my dad was in a drunken rage. The old farmhouse had a tiny bathroom added along a wall in the kitchen/dining area. The location was not ideal, but indoor potties were a fairly new invention at the time in southern Missouri. I do not know exactly how old I was, and this is my only memory of living there. As my dad became violent, I made my way into the tiny bathroom and even locked the door with a latch on the inside. Once my dad determined I had locked myself in the bathroom, he beat on the door, threatening and cussing at me to unlock it. Finally, he calmed down some and tried reasoning with me. He assured me that if I would unlock the door, he would not spank me for locking it. So, I unlocked the door.

Unfortunately, during the ordeal, I peed in my pants. The good news was I did not get a licking for locking the door, as promised. But my dad worked me over in a drunken rage for wetting my pants.

Mom tried to stop him from beating me, which resulted in her being beaten up as well. I was just a young child, and I doubt I had great powers of reason that early. However, I was beginning to discern patterns; I could see that alcohol was distinctly linked to terrible and painful events in my life.

My third and the last memory of my dad when I was a young child occurred at the house of my mom's parents. The divorce was final, and Mom had left me with her mom, my grandma Tennie. My dad showed up while I was playing in the front yard. Grandma came out and told my dad that he was drunk, and she would not let him take me. We were standing on a concrete sidewalk going to the front steps of the house. Grandma held one of my arms, my dad held the other, and both were pulling in opposite directions.

Then we all looked up and saw a car coming our way, about a half a mile out on the gravel road. It was my grandpa Luther, coming home from work. Grandma let go of me. She told my dad to take me and leave quickly, as Luther would likely kill him. So, one of my many rides with a drunken driver ensued. I do not remember what happened after that, other than flying down the old, dusty gravel roads.

Grandpa was normally good-natured. However, he could have a bad temper when riled and was prone to violence when he felt justified—and protecting family was a valid justification. My sister Glenda shared her recollection of another time my dad was drunk and took me away:

The reason Grandpa would have likely killed Junior was because he had let him take Jimmy once but later regretted doing so. Prior to the above event, Jimmy's dad and Grandpa had an altercation on the embankment to the road in front of the house. As a young child, Jimmy was hanging on for dear life with his arms around Grandpa's neck, begging and pleading to stay with Grandpa, while Junior was pulling Jimmy's ankles. Grandpa let go as he said, "Junior would have physically harmed Jimmy with the force Junior was pulling." When Jimmy and his drunken dad drove off, Grandpa said, "I should have killed him." Grandpa sat on the front porch and cried with Grandma and me. This is the only time I can remember ever seeing Grandpa crying.

Grandpa's threat was not idle chatter. It turned out he had a green light to end the problems my dad was causing: the county sheriff told my grandpa that if he ever needed to take care of my dad, to just make sure it looked like an accident or self-defense.

So begins the memory lane of my life. For many years, I tried to forget my childhood experiences, but eventually, by God's grace, I learned I had to forgive those in my life who had failed in their roles. I am no shrink. However, I have concluded that one should acknowledge traumatic experiences and be able to look back and accept whatever happened without angst or animosity. According to Scripture, peace is the conclusion of that process. Jesus Christ is the Prince of Peace, and it is Christ who brings peace through healing.

One Christmas day, after I was already grown and married, I received a diary book which had some general questions in the front of it. One prompt was to write about your first memory. At that point in time, I closed the book and never opened it again, as that was an area I did not want to visit. Just the thought made anxiety swell within me. After a few years of marriage, I told some of my childhood stories to my wife. I found dealing with problems of the past is better than trying to pretend they never existed. Thus, the healing process began in which God has mercifully granted me peace.

Below are lyrics to the chorus of a song that God gave me about emotional or spiritual wounds acquired in our earthly journey. Usually, the greater the wound, the greater the associated pain. Once a wound is healed, the pain should go away, but likely a scar will remain. The chorus below attempts to convey the message that God can heal any wound and he deserves the glory for the healing.

> *Behind every scar there's a story – Behind every healing lies God's glory*
> *Healed wounds once so tender – Help God's children remember*
> *You thought you weren't gonna make it thru – But God had more plans for you*
> *And it just might be – Another hurting soul needs to see*
> *Your scar and hear your story – Of your healing and of God's glory*

One of my goals in writing this story is to show some of the wounds in my life which God has so graciously healed. Of course, some wounds are so small they heal and leave no scar at all. We soon forget those wounds. Many have major wounds which have never healed, and I encourage those to seek the Great Physician who has the healing balm of Gilead. Of course, major wounds, even if healed, will likely leave scars and will never be completely forgotten.

Perhaps God allows scarring so others can see healed wounds and know life can go on without the hurt of an open sore. Such has been the case in my life. Overall, I had an awful childhood. However, God has blessed me with a wonderful wife, children, and grandchildren. My childhood wounds no longer have the pain of an open sore. My wounds are scars now and have mostly healed, although I carried my childhood wounds for many years into adulthood before the healing process ever began.

If you have painful wounds from life, my prayer is that you will experience healing from God and even be willing to let others receive help from your healed wounds—and I hope you will commence the healing process sooner than I did. Indeed, I hope my story will help you avoid some of the wounds of life that I have experienced. I will share how God has led my wife and me to raise a family. God has been merciful to give direction to the learning process of parenting, which I believe has been rewarding in our life. Of course, how God has directed us may not be his will for your life, but I hope you will consider the principles God has given us.

A Little Calm Before the Storm

After my mom and dad divorced, I had a brief break before the worst storms in my life would settle in. However, this time was still somewhat eventful. My dad had a rich aunt who passed away and left him with some wealth. He did not let my mom know, as he did not want her to get anything in the divorce settlement, which was what ended up happening. My mom got custody of me, but my dad had some legal rights to take me, about which I have already mentioned.

For a couple of years after the divorce, my dad would try to find me to take me with him. I doubt he had much interest in me, but his goal was to irritate my mom. Of course, he was always drunk, so I lived a life of hiding. I was to stay out of sight from the roads and driveways. If he could not find me, he could not take me. Whoever talked with my dad would tell him they did not know where I was. (Since I was hiding, they did not know exactly where I was.)

Mom was a schoolteacher during the school year, and she worked at Lily Tulip (a cup manufacturer) during the summer in Springfield, Missouri. She had to work to support us, as she received no child support. The goal was to keep me from my dad, as my safety was at considerable risk if he found me because of his inebriated condition. I bounced around to many places. I always had to be careful to make sure my dad was not around. If he showed up, I was to hide. When he showed up, I hid in cornfields, in attics, in closets, under beds, in sheds, behind trees, and in tall grass fields—and I stayed there until I could hear him tearing out in his car.

Once, I was at Grandma Tennie's, and my mom's youngest brother, Thurman, was there as well. A neighbor stopped and told us my dad was in town at the tavern and was coming to get me. So, Thurman took me to the county sheriff's office to inform them of the situation and asked if they could detain him for a while. Thurman parked his old Chevy coupe on a downhill slope in front of the police station. When my uncle and I came out of the courthouse to leave, his car would not start. We went back to the jail to get help to push the car up enough that he could coast down the hill and hopefully start the car. The sheriff had to let the jailbirds out to give us a push, which I thought was really cool. We took off down the hill, my uncle popped the clutch, and off we went.

Sometimes I stayed with my mom's youngest sister, Laveta, in Springfield, Missouri, and that was great, as her son Bruce was just younger than me. We always enjoyed playing together. Other times I stayed with Mom's older brother Herman near Cabool, Missouri, which was great, as I had Cousin Margaret Ann there to play with as well.

When I was with Grandma Tennie, my older sister Glenda was there to play with. Glenda and I spent many hours playing and often fishing in a small pond close to the house. We caught nothing as the pond had no fish in it, but we enjoyed the experience. Glenda was rather imaginative and liked to do stunts, such as riding a bike with me standing on her shoulders or on the handlebars. I was a featherweight, which made our circus-like stunts easier to perform. Grandpa Luther had several horses, but one old horse, Selam, was perfect for Glenda and me to play on. Selam moved very little, but never seemed to mind the two of us climbing all over him. I also played checkers, Chinese checkers, and dominoes with Grandma and Grandpa.

Those were good times in my childhood. However, it was all colored by the stress and fear involved in trying to avoid a drunken dad. Today, we live in an era of changing family norms. I can tell you that as a young boy, I would have loved nothing better than a secure home with a loving mom and dad.

However, at this point in my dad's life, he was drunk almost full time. Other than the memories I've already shared, I do not remember my dad any until I was about seven years old. My grandmother Kissock came and got me, as my dad had suffered a massive stroke. The doctors did not expect him to live, even though he was in his thirties. However, he lived to be sixty-four years old. He would never walk again, as his left side was totally paralyzed. His mind was damaged from the stroke, and his speech was very difficult to understand.

The stroke stopped him from drinking, as he could not get booze. It also left him unable to be any kind of father or even able to carry on a reasonable conversation.

I never knew my dad while he was sober or of a sound mind. At first, he was always drunk. Later, he was always impaired.

Never having had the chance to know a parent personally is a great loss.

I heard an evangelist give his testimony, saying that he grew up in foster care and stayed in something like fifteen different homes. He mentioned that the worst part was he never knew when he would move on. So, he kept his bags packed.

While I was not in official foster care, I could identify with that evangelist, and God allowed me to write the following song:

Throw Them Travelin' Bags Away

Verse 1:
His bags are packed again – He knows soon he'll be gone
He just never knows when – He will be movin' on
Just a child without a home – No one to call his own
But by God's grace there'll come a day – He'll hear his heavenly Father
say

Chorus:
Child, you can throw them travelin' bags away – You've a home now
where you can stay
Brothers and sisters aplenty – A great big family
Safe secure – With the Savior
And a Father who will always be – There for eternity

Verse 2:
This boy is now a man – With his wife and children
Journeying thru this land – On their way to heaven
Though in Christ he's found sweet peace – Those childhood memories
Leave this man longing for the day – He'll hear his heavenly Father
say

(Chorus Repeats)

In a One-Room Country School

I wound up at my mom's parent's house when the time arrived to begin the first grade. Note, this was before kindergarten existed in our area. This was the best year of my childhood, as I stayed in one place and had basic safety at my grandparents' home. My dad had somewhat given up on finding me.

However, unbeknownst to me, the weather patterns were going to be quite unfavorable after this one-school-year-long break.

I began my public education in a one-room country school. The one-room country school is an antique. However, I believe public education would be better if schools had stayed more decentralized, thus allowing more parental or local control. They appropriated the divide-and-conquer principle in the one-room country school. It is much easier to control a handful of kids than hundreds or thousands. The one-room country school was indeed a community affair. Just neighbors and those from our community were in attendance.

The school only had one building, and, as I've indicated, it was just one open room. I later attended other one-room country schools which had about twenty to forty students. In the one-room country school, one teacher taught all grades. In my seventh-grade year, I would attend a town school where I made good grades, and I would eventually graduate from college with honors. Thus, I have no qualms about the limited resources of a one-room country school being able to provide a quality education. Quite the contrary: The one-room country school provided an excellent educational springboard into life for me.

I will share just a few of my experiences at a one-room country school.

Grandma never had a lot of extra money, and she had to earn what little she had. However, she provided me with a Roy Rogers metal lunch box with a picture of his horse, Trigger, on the lid. Grandma packed me a large lunch, even though I was a toothpick who ate little. A parent could bring their child to school, but usually everybody walked. Glenda and I walked just over a mile to school.

On my first day of school, when lunchtime came, I would eat outside. The only other boy in my class came out with me, but he had little or nothing with him to eat. When I opened my lunch box full of food, he reached in and helped himself. At six years of age, I decided his actions were inappropriate, so I picked my lunch box up by the handle and smacked him over the head with it. He left crying straight to the teacher. First day of school and I am in trouble. The teacher was a great teacher, and she let me know I could not hit other students with my lunch box, or I would be in big trouble. In fact, she asked if I wanted all of my lunch, and, of course, I did not. She explained to me the other student did not bring a large lunch and it would be nice of me to share some of mine. So, I and the former victim of my attack became best buddies—which worked out well for me, as Grandma thought I was eating all my lunch! Additionally, I learned a valuable lesson about helping others in need.

God eventually blessed my wife and me with several children, and he led us into homeschooling, which has many similarities to the one-room country school. In homeschooling, there is usually one primary teacher (one parent—usually the mom) and students of varying ages. Homeschoolers learn to work somewhat independently, as one teacher cannot spend all their time with each student. Such was the case in the one-room country school, as the teacher was there to help and instruct, but students had to learn to work on their own. Public schools today offer a peer setting for the student. Such a setting affords little interaction with students in different grades. Not so in homeschooling or in the one-room country school; there, everybody worked together and played together. I believe not being overly peer oriented is a good thing, as it mimics real life.

In the one-room country school, older students would sometimes help younger students, thus developing skills in instruction. I believe I learned a lot in my early grades as I watched older students do spelling, math, etc. on the chalkboard in front of the school. Seeing and hearing the lessons from grades ahead helped to better prepare me for my later grades.

The one-room country school was also a place where God was welcome as we read the Bible and prayed. Sometimes during roll call, each student was asked to quote a Scripture verse when their name was called. I cannot tell you how many times the verse quoted ended up being the shortest one in the Bible: "Jesus wept"! Every day began with the Pledge of Allegiance. We had a metal flagpole which displayed Old Glory. The pole also provided a challenge for the guys to shimmy up and then slide back down.

Every one-room country school had at least one large spanking paddle. After my first grade, I would attend one-room country schools in which my mom was the teacher. Several times, I witnessed her having a large teenage guy bend over her desk as she administered the board of education to the seat of understanding. Any student receiving discipline at school would likely get the same at home. Parents supported the teacher in disciplinary actions. The teacher quickly nipped disciplinary problems in the bud, so to speak.

Recess was, of course, my favorite. We played dodge ball, Red Rover, tag, hide-and-seek, marbles, jacks, pick-up sticks, etc. We had a swing set and slide. A basketball hoop was available but was difficult to use on dirt and gravel. Snow was wonderful as we had snowball fights and built forts if there was enough snow. However, the main sporting event was softball. We had many softball games. Once a year, all the one-room country schools in the Houston area would compete in various sports for ribbons. The big one was the softball tournament. I played on at least one team which won the tournament.

One point I want to make clear is that in most of the events, everybody played some, except for the tournament games. In softball, the younger students would play some near the end of the game or maybe after the game. We threw easy pitches to the early grade students and often a bad throw to first, so they even got a hit. It was more important to make sure everyone felt some success than it was to only win. Obviously, a first grader cannot compete with an eighteen-year-old, but we all learned to get along like family.

Another important event at the one-room school was the annual Christmas play. There were several scripted plays we used. Everyone in the school would perform in costume. Note, this was a big event as there were no other theatrical performances in our small community. Everyone in the school was neighbors or relatives.

Not all was puritanical in the one-room country school. We had paper wads. Small snakes were plentiful and usually worked to scare the girls. Behind the school grounds were woods, which sloped downhill to a small creek. Grapevines were plentiful and the guys would try to swing on them in Tarzan fashion. The older guys would frequently light up a piece of grapevine to smoke. (The principal attraction was that they were free for the taking and the dried vines are hollow, thus allowing smoke inhalation kind of like a cigarette.)

Poison ivy was abundant in the nearby woods. Once we had a young guy from the city who had moved to our area and attended our country school. He did not know the ill effects of poison ivy. We encouraged him to wipe some on his arms. He did so and turned out to be allergic to such. I was one perpetrator in the prank. As a child, I was not allergic to poison ivy, but later in adulthood, I lost my immunity. Perhaps divine retribution?

As with many aspects of my life, God gave me a song about my one-room country school experiences:

That One-Room Country School

Verse 1:
Now I look back with joy – When as a six-year-old boy
I commenced my education – In a one-room institution
Just for our community – Seemed a lot like family
We did our three Rs you see – Didn't take a lot of money
We all got along together – Learned to help one another

Chorus:
In that one-room country school – The teacher had the rule
You could still get the paddle – You could even read the Bible
In the pledge we could say – Under God and even pray
We didn't need the NEA – Parents had their say
Now I know it's different today – I still like that old country school way

Verse 2:
To school we'd come walkin' – That old stove was a smokin'
Our water came from a well – The restrooms now I'll not tell
The times I liked best – Was when we had recess
Red Rover, Red Rover – I'm a comin' right over
The big kids to the small – Would join right in softball

(Chorus Repeats)

Verse 3:
We had to leave mighty early – It made a long day's journey
They'd shut our school down – Said they'd bus us to town
It was all a lot bigger – But I still kinda figure
That I got a lot more – And I am the better for
That school in the country – Where we were more like family

(Chorus Repeats)

Yes, there were some sunny days in the springtime of my life—days of learning and play and friendship and fun. With my parents' divorce and my dad's absence, I had a life that was largely free from violence and fear for my first year of school. We were out of the frying pan.

What I didn't know yet was that the old saying was true: out of the frying pan, into the fire.

My mother's second marriage was over. But the violence of her third marriage was about to begin.

2

---∞---

The Third Try Is Not the Charm

The storm clouds of life were definitely gathering, with something as simple as where my mom purchased gas in Springfield, Missouri. The attendant who pumped the gas, Leonard Holloway, would soon be my mom's third husband.

Mom's parents, her siblings, and others begged her not to marry Leonard, but she did it anyway.

My mom is a good woman. I never saw her touch a drop of liquor and she has always tried to help those in need. She has a gentle and loving spirit about her, but she seriously lacked wisdom in choosing what is supposed to be a life mate. Whether or not she knew it, she had just married her third drunk.

I am no rocket scientist (although I did major in aerospace engineering for one year in college). However, when you have just had two marriages go south primarily due to booze, I would think you might not pick a third man who was addicted to the same toxin. Of course, Leonard was on his best behavior during their brief courtship. Others saw Leonard's true colors, but Mom did not. Leonard, a grown man, did not own a car or possessions beyond the clothes on his back. His occupation at the time was pumping gas, which was one step above unemployment. He was an ex-marine, which perhaps should have caused some alarm to anyone familiar with the possible behavioral patterns of a jarhead. What could possibly go wrong?

As I said earlier, I am no shrink, but I am guessing Leonard's physical presence ensured my dad would no longer be an issue (this was before my dad had his stroke). Leonard was very strong and was a trained killer, thanks to the Marine Corps. Leonard had been a machine gunner during WWII in the Pacific. He had a good sense of humor and was quite self-confident. However, no one in the family but Mom saw him as marrying material because of his lack of character. He appeared to have lived a rough life, and he had.

During this era, divorce was not common, and I suppose Mom may have thought she would not find a better spouse. She already had more than one divorce, and she had two children. Unfortunately, she was on a downhill slide with the liquor problem. Her first husband was not violent when drunk. Her second husband was violent, but not to the extreme of her third ex-marine husband.

When Mom married Leonard, I was six years old.

Leonard had a rough childhood himself growing up in West Plains, Missouri. He didn't have much of a father figure in his childhood, and he began working when about eight years old, doing whatever he could to help provide for his family. Eventually, he found work carrying five-gallon buckets of concrete for construction. Such strenuous labor likely helped to develop his extraordinary strength—though most of his brothers were exceptionally strong as well, so his strength may have just been genetic. Leonard started smoking when he was so young he could not remember a time when he was not smoking. He grew up rough, which well-suited him for the Marines. He boxed in the Marines and won several medals. Besides his strength, he was ambidextrous, with catlike reflexes. He could kickbox as well. Leonard survived WWII and received an honorable discharge. He had trouble finding work, so he reenlisted in the Marines and was a Drill Instructor for several years.

My life has been a learning process. To any six-year-old boy, I can say with certainty that you do not want your mom to make a former Marine Drill Instructor your stepdad. Actually, I can testify that I learned invaluable lessons in discipline from Leonard, but I cannot say there was much fun in the process. His favorite quote to me was that when he told me to jump, my job was to jump. When he told me to come down, then I could come down. I would eventually enlist in the United States Air Force. I did not consider the Marine Corps, as I had all the Marine experiences I wanted as a child.

Mom and Leonard married while I was in the first grade. I got to finish the school year out by staying with Glenda, Grandma, and Grandpa. However, as soon as the school year ended, I began active duty with Leonard.

I am inserting a disclaimer here that my goal in writing this story is not to impugn the character of anyone. I'll share more about the favorable traits of both Leonard and of my dad. However, their actions are what they were to a young child.

I am also guessing some stories I will share could generate some skepticism about their credibility. All I can say is my mom is alive at the time of this writing about my childhood. She is also of a sound mind and witnessed most of the childhood events that I have recorded. In fact, Mom said she would like to sign her name to a copy of this story with the statement that everything written about my childhood is the truth. Glenda is also alive and has witnessed many of these stories. Mom and Glenda have both read these childhood stories and agree to their accuracy. In fact, Glenda's first comment after reading my childhood story was that I was way too nice and did not convey how bad the circumstances were. Other members of the family have also witnessed many of these stories that I will share.

Memories, especially childhood memories, can be faulty, but I have taken great effort to share the memory lane of my life accurately. I have established most of my childhood stories by at least two or more witnesses.

Now, let's go back to my mother's husbands and the addiction that held them all captive. My dad was a B-17 flight engineer/aerial gunner in WWII. He survived the war but came home with a drinking problem and PTSD issues. Many times, while my mom was still with my dad, he would take his service pistol and shoot at airplanes flying overhead. He was also drunk while doing this. Fortunately, he hit no airplanes that we know of.

However, he did once hit some livestock. Somehow, while drunk, my dad mistakenly shot the bull his dad owned for their beef cattle. He was quite upset that he had killed the bull, because it meant he would have to buy another one. To add salt to the wound, this was during the summer. Butchering was usually done in the winter—in cold weather. My dad would have to buy a freezer to put the bull in to keep from losing all the meat from his accidental shooting.

Alcohol often costs more than the initial purchase.

WWII likely had similar effects on Leonard as it did on my dad. Both of them at times showed some redeeming qualities. However, life circumstances such as WWII and booze magnified their sin nature to manifest a very vile behavior. I direct most of my animosity towards the alcohol that fueled their actions, rather than holding them totally accountable for their vile behavior.

Glenda's dad also served in WWII and came home with a drinking problem but was a very personable guy when sober. He did not have the violent behavior of my dad or Leonard. Although he was no stranger to barroom brawling, as he was both good sized and strong, he was not violent with my mom or Glenda. He lived a long life, and he struggled with the liquor bottle for most of it.

In any race, it is best to run the entire race well. However, I believe that, in the race of life, if you cannot run the entire race well, it is best to at least finish the race well. My dad finished the race somewhat better than he started it, in that he stopped drinking, even though that was likely because of his disabling stroke. Surprisingly, Leonard finished the race well too—but I will make you keep reading to find out how.

My dad and Glenda's dad had always vowed they would kill the other one if they ever met. I am not sure why, as both had married the same woman, and neither seemed to care any for her. While Aunt Laveta lived in Springfield, Mom got word that my dad and Glenda's dad were both stopping by Aunt Laveta's house at the same time. Neither knew they were about to meet for the first time. Mom left to avoid the fireworks, leaving Aunt Laveta there to referee the fight.

The first husband meeting the second husband—it should have been a brawl for the ages. Upon their arrival, though, they were both under the influence, and they chose to go drink some more rather than fight.

Alcohol's effects, as always, were unpredictable.

The Honeymoon?

Another of Leonard's character flaws was his inability to hold on to a dollar. To make matters worse, he would run through whatever money he had and there would be nothing to show for it. Of course, a big part of that was because of his smoking and drinking. We lived mostly around Houston, Missouri, and we often wound up moving when the rent was due.

I had a few good times with Leonard, as he liked to fish, and we had an occasional good fishing trip. However, the good times were insignificant compared to the not-so-good times. Mom continued to teach and did not make big money but kept us fed and helped meet minimum needs. To keep Leonard from spending everything, Mom would usually hide some money back for unexpected expenses. Mom and I have commented to each other several times that it was a very good thing Leonard did not have a credit card back then. Leonard was a hard worker, but with his drinking problem, he had trouble finding and keeping a job.

After a few years of bouncing around with various jobs, the milk processing plant in Cabool, Missouri, hired Leonard. Most considered the plant to be one of the best places to work in the area. The plant was not normally tolerant of employees with issues, since there was always a long line of applicants wanting to work there. Standard protocol at the plant was to fire anyone troublesome, but they never fired Leonard, even though he would frequently go on a drinking binge for a few days and just disappear. The company's position was that he could outwork any three men there. He, in fact, worked there until he retired with a pension.

I don't know how Mom and Leonard managed it. However, a giant break in my life occurred when they bought a small farm about a quarter mile from Grandpa Luther's farm. The farmland was poor. The house was old and in disrepair. Perhaps a bad omen was the fact that the prior longtime owner, Jack, had a drinking problem. Jack left thousands of empty liquor bottles in piles around the place, and those bottles are the only good thing I associate with liquor, because they made great targets. I would eventually break most of them either by throwing rocks or by shooting a BB gun or a .22 rifle at them.

Jack was not violent when drunk, but because of his drinking problem, he had trouble providing for his family. Once, Jack's wife, Sylvia, came crying to Grandma Tennie.

Sylvia and Jack had gotten into an argument at their old farmhouse. It was a cold winter day. While drunk, Jack had taken all of his clothes off and thrown them in the wood stove. Keep in mind that they had almost nothing because of booze, and Jack managed to burn up the clothes he was wearing. Alcohol can produce such wonderful results!

The giant benefit for me of the farm purchase was the fact I could see Grandma, Grandpa, and Glenda a lot more than if we had not lived close. Usually, when Leonard was home, I was too. However, when he was at work or on a drinking binge, I could spend time at Grandma and Grandpa's farm.

God has moved miraculously many times in my life, especially in the real estate arena, and that was a prime instance of his grace to me. This farm was the best location for me to find some shelter from the storms of life coming my way. Grandma and Grandpa were my refuge during this turbulent time in my life—and a refuge of sanity would be crucial for me to weather the coming storms.

California Here I Come

Even though Mom and Leonard had managed to buy that farmhouse near my grandparents, money was still a constant issue in our lives. Leonard lived life, as the old saying goes, with champagne taste on a beer budget, and one memorable and uncomfortable trip in my childhood proved that this was a loser as a financial strategy.

Leonard usually had a late-model car, as he could finance them, and he had just acquired a late-model brown Ford Falcon station wagon. He declared he was going to take us all to Disneyland in California. This was quite an event, as we were a redneck hillbilly band and had never traveled much or known any great entertainment venues. Glenda was joining us, although she rarely interacted with Leonard. We loaded up and set off to California via the southern route.

On our first night, we stayed in a cheap motel and encountered a dust storm. We had sand in and on everything. Money was already running low, and we had barely begun our journey. After our first night's rest, we drove nonstop to Phoenix, where one of Leonard's brothers lived. We stayed there for a few days. We did not get to see the Grand Canyon as we passed it during the night. Leonard's brother and family were rather unique (they were no strangers to family dysfunction either) but seemed glad to see us. They provided a place for us to sleep but offered us little to eat—par for the course on this shoestring trip.

We finally moved on towards our final destination of Disneyland. We did not have air conditioning in our car, but crossing the scorching desert in summer was going to be worth it for the reward of Disneyland. Finally, the big day arrived. We parked in a Disney lot and rode the Monorail to the main gate. Unfortunately, the financial funds required to enter the Kingdom were not available. All we got to do was peek in as best we could and then ride the Monorail back to our car. Leonard had fulfilled his promise of taking us to Disneyland. Never mind that we'd been expecting something more than peeking through the gates.

Then we drove across the Mexican border to Tijuana. My mom has a dark complexion and has somewhat of a Hispanic look. The border agents tested Mom thoroughly when we came back into the States to verify her citizenship. Fortunately, she knew her American history and geography or we might have had to leave her in Mexico. (This was before open borders!)

Leonard had a marine buddy in California who we spent some time with. They fed us some at his house and even let us pick a bag full of oranges from a tree in their front yard—which was a blessing, as Leonard was out of money and was uncertain what we were going to do. Fortunately, Mom, as was her habit, had some cash hid back, and it was barely enough for us to get back home. We bought some sliced bread, bologna, and cold hot dogs to eat on the straight drive through back home. Plus, we had the bag of oranges. Mom had colon problems and ate a hot dog, which made her extremely sick by the time we got back to Missouri.

We had stopped at a gas station in Idaho. When Leonard started the car, it backfired and caught the gas in the carburetor on fire. The air cleaner assembly for the carburetor was missing. Unfortunately, we had parked right behind a large gas tanker truck. We jumped out and ran, fearing the car and tanker might blow up. Leonard ran to the gas station and grabbed a fire extinguisher. He somehow got the red-hot hood up and sprayed the engine, which put the fire out. The formerly brown hood had gotten so hot the paint had melted, and the hood was now black and had bubbled up from the heat. Also, the engine was now white from the fire extinguisher chemicals. Somewhat miraculously, Leonard started the car up, and it seemed to run, so we continued on our way. Glenda was quite hesitant to get back in the car, but she finally did.

We came back through the Rockies, and we got to see the mountains, at least during daylight hours.

Thus, another valuable lesson I learned from Leonard was the importance of managing money. Hopefully, Leonard's intention on the trip was honorable, but the lack of financial resources made the big trip considerably less than ideal. Mom told me several years later that she had always wondered if Leonard's goal was for us to stay in California permanently to get away from Mom's family. If so, Mom's hidden green cash foiled his plan. Either way, Leonard could not manage money. I do not remember Leonard taking us on any other trips.

I have not accumulated great wealth in this life, but I have tried to manage what I have and use sound financial discretion. God has always met our needs. My mom's parents gave me a positive example of trying to avoid debt and being financially responsible. I have clearly chosen their example as the one to follow, but I have to admit that Leonard taught me valuable lessons on how not to manage money.

In a Lake of Milk

Working for money is no disgrace. It's honorable to labor to buy the things you (and your family) need for life. Money isn't the only thing people work for, however. Sometimes you find yourself working not to gain anything valuable but simply to try to prevent disaster. That was the position I found myself in more and more often now that we were living with a man whose temper was both explosive and dangerous.

The saying "no need to cry about spilled milk" was likely coined by someone who has never cleaned up as much spilled milk as I have. I'll provide more details shortly. Leonard's rages and drunkenness were becoming commonplace at this point. The brief honeymoon was over. His behavior was erratic, and the consequences were always bad. While I always felt basically helpless during Leonard's profanity-laced temper eruptions, I was fully aware of the realities at hand. There was always a chance one or more of us would not survive. If a flying coffee cup thrown at major-league pitching speed hits you upside the head, you are not likely to survive. For whatever reason, the man loved to throw household items while in a drunken rage. Watching out for flying objects became a serious concern in our home.

After the arrival of my younger sisters, Tennie and Nita, I would usually take them outside during Leonard's rages. I do not believe Leonard would have intentionally hurt them, but with furniture, plates, and almost anything flying, no one was safe. It was ironic: Leonard expected a clean house. He liked everything in perfect order, typical Marine protocol. Yet, when he was in one of his raging fits, he would destroy the house. Mom worked full time, and she liked everything in order, but she was not a super-neat housekeeper by nature. Therefore, I tried to keep everything super neat, hoping to prevent a blowup. However, it wasn't something any of us could actually prevent, and when Leonard finally did blow up, I knew I was in for a lot of work. Mom would usually be emotionally and physically wiped out from the altercation, so afterwards, I would try to put the shambles back together.

Only five rooms were in our old house, which was in the shape of a boot. The toe of the boot was where my bedroom was situated. The heel of the boot was the living room. Mom and Leonard's bedroom was just above the living room. My younger sisters slept in this bedroom as well. The kitchen/dining room, which was fairly good sized, connected to this bedroom. To get from the living room to the kitchen, one had to go through Mom and Leonard's bedroom or go outside and come back in through the kitchen door. A small bathroom was attached to the kitchen, topping off the boot. The entire house had a linoleum floor covering which was worn but functional.

Leonard did not always destroy my bedroom in his rages but would always hit the living room by flipping over most of the furniture except for the TV. He liked to watch TV. He would knock down items hanging on the walls. The piece of furniture which took the worst of the damage was the coffee table. Leonard converted many a coffee table into mostly toothpicks. He would usually replace them as he drank a lot of coffee and, of course, needed a coffee table.

In Leonard and Mom's bedroom, he would take all the hanging clothes from the closet and throw them into the yard. He would pull the drawers out of the dresser and dump them on the floor or throw them into the yard. The chest of drawers would receive the same treatment. He would rake everything off the top of the dresser and the chest of drawers. When he hit my bedroom, he followed the same protocol.

However, he saved his finest rearrangements for the kitchen. The dishes mostly ended up on the floor. The only thing that kept us from not having bowls, plates, cups, etc. was that we had a set of Melmac (hard plastic) dishes that were nearly indestructible as advertised. If we could have recorded a TV commercial showing the durability of Melmac dishes, we might have made a fortune. Leonard would dump our silverware onto the floor, but the grand finale was the refrigerator. We lived in the country where we got milk directly from the farmer in gallon jars. Leonard would rake out the refrigerator's contents onto the floor, causing glass jars to break. Two gallons of milk created what appeared to be a small lake. It was not a milkshake, but a milk lake. All the broken glass, other food from the refrigerator, and whatever else landed on the floor made quite a mess, to say the least.

On the positive side, Leonard would usually tear out in the car after the damage was done. He would usually be gone a few days before returning to the scene of the crime. Mom had some time to emotionally and physically pull herself together, and I had some time to put the house back together as best I could.

Leonard made his money in a place that processed milk. Much like his money, though, the milk in our house did not stay where it should.

Milk and money: both of them were thrown away and wasted in our household. It's ironic that the money that could have bought us more food was turned into alcohol, a liquid that did us no good at all, while the nutritious liquid that could have done us some good often never got a chance to make it to our bellies.

Once again, proof that alcohol's results are often considerably less than good.

3

Hercules?

A very small and weak person can have serious anger issues, but serious anger issues in a large and strong person create an immediate threat of violence that deadens the surrounding atmosphere. The large and strong person doesn't even need a weapon in order to do harm—his fists are quite enough on their own.

This is something I continued to learn during my mother's third marriage.

I have often wondered why a drunken man chooses to use his physical dominance over a woman or a child who can offer little retaliation. Apparently, alcohol blurs his ability to discern whether the fight he's engaging in is an honorable one—or maybe it just impairs his ability to care.

I have mentioned Leonard's extraordinary strength, and I will give a couple of examples. Mom's parents lived in the country and had a deep well which provided drinking water. To get water, one had to drop an elongated, galvanized well bucket into the well via a pulley and a long rope. They also had a cistern which collected rainwater from the house roof. The cistern was used via a small red handled pump in the kitchen. Of course, frogs, occasionally a dead mouse, bugs, etc. could be found in the cistern. We used this water for non-drinking water.

Leonard had some knowledge about plumbing, and he decided he was going to install running water in Grandma and Grandpa's house. He would install a septic tank and lateral drains for a bathroom. To have running water, he would install a well pump. Mom had saved up some money, and she would pay for it. The task would be completed by hand digging with a pick and shovel. I was not really big, so I do not believe I contributed a great deal, but I tried. In reality, most of the hard Missouri red, rocky clay full of tree roots was dug out by hand by Leonard Holloway. The digging alone was quite a feat, and Leonard did it in the heat of summer.

The septic tank was a large, round, heavy metal tank coated with tar. I am guessing the tank was about eight feet long and about five to six feet in diameter. A truck delivered the tank, and it had a crane to unload the tank. Besides hand digging a hole big enough to fit the septic tank in, all the laterals were hand dug as well. I have never seen one man undertake such a physically demanding task, but Leonard did it with what seemed like superhuman strength. After the digging was complete, Leonard and I tried to roll the septic tank into the newly dug hole. However, one end of the tank fell in first, and the other end of the tank was caught at the top of the hole. Leonard and I tried everything we could think of to get the stuck end of the tank up so we could scoot the tank enough to drop it in as desired. Both of us tried to lift the end stuck in the hole, but we could not even budge it. We tied ropes around it and used long boards to pry the tank up, but it was stuck or lodged, and, once again, we could not budge it.

We finally went in the house. Leonard told Grandma and Mom that we would need a tow truck to come out to lift the tank with the ropes we had around it. Grandma complained they had no money. Mom joined in that she had spent all she had on buying the equipment. Leonard always had a short temper fuse, and soon he was in a rage and tore outside. We all followed. With the adrenaline flowing, Leonard ran straight to the jammed tank and put both hands into the inlet hole. Then he yanked the entire tank up into the air, held the tank horizontally, and slowly lowered it into the hole he had dug. Grandma, Mom, and I were totally silent and in disbelief at what we had just witnessed. Note, Leonard and I together could not even budge the tank before the rage-induced adrenaline.

I do not know the force required to lift the tank, but Leonard plus adrenaline made it look easy. Glenda's recollection was the weight of the tank was over five hundred pounds. I do not remember what the tank weighed. I looked up comparably sized metal tanks today, and they begin at about nine hundred pounds and go up, depending on the thickness of the metal.

The second strength story is not as positive a story, but still shows Leonard's amazing strength. Leonard was drunk and in a rage. He had torn the house up as usual, and somehow he and Mom wound up outside. (Normally, Leonard and Mom kept the fighting inside the house.) Leonard backed Mom up against the front passenger side door of our 1958 Plymouth Fury. I was also outside and witnessed the entire event. Leonard had both hands on the car door, with his arms touching my mom's waist, boxing her in. Suddenly, he reared his right arm back with a clenched fist, intending to deliver a stomach blow to Mom, who was petite and skinny. Fortunately, she saw his fist coming at her. Just in the nick of time she turned sideways, pressing her stomach against Leonard's left arm as he punched with his right, and the car door absorbed the punch.

The blow would have been lethal: Leonard's fist hit the outside of the car door, smashing or denting it to the point of touching the inside panel of the door. I guess the door was five to six inches thick. Fortunately, the window was up, or the glass would have been broken. They made cars of that vintage with fairly heavy metal, but Leonard's hand showed no sign of injury. I still shudder to think of what would have happened if Mom had not dodged the intended stomach blow. No wonder he won several medals for boxing while in the Marines.

Later, Leonard and I removed the inside panel of the door, and then used a maul to beat the outside of the door out enough so we could lower the window.

Leonard's strength was incredible, but some of his brothers were as strong as or maybe even stronger. One of his brothers in West Plains, Missouri, came across a car with the front end stuck in a ditch. Leonard's brother simply picked up the front end of the car and set it back on the shoulder of the road. This was a compact car, but nonetheless, it was no small feat. The police arrested a different brother of Leonard's in West Plains and placed him in jail. Leonard was at home in Cabool. The West Plains police called him to come get his brother because he was destroying his jail cell. They trusted Leonard could safely get him out of the jail. Leonard did as they requested. His brother had smashed his bed into a metal ball, ripped the toilet stool up, and taken the sink off the wall. He was working on breaking the bars. Leonard got him safely out of the jail.

In a Cloud of Dust!

As I said, the violence usually stayed in the house, but I remember one time when it happened on the road. Leonard had a marine buddy visiting with us. One morning, they dropped Mom and me off at the one-room country school of Rocky Branch, between Houston and Cabool, where Mom was teaching. I was in the third grade, so I would have been eight years old. It seemed likely that two old marine drinking buddies spending the day together meant turbulent weather ahead. Sure enough, Leonard and his buddy showed up at the end of the school day to take us home. Not surprisingly, both of them were drunk. Mom wanted to drive, but Leonard would have nothing to do with that idea, as he was more than able to drive, in his opinion.

We were driving the yellow 1958 Plymouth Fury that could fly (V8 with a four-barrel carburetor). Leonard put the pedal to the metal on the old gravel roads. We were on one long stretch of the road that was fairly straight but had several hills. I was in the back seat with the drinking buddy. Mom and Leonard were in the front seat.

I am not sure how, but Leonard drove drunk a lot and had no major accident that I am aware of. I always thought he could have been a great racecar driver (if sober). However, on this day and on gravel roads, he was keeping the car on the road but was topping hills at or near triple-digit speed and often on the wrong side of the road. He always drove fast, especially when drunk.

Mom was screaming that Leonard was going to kill all of us. The weather was hot, so we had the windows down. Suddenly, Mom reached over, turned the ignition off, pulled the key out, and threw it out the window of her door. You cannot do that to cars nowadays, but you could back then. Leonard, with his right hand, immediately grabbed Mom's left arm and started twisting it into a corkscrew to the point that she was screaming out of control in pain. The car was slowing down as the engine was off. Leonard turned to me and said I had better find the key fast or he would twist her arm completely off. Of course, I am omitting the profanity used.

As the car was nearing a complete stop a considerable distance from where Mom threw the key out, I hit the gravel road, running like a wild man. I had no idea where we were when Mom threw the key out, and the ditch was full of weeds. The dust from the gravel road, I am guessing, would rival a

London fog. With Mom's excruciating screams loud and clear, I ran as fast as I could, with my eyes focused on anything that might be shiny. I believe God Almighty directed my feet and eyes that day as I found the key reasonably quick. Immediately, I started screaming as loud as I could that I had the key and began my sprint back to the car. I had the presence of mind to open Mom's door. Next, I held the key such that Leonard would let loose of Mom's arm to take the key, which he did. Next, I grabbed Mom's other arm and pulled her out of the car. Leonard was starting the engine. The door I had gotten out of and Mom's door were still open as Leonard tore out, without Mom and me, throwing gravel and creating another dust storm.

There we stood in a cloud of dust. Mom was still bawling from having her arm nearly twisted off. I was somewhat winded myself. We were out in the country, standing in a ditch, encrusted with road dust, and not really close to anything. The closest house belonged to someone we knew who had a telephone, so we began our long walk to the house. Upon arrival at the house, I knocked on the door. Rather awkwardly, Mom asked to use the telephone and called Uncle Herman, as he lived fairly close. His wife, my aunt Jackie, came and got us.

It turns out that wasn't the first time Mom had resorted to such desperate measures to stop someone. Years later, Mom told me that my dad once found me in the front yard of Mom's best friend, Mary. My dad was going to take me with him. Mom ran to his car, yanked the key out, and threw it into a cow pasture. When my dad went to find the key, Mom, Mary, and I all went in the house and locked it such that my dad finally left alone.

The sad thing was that Mom's friend Mary had also married a man with a drinking problem. Her husband was not physically abusive but left her with a difficult life because of the woeful effect of drunkenness.

It was a pattern I saw over and over again in my youth.

Playing Hide-and-Seek

Leonard's volcanic temper eruptions made life like living on pins and needles. There seemed to be no rhyme or reason, but you knew you were going to be stuck, eventually. One eruption sticks clearly in my mind. Leonard seemed to be in an above-average rage and was in the standard process of tearing the house up. I had taken my younger sisters outside and decided maybe I should hide them, as this time seemed ominous to me. We had a few small sheds outside, so I picked one with several packed boxes inside and moved some around so I could set my sisters behind them. They were probably about two and four years of age. While I was hiding my sisters, I heard a blood-curdling scream which ended abruptly. My gut told me he had finally done it. I expected the worst. With the girls hidden, I told them we were playing hide-and-seek and if their dad came in the shed to not make a sound or they would lose the game. I thought Leonard might want to take them with him if Mom was not alive, as he would be running from the law. My hope was Leonard would not find them before leaving.

I was going to go in the house and find out what had happened. I had not heard another sound, so I took off running to the house. Just as I came around the back of the house, Leonard started the car and was tearing out as usual. I hesitated but went into the house despite my fear of what I might find. I felt sick to my stomach. As just stated, I expected the worst. I stepped in through the kitchen door to find the usual upheaval and did not spot Mom at first. We had a small deep freeze behind the kitchen table at the far end of the dining room. I finally spotted her sitting in the corner behind the table. She had her back up against the deep freeze, not making a sound. She was sitting with her knees pulled up in front of her and her head face down on her knees. I walked through the milk and was relieved, as she appeared to be alive. I asked if she was okay. She did not even raise her head but muffled, "Yeah." The affirmation of my question did not really mean she was okay, but rather that she was alive. Her hurt would last much longer than the time required for the bruises to go away. The hurt ran much deeper than the bruises.

Mom had survived once again. However, in my heart, I fully expected someday to find her dead from domestic abuse. I anguished in dreadful anticipation of such a day. To say I have disdain for any man who physically harms a woman would be a gigantic understatement. Every man is responsible for his own actions, but I have targeted my hatred more toward the alcohol that so readily exposes the vileness that is in some men's heart. I know alcohol abstinence is a rarity in the times in which we live. However, to my readers who are young ladies, I would encourage you each to find a man who will vow to never drink alcohol, to ensure avoiding the misery of living with a drunken, abusive man.

Note, in looking back on this event, I certainly lay no claim that my strategy of hiding my young sisters was a good plan. However, such is what came to my mind amidst the chaos of a life which was quite unscripted.

The Road Not Taken

Robert Frost's poem "The Road Not Taken" illustrates the reality that we have a choice with each fork in the road of life. We can only ponder how life would have played out differently had we trod a different fork. Amidst life's storms with a drunken madman, a unique fork in the road appeared in my mom's life. We were at the farm, and a man who lived in Cabool showed up at our house one day while Leonard was at work. Mom knew the man but not well. He was a successful businessman and seemed to be a decent fellow. He showed up with a proposition. Somehow, he knew of the mess we were in with Leonard. The visitor told Mom he had some wealth. He proposed that if Mom would leave Leonard, he would take care of her and her children. He promised to treat all of us very well. Mom assured him Leonard would kill him and all of us if she did such a thing. He was willing to take the risk. However, Mom assured him she could not take the risk and turned down his offer. Mom worried for months that Leonard would find out about the visit and kill the man. As far as we know, Leonard never knew about the visitor or the proposition. We will never know the outcome if Mom had traversed that fork in the road of her life.

Seeing Stars in the Daytime

Avoiding provocation of Leonard was a priority for me. In most of his drunken rages, Mom was the focus of his rage, but especially when I was younger, Leonard administered discipline to me in the form of a beating. Once, Mom tried to stop him, and he beat her up as well, so I tried my best to avoid any behavior that might provoke his wrath towards me. However, on two occasions, I got more than just a beating. He was not drunk either time, but he always had a short-fuse temper.

We had an old push mower that I mowed with, and the pull cord broke so I could not start it. Leonard told me to fix it. I was about eight or nine years old. We did not have many tools, and I did not know how to fix it, but I worked on it to no avail. On arriving home from work, Leonard went straight to the shed where I was working on the mower. As he walked up to me, he could tell I had not fixed it, so he backhanded me in the face. The next thing I knew, I was seeing bright lights amidst a dark background. The colors were pretty and seemed somewhat like shiny stars on a dark night. After regaining consciousness, I realized I had been coldcocked.

The other time was somewhat my fault. I was playing marbles behind the back end of our old house. I had been shooting the marbles with my thumb, which is the proper way to shoot a marble. For whatever reason, I tossed a marble at the same time Leonard came around the corner of the house. He told me to shoot the marble with my thumb. Later, he came back by, and I was shooting with my thumb. Some time had passed, and I thought Leonard was in the house. Once again, I tossed a marble; once again, Leonard popped around the corner of the house. He probably expected I would toss one again and was watching, but I did not see him. I knew I was in trouble, as I had just disobeyed a direct order. I stood at attention to receive another backhand to the face. This time I saw more lights and was out for quite a while. I finally came to, once again horizontal, with a headache and a respectful distance from where I last remembered being. No wonder I never became a rocket scientist!

Both times Leonard knocked me out, I started hearing sound before anything else. I could hear birds chirping before I could see or move. I don't know if that is common, but that is how being knocked out worked for me.

That was life with a man who drank and got angry easily: you learned through experience things you never wanted to know. Additionally, I lost my childhood years of simply playing and having some fun, as survival trumps pleasure.

My learning days, at that point, were very far from an end.

4

You're a Marine Now!

As I mentioned earlier, I was six years old when my mother married Leonard. I may be the youngest person to have involuntarily enlisted in the Marine Corps. Glenda would mostly stay with Mom's parents, but I was soon to become a marine. To be a marine, one has to complete boot camp. Somewhere in my many years of training with Leonard, I extended far beyond boot camp.

Leonard got out of the Marines, but the Marines never got out of Leonard. He always dressed sharp and kept a Marine haircut. Of course, there is nothing wrong with such behavior, but I got my craw full of many other Marine customs. I had to address him with a militaristic "Sir" and often stand at attention. Dress shoes had to have a military shine. Occasionally he would pull a white-glove inspection on my bedroom, including the bouncing-a-quarter trick on my bed. Our old house sat very close to a gravel road. Keeping a bedroom dust-free was nearly impossible. My bedroom windows were loose enough to let snow accumulate on the floor in winter when we had blowing snow. If snow could get in, dust from the gravel road certainly could as well. In the summer, the windows were open, as that was the only way to cool the house. The screens we had were so full of holes, they were practically useless. In fact, we once trapped a snake crawling in the window when we closed the window at bedtime. The snake nearly scared Mom to death before it was removed.

One Marine example I will share relates to lawn mowing. We had a large yard—I would guess between one to two acres. I was eight years old when we moved to the farm. Leonard promptly assigned me mowing duty. He would give me the order to mow the next day, and he would add he wanted all the grass cut. That meant every blade of grass, including around trees, sheds, the house, fences, etc. The only exception was the ditch by the road. No one in our area mowed the ditches by the gravel road in those days.

That particular ditch ended up being very significant in my life, as I will explain later.

We did not have a weed eater or clippers other than my hands. The push mowing took most of the day. After mowing, I would try to pull the grass around everything, but of course, getting every blade was close to impossible. When Leonard would get home from work, he would inspect my mowing. Below is a typical dialog when he found a blade of uncut grass (Leonard's profanity omitted):

> Leonard, *pointing at the uncut blade of grass*: What did I tell you to do?
> Me, *standing at attention*: Cut all the grass, Sir.
> Leonard: What did you do?
> Me, *still at attention*: I cut most of the grass, Sir.
> Leonard: Did you cut this blade of grass?
> Me, *still at attention*: No, Sir!
> Leonard: Tomorrow, I want you to mow the entire yard again and cut every blade of grass this time. Do you understand me?
> Me, *still at attention and answering with emphasis*: Yes, Sir!

Note, not answering with emphasis could have been enough for a more extensive punishment. Usually, I did not have to mow a third time. Out of fear that Leonard would somehow find out I had not obeyed his order, I would mow it all again. I am not sure what the consequences would have been if I'd been caught not obeying his order, but I did not want to find out.

I still believe Leonard was extreme to the point of being ridiculous and cruel. However, I learned from him the concept of following orders, which is not a bad thing. Later, I would play football and eventually join the Air Force. Knowing how to follow orders was of benefit for both of those ventures.

I did so much servanthood to Leonard that now, as an adult myself, I rarely ask my wife or children to do menial tasks for me. I do not want to be such a tyrant. If I want something to drink, I will get it myself.

The Ugly Stepchild

My older sister, Glenda, would visit sometimes. However, she lived with Grandma Tennie and Grandpa Luther. They were the ones who raised her. Glenda is rather strong-willed. She and Leonard did not get along at all. All sides agreed she would not live with Mom and Leonard. Rhetorically speaking, I came with the deal as the ugly stepchild to Leonard. I do not know if Leonard wanted a son, but I am certain I was not the son he would have wanted.

The truth was, Leonard actually had a son from a previous marriage. Later, I will tell some of my stepbrother's story. Leonard showed little interest in his biological son, and I knew I didn't meet his expectations as a son. I have seen this bumper sticker: ***My kid can beat up your honor student.*** That's the kind of son Leonard wanted. While I was trying to be an honor student, Leonard urged me to be a bully and get into fights. I involved myself in a few fights to make him happy, but it was just not my thing.

Besides all the ridiculous demands, trying to avoid his blowups, being a personal slave, trying to stay alive, taking care of my younger sisters, and cleaning up all of Leonard's messes, I had the constant insults of how disappointing I was to him. I sometimes had to sneak around to study, as Leonard thought all that book stuff was for sissies.

Speaking of sissies reminds me of the subject of music. I was born with a love of music. I enjoyed singing at a very young age. Leonard believed music was for the female gender, and he was not having a sissy son playing, singing, or even listening to music. I was strictly forbidden to listen to the radio, as radio programming primarily played music in that era. Leonard's look at me signaled it was time to leave when music or singing played on the TV. So, I would leave the living room.

After I left home and Leonard's authority, I got a guitar, and I have been hummin' and strummin' ever since. However, one of my largest regrets in life is the fact I did not get started with music as a child. My uncle Thurman was a near child prodigy with the piano, and he taught hundreds (if not thousands) how to play the piano. Uncle Thurman offered to give me piano lessons at Grandpa Luther's house. I knew not to ask Leonard, as he would not approve, and I knew I was taking an enormous risk, but I jumped at the chance. I desperately wanted to play an instrument. Grandpa played the banjo, and he started giving me banjo lessons. I do not know how, but Leonard quickly found out, and that was the end of all that. I don't remember Leonard administering any physical punishment, but I never touched a musical instrument again while living with Leonard, so dire was his warning.

I didn't want broken fingers.

If I was ever caught playing an instrument again, that's what I was promised.

God blessed my wife and me with children who loved music as well, and they had instruments and sang together while growing up. The baffling thing is Leonard enjoyed our kids (even the guys) playing and singing music. Such was not the case when I was young.

I was wrong to nurture it, but I grew up with an intense hatred for Leonard. That burning hatred would last for many years, even some years after I was married. Eventually, God smote my heart, and I had to get over it. Life is not always fair. I can honestly say I learned a lot from Leonard. Much of what I learned was from him doing wrong, but I still learned many valuable lessons. Much of my experience with Leonard has served as motivation throughout my life. God can use bad things in life for good.

Two Cuties

Speaking of good things—not good things that you learn from the bad things, but two events that were good altogether to me—I was eight years old when my sister Tennie was born and ten when Nita was born.

Tennie and Nita were two bright spots in an otherwise bleak childhood with Leonard. Mom was usually worn out from working and abuse. I enjoyed helping take care of the girls. Tennie was born with long black hair and was so doll-like that everyone fussed over her when we were out in public. Nita was a cute blondie, outgoing and comical in her actions. They were both a lot of fun. They were good babies as long as they had a dry diaper, which was rare. We had no disposables back then. Also, we did not have a washer/dryer, so we spent many an hour in a laundromat washing, drying, and folding diapers. Tennie was always athletic. She could play croquet with adults when she was quite young. I would play all kinds of games with them.

They provided a lot of enjoyment in my life. At that time, I was Bub to them and still am today.

I was also Mom #2 to them, as I took care of them and made it a priority to protect them from harm.

That was a big job for a young boy, and though I could often do the first, the second—protection from harm—was beyond my ability to guarantee.

The Question I Have Never Answered

I am sure others involved with domestic abuse have wrestled with the same question: "Why did I never report the abuse?" We did not even have a telephone, let alone an abuse hotline number. Additionally, reporting an abuser raises the danger level significantly if caught by the abuser. Thus, I placed my focus on managing the mess as best I could. I put enormous effort into trying to prevent the blowups. Leonard would often blow up if there was not enough food at a meal. I often left the table hungry as I passed up food in hopes that if Leonard had larger portions, it might help to avoid a rage incident. Of course, his smoking, drinking, and tearing everything up is why the cupboards were usually bare. I jumped at his command to humor him, whether he wanted the TV channel changed (I was the remote control) or a cup of coffee (I was his personal servant). All the while, I had to contend with his personal insults to me. As mentioned earlier, I tried to keep the old house looking as neat as possible. I was doing my best to protect my mother and my little sisters from harm.

However, what is a scrawny kid supposed to do when his mom is being beaten and the perpetrator is an ex-marine—a Marine-trained killer? Direct confrontation never seemed like a viable solution, but perhaps I should have tried. That thought still troubles me. I spent many an hour at night in bed contemplating options. Between drunk driving, flying coffee cups, being coldcocked, and Mom being beaten, there was a good chance someone was going to die.

These are ugly memories. However, when the focus of life becomes survival, life can become ugly. I had a single-shot .22 rifle that only shot one short shell without reloading. I was a good shot but could not convince myself one small caliber .22 short shell would stop Leonard. There was another option I weighed many times at night. In Mom and Leonard's closet, Leonard kept a loaded .45 revolver on the top shelf. He never showed me the gun. My belief was he did not want anyone to have familiarity with it. I had never shot a pistol. I contemplated ending our dilemma many times with that revolver. If I failed, I was certain I would not survive. I pondered the legal ramifications if I were successful, such as life in prison. In my bed at nighttime, I played scenario after scenario over and over in my mind. I never executed the plan. I believe it worked out for the best that I did not. However, if someone other than myself had died from Leonard's violence, then I would have lived with the guilt of knowing that I might have prevented it.

I certainly lay no claim that such thoughts were good, but desperate situations evoke desperate thoughts. Constantly living with the threat of death or harm is a horrible weight. Senseless bruises on your mother are a horrible sight. Constantly having to filter every action and word to minimize the likelihood of a rage incident is a horrible task. Hopelessness is a horrible feeling. I lack words to describe the misery of living for years in fear and with the wonder of how this nightmare would end. I will not repeat the stories of the many blowups, as they were often about the same. Leonard would tear the house up, beat Mom up, and then tear out in the car. I would try to clean the mess up.

I had never told Glenda about my planning to end our problem with Leonard until I began writing this story. She informed me she was doing the same thing, but that she never determined a way to be successful at it, either. In fact, Glenda said that as a child, she often prayed that Leonard would just die. I will discuss the subject of marriage much more. I cannot emphasize enough the importance of marrying the right person to avoid such a dreadful situation. Additional insurance against such is to have an alcohol-free home.

Despite the home I lived in, I did have more than a glimpse into a house where marriage was a blessing and where a husband and wife worked together to build a life that nurtured themselves and others.

That house was the house of my grandparents. It was a refuge for me as a boy, and I'll share about that haven of peace in the next chapter.

5

Grandma Tennie and Grandpa Luther

Two of the most important individuals in my life as a child were Grandma Tennie and Grandpa Luther. Many times, I sought refuge there while living with my dad and with Leonard. If not for that refuge, I am not sure how I would have weathered the storms of my childhood.

I believe there are two kinds of people. There are characters and then there are all the rest of us. Characters clearly stand out in life. Characters are cut from a different cloth than most people. There is nothing wrong with being a character or not being one. With Grandma and Grandpa, the latter was the character. Although Grandma was one of my most admired people, I was closer to Grandpa than to anyone else growing up. Born around the turn of the twentieth century, they represented a unique generation. Both of them knew life before most of the modern inventions, yet lived to see so much change in the world. They experienced raising a family during the Great Depression. Both of them were fiercely independent (from handouts). They exemplified self-sufficient, rugged individualism and personal responsibility—qualities that today are a scarce commodity, I believe. Note, I am not referring to those qualities as trust in the power of themselves, but rather individuals who recognized they were responsible for their lives, which included trusting in God as opposed to trusting in others or the government for their survival.

Grandma Tennie

I concluded many years ago that Grandma Tennie is the hardest-working woman I have ever known. She always had gray hair as I remember her. She was of a stocky frame and fairly strong from years of hard work. Neither she nor Grandpa were without imperfections, but you could not accuse Grandma of being slothful or lazy. Her primary role was to provide food, clothing, and care for her family. She was a mama bear to her family. She always had a cake baked with a gift for birthdays and Christmas when I was a child. Grandma was a big believer in getting an education to get ahead in life. She conveyed that concept to me more than anyone else did.

Grandma and Grandpa bought a few food items in town, but Grandma preserved or canned most of the food for the year. A special treat from the grocery store was Kellogg's Cornflakes. Grandma kept a cellar full of canned food in case of a bad gardening year or even years. Grandma would occasionally play a game of Chinese checkers or dominoes in the evening, but most of her time was all about work. She raised chickens for food and profit. Chicken or squirrel was the main meat staple of our diet. If company came unexpectedly, Grandma would tell me which chicken to catch, and she would have it in the frying pan in no time at all. She sold eggs as a source of income. She also ordered jewelry, which had to be assembled and then sold for income.

Grandma Tennie was certainly a master gardener. Glenda and I would help with the planting and especially with the weeding. Grandma started her own plants and knew how to fertilize and cultivate the large family garden. Grandpa would plow the sizeable garden in the spring using a team of horses and then disk it, but after that, Grandma took over. In the fall, Grandpa and I would dig potatoes for storage in a shed to last most, if not all, the winter months. Grandma not only raised enough garden vegetables for eating all summer, she would can or freeze enough to last until next year's garden. She would also keep seed from most of the vegetables to have for planting next year's garden. She always had onions, squash, and pumpkin available all winter from the garden. A big highlight of the year was when the seed catalogs came in the mail. Grandma would not order a lot, but usually a few items. We enjoyed looking at all the colorful pictures of vegetables, flowers, and trees in the catalogs.

I believe Grandma's pride and joy of all her labors was her large orchard. She had planted it and maintained it. She had trees which bore fruit early and trees which bore fruit late, so that there was fruit until winter arrived. We ate a lot of it fresh, but she would can and freeze fruit as well. Besides the vegetable garden and orchard, Grandma kept a small vineyard. While some of the grapes were suitable for eating, most of them were used to make canned grape juice. We had grape juice all winter. Grandma cooked and canned most of her food on a wood cookstove. However, when I was young, she acquired a gas cookstove, but for additional heat in the wintertime, she would often still use her wood cookstove.

Grandma was also in charge of all medical care. I don't believe she had any formal medical training, but for several years, she was a midwife. Once I stepped on a nail which resulted in a red streak running up my leg, showing infection. Grandma placed a large piece of salted pork fat on the sore and wrapped cloths around to keep the fat in place. The infection soon cleared up as presumably the salty fat sucked the infection out.

With the income Grandma made, she purchased a black-and-white camera, which was not very common. She made sure all birthdays and special events came with a picture. Grandma was skilled at sewing, making clothes and quilts.

I am guessing my mom bought Grandma an electric wringer washing machine. She just put water in the tub to wash the clothes by agitation. When the clothes were clean, we could run them through the two rollers that would wring most of the water out of the clothes. It was quite easy to get an arm in the wringer, and I managed to do it. I got my fingers too close and soon my entire arm was in the wringer. In time, I eventually outgrew the flat-arm syndrome.

One time Grandma had me all ready to go to church with a clean white shirt and bow tie. I went to the barn to check on Grandpa. It had recently rained, which left the barn lot quite a mess from all the cow manure. To navigate the barn lot, Grandpa had several boards laid out to walk on. You might guess what is coming next. I slipped on one board and face-planted into the poopy, soupy barn lot. Grandma was not a happy camper. This was before the indoor bathroom. We had to use a round outdoor washtub for bathing. Water had to be taken from the cistern or well. Grandma cleaned me up. I repeated the trick another time with the same results. Those wet boards could be slick.

Mom told the story that one Christmas during the Great Depression, her parents told all the children they had no money to buy presents for them. However, after all the children were in bed on Christmas Eve, they could hear their mom working in the kitchen. The next morning, they had popcorn balls made with molasses, which was a special treat, so they had a surprise. My mom also mentioned that while times were difficult during the Great Depression, they always had food, clothing, and housing. She also said they were a happy family.

Grandma was a woman of great faith. She would begin her day on her knees and was faithful in her service to God. I heard her more than once name my name before the throne of grace in her early morning prayers. Only God knows how much

Grandma's prayers affected my life. Perhaps I might not have survived one of the car rides with a drunk driver if not for the prayers of Grandma, or possibly a flying coffee cup might have done me in. More important than survival in this temporal world is preparation for eternal life. Such were Grandma's prayers for me. I will discuss more about this later. God gave me the song below. I clearly know the importance of a praying grandma.

The Prayers of Grandma

Verse 1:

It wasn't easy you see – For her to bend on her knees
But she'd bow her face – Before the throne of grace
From the years her hair was gray – And from the years she knew how
to pray
She brought my name before – Her Lord and Savior
She interceded for me – For my soul with God she would plead

Chorus:

When I look back on my youth – So many others never found the
Truth
I could have been – One of those who died in their sin
But God saved my soul – And I praise him so
And I'm here to tell – The difference between heaven and hell
For me was – The prayers of Grandma

Verse 2:

We are so busy today – Sometimes too busy to pray
But our youth still need – Someone to intercede
Someone who with God will plead – The difference will be eternity
Now who will pray for them – Lift up the children
Prayers of importunity – Just like Grandma prayed for me

(Chorus Repeats)

A Cunning Grandma

I was a baby when Mom first left me at her parent's house. When Grandpa came home from work, I surprised him with my presence. Grandma told him it looked like Oneta's second marriage was not working out well. Grandpa did not perceive the news as good. Grandma and Grandpa had raised their own five children during a very difficult era. Now they were aging and raising Glenda, my mom's first child. They never had a substantial income, and now, here was the possibility of having to raise another child. Grandpa was obviously not happy with my presence. He declared, "Oneta had her own children. She needs to raise her own children."

Grandma was holding me, and upon hearing her husband's outburst, she handed me to Grandpa. She told him she had to take care of her chickens and do her chores so he could watch me while she was outside.

As Grandma expected, when she returned from doing her chores, Grandpa was having quite a time playing with me. He was doing the usual baby talk, and I was smiling from ear to ear. I wound up staying with Grandma and Grandpa often. Grandma told me she never heard another cross word from Grandpa about my presence. Instead, he was always glad to see me. His bark was clearly worse than his bite.

Grandpa Luther

As stated earlier, Grandpa was a character. He had a friendly nature and seemed to enjoy life. The best part for me was that he was still a kid at heart. Even in his late fifties and early sixties, he would challenge me to a foot race. We would see who could skip rocks the furthest on a pond. We would squirrel hunt together. Occasionally, we would sneak to a neighbor's pond for fishing. Many a summer evening, we would gig frogs after dark using a flashlight and a barbed gig on a long pole at several ponds. Grandma could fry frog legs for breakfast in a way that made them a real delicacy.

One day, as Grandpa and I walked up the old gravel road to their house, we saw one of Grandma's guineas perched on a fence post. We were a good distance from the bird. Grandpa challenged me to see who could come the closest to hitting the guinea with a rock. The bird was undisturbed by my throw. Grandpa made his throw and, to the surprise of both of us, the rock hit the guinea in the head. The bird dropped like a rock. We couldn't let the meat go to waste, even though Grandpa knew he was in trouble with Grandma. I took the bird to Grandma and told her what happened. She was not amused.

Grandpa was no stranger to hard work as he farmed and was a carpenter. He would milk early, work all day as a carpenter, then come home to milk again and do other farm chores. If possible, I would work right by his side. Grandpa built several large hay barns for farmers. One of his trademarks was when he got the main beam in place at the peak of the barn roof, he would dance a jig back and forth on the beam considerably high in the air. Grandpa was a character. He was not a really big man but was strong in his own right. On Saturdays, we would go to Houston to purchase feed for the milk cows and horses in one-hundred-pound feedbags. Once we got home, he would stand two bags up on the end of his old pickup bed. He would lean over so he could pick each bag up on his shoulders with arms wrapped around each bag. He would carry two hundred pounds of feed over a distance of about one hundred feet, which included stepping over a fence. Once emptied, the feed sacks would go to Grandma to use for sewing or making clothes.

Grandpa had an outgoing personality and knew about everybody in the county. However, he could be rather

cantankerous. He carried a business card in his wallet. I still
have the card, which has the following on the back:

> 5000 years ago, Moses said, "Pack up your camel, pick up your shovel,
> mount your ass, and I will lead you to the Promised Land."
> 5000 years later, F. D. Roosevelt said, "Lay down your shovel, sit on
> your ass, and light up a Camel, this is the Promised Land."

Before purchasing feed on Saturdays in Houston, Grandpa
would walk down one side of the main street to just meet and
talk with folks and have a good time. Once at the end of the
street, he would come back up the other side doing the same. If
he ran into someone whom he knew was a diehard Democrat,
he would ask him or her to read his business card. He seemed
to enjoy irritating Democrats but somehow seemed to still
maintain a good relationship with everyone. Politically, he was
conservative and opposed to a massive welfare state. He and
Grandma were testimonies that if you worked hard and with
God's blessings, you could survive without handouts. Neither
he nor Grandma took any government handouts during the
Great Depression.

I believe family should take care of family as the first level
of societal support. If there is no family, then the church should
be the next disperser of benevolence, but the church has not
done such, so the government has taken over. However, I agree
with Grandpa that the welfare state is far too out of control and
people should work for what they have, if at all possible. My
mom told me the first time she ever tasted peanut butter was
when she traded sandwiches at school. The trade was with a
student whose family was getting peanut butter from
government assistance.

Grandpa was skilled at using his bullwhip and could snap it
to sound like a firecracker. He would use his whip to herd cattle
and horses. He could lasso a calf from a horse. Grandpa was a

cowboy. He carried a certain swagger that set him apart from the crowd. Sometimes, on horseback, he would move the cows down the road in front of the house, and he would use his bullwhip to help herd them. Occasionally, Glenda and I would lie down behind a lilac bush in the front yard and shoot our BB guns at the bull as Grandpa would drive the herd down the gravel road. The BB gun had enough pop to it, the bull would jump when hit. Grandpa would pop his whip to get the bull to settle down. I am not sure if he ever found out about our rather mischievous deed. The bull was normally gentle, and Grandpa would often ride him bareback. Once Grandpa and I found a long snake slithering through the grass. Grandpa picked it up by the tail and popped it like a bullwhip, giving the snake a fatal whiplash.

Grandpa seemed to have honed the capacity for enjoying life. He balanced hard work with enjoyment, like dancing on a barn beam. I learned from him that life requires lots of hard work, but it is important to stop and smell the roses, as the old saying goes. I do not believe life was drudgery to him. Grandma was a worker bee, and while she enjoyed life, she seemed to always be on top of her work schedule. Whereas Grandpa did not keep his farm a showplace. The fences were usually in poor condition. Grandpa built their house. Yet, like the shoe cobbler whose children run barefoot, he never finished the exterior rocking. Houses that did have that exterior rocking were called Ozark Giraffe houses because of the color of the Missouri slab rock used. He did work as a carpenter and farmed as well but would usually find time to play his banjo or go horseback riding to just have some fun.

Grandpa loved music. He loved to play his banjo while sitting on the front porch, swinging and singing. He was self-taught on playing the piano, but he only played the black keys. Many claimed him to be the best bass singer in the area, and many considered him the best tenor singer in the area. He came from a large family. They had little, but all the children learned to sing and read music (shaped notes). I was born with a love for music, or perhaps I just adopted Grandpa's love for music. He sang gospel music, and I believe his two favorites were "The Unclouded Day" and "I'm a Millionaire." He also sang a lot of old folk/country songs, like "On Top of Old Smokey" and "Red River Valley." Also, Grandpa yodeled with a passion. Grandpa's talent extended to whistling when he wasn't singing or yodeling.

Grandpa grew up riding and working horses, and he never gave that up. He bought an old Allis Chalmers crank tractor not long before his death, but he still preferred to ride and work his horses. Note, a crank tractor required manually turning the engine over with a crank to start the tractor. Disengaging the crank quickly and carefully was necessary before the engine started. Not doing so could cause a broken hand or arm. I walked many a mile behind Grandpa and a team of workhorses plowing fields to be planted in corn. He had no combine, so we had to pick the corn by hand. After we picked the corn, we would cut the cornstalks by hand and make corn shocks, which we used as cattle feed in the winter. His pride and joy was a rather spirited palomino riding horse.

While Grandpa was known for riding horses, he also had a reputation for driving vehicles. He only had two speeds. One was at a complete stop and the other was wide open. Fortunately, he never had a vehicle with an engine bigger than a six-cylinder, so he had some limit on how fast he could go. Six-cylinder engines were not as powerful back then as they are today. He became well known for passing almost every vehicle he approached. If he could not pass on the left or the normal side, he would just pull over to the shoulder or in the ditch and pass on the right side. Coming to a complete stop was quite an experience with Grandpa. He was a master at running wide open and then slamming on his brakes at the last second to come to a fishtailing, screeching halt at just the right spot. Everybody thought he would kill himself driving so crazy, but to my knowledge, he never had a vehicle accident.

I cannot say Grandpa was a visionary with technology. He saw no need to get electricity in their house. They had kerosene lamps and lanterns. However, once he had electricity and even a TV, he loved heavyweight boxing and *Bonanza*. As with electricity, he had no desire for indoor running water and an indoor bathroom. He had built a two-holer outhouse, which seemed quite sufficient. Once again, as he got more modern conveniences, he quickly decided soaking and singing in the bathtub was quite enjoyable.

I can say Grandma and Grandpa were classic examples of showing financial responsibility. They had to borrow money to buy the farm they lived on but paid it off as soon as possible and then never borrowed money again. I have chosen to pattern my financial life after their example.

I mentioned earlier that Grandma and Grandpa were not without imperfections. There was never any physical violence, and I never worried about them divorcing, but they did have rather intense arguments. To the best of my memory, they usually bickered over money. Grandma thought she should have some share of Grandpa's income, but Grandpa did not agree. They would occasionally have their heated encounters. Yet, most of the time, they got along well.

Their home seemed like a haven of security compared to my volatile home life with Leonard. However, I did receive disciplinary training at Grandma and Grandpa's home. Several times my posterior would have an encounter with a small peach tree branch, but I never had fear of abuse. Note, disciplinary training is good; abuse is not.

My Darkest Hour

Bottom line for me was that Grandpa Luther was the closest thing to a good father image I ever had. As bleak as life was at home with Leonard, life was exciting with Grandpa. Grandpa knew how Leonard was, but he stayed friendly with him as he felt he could accomplish more on friendly terms than not. Leonard liked and respected Grandpa. He did not know Grandpa had threatened to kill him many times. Sometimes Grandpa could talk Leonard into letting me do something that would not have happened otherwise, like going to town on Saturday with Grandpa for shopping. I always believed that, if need be, Grandpa was likely the only person who could have stood up to Leonard.

In October 1965, I spent part of one Saturday morning with Grandpa. In the fall, I would pick up walnuts. That day, Grandpa and I loaded up the walnuts in his pickup and took them to Houston to sell.

That was the last time I spent time with Grandpa, as he soon became very sick. He would soon die at the Houston hospital from a heart attack.

That is the darkest moment of my life. My only genuine joy in life was suddenly and unexpectedly gone. Grandpa was my refuge from Leonard, and now all hope seemed gone. In what was an unsafe world, I felt safe with Grandpa. Losing a loved one is never painless, but I felt in my heart that I would not survive Leonard now. I thought there was no one in my world I could run to in time of need.

My life with Leonard was bad, and then the worst possible thing happened. God took my grandpa. Some lose a loved one after many good years. I was thirteen years old and was usually only with Grandpa when Leonard was at work or on a drinking binge. Grandpa seemed to be my only hope, and yet God took him home. I have no positive memories of my dad. In fact, I lived my early years hiding from him. I was a captive slave to Leonard. I had to do exactly as ordered or suffer the consequences. Plus, I lived with the constant fear Leonard would eventually kill some of us in one of his drunken madman rages. Now God had taken away the only positive outlet or hope I had.

Today, I can say I am thankful for Grandpa Luther and for the good times I had with him. Cherish the good things God gives, for we know not when they will cease to be. Now I can look at the positive side and not just the loss. I did not realize God was my real refuge and his provision is sufficient. Presently, I have not lost a spouse or a child, so I cannot speak exactly about such a loss, but I can say that God knows what he is doing. We do not know what God has planned. Unbeknownst to me, God had more building plans in my life. God had a plan for my future that I was unaware of.

So much in my life depended on Grandpa being there that mentally I did not want to accept the reality of his death. A huge crowd attended his funeral. I saw him in the casket and saw his casket over his gravesite. Many a time at night, in bed, I would try to imagine some way around the reality of his death. Eventually, in time, I would accept Grandpa's death. I could reconcile the fact that I witnessed him in the casket, and I know well the place his physical body rests even today.

Later in my life, I heard a funeral home owner share some thoughts on a traditional funeral versus cremation. His primary concern about cremation was the importance of bringing closure for the death of a loved one. I could readily identify with the director's conclusion based on my experience with the death of Grandpa Luther. I will share the director's story later.

Grandpa had an old hound dog that howled at night for weeks after Grandpa's death. Seemingly, even the dog had difficulty accepting the loss of his master.

6

Early to Rise

Grandpa's sudden death created an immediate problem due to the fact that the cows still had to be milked. I had often helped with milking, so I knew how to do it. However, Glenda and Thurman did the first days' milking after Grandpa's death. They thought I should stay with Mom. The loss of her dad was very difficult for her. I am guessing she was experiencing the same emotions I was. She knew Grandpa had some influence with Leonard, but now that was gone.

Cows are not very social creatures by nature, and especially with unfamiliar people. Grandpa and I were the only two people the cows were used to being around. So, on the first morning of milking, the cows did not want to come into the barn for Glenda or Thurman. It was as if they realized something was not right. Then Glenda tried a curse phrase that Grandpa commonly used to reference the herd, and that worked like a charm. I suppose the cows knew something was not normal, but at least these two knew the secret code. I soon worked myself into the milking schedule. When Thurman returned to teaching, I did the milking by myself for a while.

I was thirteen at the time and, of course, in school. Our one-room country school had been closed. Glenda and I rode a bus to Cabool for school. Going directly to Cabool was about sixteen miles, but our route seemed like a hundred miles traveling down mostly narrow country gravel roads. Great-

Uncle Calvin, brother to Grandma Tennie, drove the school bus. He was a good guy but also a strict disciplinarian and would not wait much for anybody. I was the third stop on the route and the bus arrived just a little after 6 a.m. In order for me to do the milking, I got up by or before 4 a.m. We had over a dozen head of cows to milk. Home was where I slept, and then I'd bike to the barn, which was about a quarter mile away. Aside from being dark and cold, the worst part of the bike ride was when I had to pass a neighbor's house. They kept a mean guard dog, which was loose at nighttime. The dog would try to bite me as I pedaled my bike.

The hardest part was that cows are creatures of habit, and at 4 a.m., they were down in the woods trying to sleep. I would have to find the herd and then woo them up to the barn with some grain or feed. Fortunately, Grandpa had recently installed an automatic milking system, which allowed me to use two portable milking machines. I would put feed in the stanchions and bring in three cows at a time. First, I would wash the cow's teats and then hook up a portable, automatic milker for the first cow. Then, I'd repeat the process for the second cow and hand-milk the third. I poured the collected milk through a milk strainer into a ten-gallon metal milk can.

After milking the cows, I carried full milk cans to the road for the milk haulers to pick up. A can full of milk weighed about ninety pounds. I'd take the buckets and milking equipment to Grandma's house for cleaning during the day, so we could use them for the evening milking. After the evening milking, Grandma would clean them to be ready for use the next morning. Once done milking, I would ride my bike back home and try to avoid becoming dog food. I fully imagine I smelled somewhat barnyard country, as I had little time to clean up before getting outside to catch the bus.

During deer season, Great-Uncle Calvin kept his .30-30 deer rifle with him on the school bus, just in case he saw a deer. I think it is fair to say you know you were from redneck country if your school bus driver is hunting for deer while picking up kids for school!

Likely because most of my time with Leonard was so miserable, I actually enjoyed milking. Whenever I had the chance to stay with Grandpa, I always milked with him. Any time I spent milking gave me more time away from Leonard. I guess farm life instilled in me the nature of early rising, as I have always been an early riser. I did not milk a long time by myself, as Grandma sold the cows before severe winter weather set in. We had to cut ice in ponds for drinking water for the cows when temperatures stayed below freezing, which would have been difficult to do and still go to school.

A Pit Crew Member

They consolidated all the one-room country schools in our area into area town schools. I wound up going to school in Cabool for my seventh grade through eleventh grade years. I adapted well to the larger school, but I would have rather gone to the one-room school. Coach Seals was my Physical Education instructor and our school's football coach. He was a big guy and an excellent coach, but more importantly, he was a good Christian man. As God allowed one door to close with the death of my grandpa, he brought me a new important mentor in the person of Coach Seals. He approached me one day about trying out for football for the next season. I told him I would love to, but I did not really know the rules, and I did not know if my stepdad would let me. Coach said his job was to teach me how to play, and he thought I could help the team. I assured him I would find out and let him know.

Actually, any game that had a ball in it was near heaven to me, as I loved any kind of ball game. I had a football and kicked it around a lot and played as much as one could play in a one-person game. However, now I had to ask Leonard for approval. I rarely asked anything of Leonard, because he would say no to anything I wanted. But I thought he would go for football as it fit the tough-guy stuff he liked. I popped the question, and as expected, he responded that it would be good as it should toughen me up. However, he immediately informed me that while he approved of me playing, I was on my own to get to practices and games. He would do nothing to help with that, and such was the case.

Fortunately, there was one guy on the team who drove right past our house. So, I hopped on my bike and pedaled straight to Charlie's and asked about riding with him. Charlie was a strong, strapping country boy who played tackle on the varsity team. He was rather quiet but had always seemed like a good guy. His family was definitely not wealthy. Charlie owned an old car. When I asked about riding, Charlie seemed to show some enthusiasm and was hopeful I could help some with gas. I had to inform him I had little money but would help with what I could. He said that would be great and I could help with tire repairs as well.

I knew I was going to learn how to play football, but did not know I was also going to learn a lot about fixing flat tires.

Football practice began in August before school started and was from 6 a.m. to 10 a.m. and then 6 p.m. to 10 p.m. for six days a week. When the first day of practice finally came, Charlie let me know he would be over about 4 a.m. I wondered why we were leaving so early. The drive should be less than thirty minutes. I assumed Charlie wanted to arrive early due to the strict rule against being late.

I quickly found out the reason for our early departure. We had to stop and repair a flat tire up to a half dozen times. In my new role as a member of Charlie's pit crew, I'd exit the car as it approached a stop. Then I would get the bumper jack out of the trunk and begin jacking the car up. Charlie would grab the lug bolt wrench and start taking the tire off. As soon as the tire was off, we would jump on the tire to break the bead around the rim. Charlie would pull out the inner tube, which was so patched it looked like chicken pox on the back of a child. Charlie would quickly pump up the tube enough to find the leak. Once the new patch was on, we put the tube back in the tire. Soon Charlie would put the tire and lug nuts back on. Next, he would pump that old bicycle pump like crazy. The heat from the furious pumping made the pump almost too hot to handle. I would let the jack down and put all tools in the trunk. Then off we would go for at least a few more miles until we would repeat the process again.

I believe we had some flat tires on every trip. We were not getting home until midnight to 1 a.m., and then we'd be back up and out before 4 a.m. We would have been ahead to have slept in the car.

The road we traveled was rather curvy and hilly. Whenever we would crest a hill, Charlie would turn the ignition off and push the clutch down, hoping to save gas as we coasted down the hill. Charlie knew when to turn the key back on and pop the clutch just in time to start the engine back up. We would count our change before pulling into a gas station. Then tell the attendant we wanted whatever our change added up to, like maybe eighty-eight cents, which might have been four gallons of gas. Gas was cheaper back then, but we could not afford to fill'er up.

While the ride was not without some issues, I am thankful Charlie let me ride with him, and I learned a lot about changing tires.

The Old Pigskin

Was all that bother to get to football practice worth it? Yes, a caring adult role model and a chance to gain some self-confidence were great benefits in my life at that time. Just being a part of something successful, as opposed to the dysfunctional life I had lived, was a blessing.

Coach Seals had a very successful coaching career in Cabool. In most of the games played, Cabool won and was South-Central Region Conference Champ or contender most years. The grading of schools at the time was based on the student population, ranging from 1A to 4A. Cabool was a 2A school, but we played neighboring towns, which included schools from 1A to 3A.

Preseason practice was simply rough in the hot and humid August weather. Besides all the conditioning exercises, I had to learn how to play football. Most of the guys on the team had already played some, but I was a newbie. Football to me is the consummate team sport. Every player needs to do their best to carry their own weight or do their part and, if need be, help anyone else who could use a hand. Coach thought I should try playing the end position. I did, and that is where I stayed.

After a few days of practice, every bone and muscle in my body ached. From all the strenuous exercises to all the bumps and bruises of blocking, tackling, and falling down, the body was in pain. However, I kept practicing and learning. By the end of the season, Coach told me I had a good nose for the football, and he thought I would make a good defensive end.

I enjoyed the game—that much is true. Although I believe I played with the determination to dominate to prove Leonard wrong about me not being tough. Later I will share my secret weapon which I believed helped me significantly while playing football.

There are more stories to tell about football and Coach Seals, but for now, suffice it to say that I was beginning to find my feet as a young man. From taking over my grandpa's milking job for a while, to learning to handle both tire repairs and pigskins, my teenage years were bringing even more maturity than my earlier childhood years had.

It turns out that was a good thing, because I was going to find myself on my own sooner than I expected.

7

Uncle Harlin, Aunt Irene, and Paul

When I look back on my life, I see some people who did a lot of damage to me as a child, like Leonard and my father. But I also see people who were strong pillars—people who supported me and showed me there was a different, better way to live. As I indicated above, Coach Seals was one of those pillars, and Grandpa Luther and Grandma Tennie were others. Grandpa and Grandma were not the only upright people in their family, however. Grandma Tennie's brother Harlin, his wife, Irene, and son, Paul, also played a significant role in my life.

My mom and Uncle Harlin had always been close. I do not know the origin of the nickname, but he would often call my mom *Snooks*. Uncle Harlin was a very successful farmer. He was certainly no stranger to hard work. He not only worked hard, but he worked smart. Uncle Harlin milked a large herd of Holstein cows for most of his adult life. With the help of his son, Paul, they developed a very productive milking herd. I cannot think of a more demanding and challenging profession than milking, as the job has to be done twice a day every day of the year. Sick or not, milking still has to be done. Bad weather or not, milking still has to be done. The day begins early and often ends late. However, even with all the hard work, Uncle Harlin, Aunt Irene, and Paul always had time to visit with me and were great encouragements in my life. They lived a few miles from Grandma and Grandpa.

I started driving long before the legal age, and my favorite place to go was to Uncle Harlin's. Driving without a license and underage, though technically illegal, was not a big deal where we lived at that time. Uncle Harlin had bird dogs, and sometimes he would pick me up and we would go quail hunting. I helped some on the farm with them. The first time I drove a tractor was for Uncle Harlin when I raked hay for him. I had to go through some woods to get back to the house. Somehow, I clipped one end of the rake by hitting a tree and broke a piece on the rake. I had seen Uncle Harlin get pretty mad before when working cattle. I was not looking forward to telling him what had happened. However, I told him what I had done. Additionally, I told him I would somehow pay for fixing it. He was not mad at all and said he would take care of it. In fact, he told me the only way in life to never make a mistake is to never do anything. I have never forgotten that lesson.

Aunt Irene probably read more books than most people have ever seen, but she always seemed glad to visit awhile. I spent many an hour just visiting with her. She would always want to feed me some and was a great blessing in my life.

Paul was a first cousin to my mom, but always seemed like a first cousin to me. Paul was a good-sized fellow but quite the gentle giant. He was always interested in pretty much everybody and would do whatever he could for you. While milking, Paul and I solved most of the world's problems. Unfortunately, no one heard our solutions other than the cows. Paul and I eventually took some vacation trips together. In fact, Paul would be the one to introduce me to an attractive, single schoolteacher who taught school in Raymondville, Missouri. Her name was Deanne, but she went by Dee.

I will tell more of that story later, as I would soon find myself in pursuit of this young lady's hand.

Having grown up in rural southern Missouri, surrounded by many hardworking farmers, I am undoubtedly partial to them. I think they are the best people. They know how to manage the earth's resources and livestock. Yet they nourish and cherish the values of life, family, and faith. All the farmers I grew up around knew hard work well but were still always willing to help a neighbor in need. Most of my favorite people have been hardworking farmers.

Also, one of them, Uncle Harlin, would soon be a major factor in a major turn in my life's road.

The Grand Finale

I was fourteen and tried to get away from Leonard as much as I could. However, when Leonard was home, I usually was as well. His drinking and rages seemed to never get better, just worse, as in more extreme and more frequent. On this occasion, Mom, Glenda, Tennie, Nita, and I had gone to Springfield for a couple of days as Mom had an annual teacher's meeting there. This was pleasant, as we had some time together without Leonard. We also did some shopping on Saturday, and we were running later than planned when we left Springfield.

We knew Leonard would not likely be happy with us being later than he expected. Our estimate turned out to be a gigantic understatement. He was in a drunken rage. Note, there was no reason our being later than expected should have been a concern, but a drunken mind needs little to justify a raging fit. Leonard had already torn the house up and thrown clothes outside. We arrived at dusk and knew we were in trouble when we saw household items in the front yard.

However, if not for the settling darkness, I very well would not be writing this story. Mom got out of the car first as Glenda and I lagged behind, knowing we would likely be heading into a buzz saw, which turned out to be another understatement. Mom met Leonard on the front porch. We heard Leonard from where he stood on the front porch, without him seeing us on the side of the house. We heard his less-than-congenial greeting. He told Mom he was going to kill Glenda and me with his pistol.

Kind of ironic that Leonard's plan was to kill Glenda and me with the gun that I had planned to kill him with.

Fortunately, neither one of us successfully executed the plan, but Leonard tried. I believe God directed Glenda and me to be at the exact spot where Leonard could not see us but we could hear him.

Mom had gone to the front porch as she saw Leonard there. The normal entrance to the house was through the kitchen door on the side of the house, which was close to where we parked the car. Since Leonard had not seen Glenda or me, he returned into the house through the front door. I presume he was going to welcome us (with a bang) at the kitchen door, either assuming we would be in the house or coming in there. Instead, Glenda and I ran straight ahead in front of the house and jumped into the ditch full of grass and weeds by the gravel road. We lay down in the ditch, hoping Leonard would not see us as darkness continued to settle in.

Leonard came out of the kitchen door with his pistol, looking for us. We remained motionless. When we decided Leonard was going away from us, we crawled on our bellies in the ditch to get away.

Most of Leonard's fighting was with Mom. He had threatened to kill her often and had nearly done so many times. I do not remember Leonard ever threatening to kill with a gun before, but in his drunken rage, we did not question his sincerity. I suppose he thought killing his stepchildren would hurt our mom. Not to mention he did not care for either of us. A liquor-crazed mind is a terrible waste and a great danger. The ditch we were in was opposite of the direction of Grandma's house. The ditch afforded some protection from sight or gunfire if Leonard detected us getting away.

After crawling far enough, we felt Leonard could not see us in the settling darkness; we stood and ran to neighbors, Walt and Zola, who lived over a quarter mile away.

Walt was a first cousin to my mom, and I have always thought of him as being the hardest-working man I have ever known. He milked a large herd of cows his entire adult life. For many years, he milked by hand. Once when I was a younger kid, I was running by him and he reached out and grabbed me by the shoulder; I realized his hands were like a vise. Fortunately, Walt was good-natured and was one of those good, hardworking farmer types. Likewise, his wife Zola was a hardworking, kind soul as well. Glenda and I went to their house and explained to Zola that Leonard was in a drunken rage, and he had threatened to kill us. Walt was still milking. We were not sure what to do, so we asked Zola if she would drive us over to Uncle Harlin's, and she did. She drove a long way around on narrow gravel back roads to avoid driving by Mom and Leonard's house. We thought Leonard might stop her, suspecting we might be with her. Everybody knew everybody's vehicle out in the country at that time.

Upon arrival at Uncle Harlin's, we explained the situation. He already knew some about Leonard's problems with alcohol and his rages. Some time had passed; Uncle Harlin, Glenda, and I were out in the front yard as Mom drove up. She got out of her car and said Leonard was over his rage, and it was okay for us to come home. Glenda had already told me we were not going back, as Leonard would eventually kill one or both of us. She told Mom the same thing and said she should separate from Leonard for safety's sake. Glenda told Mom she would stay with her if she would leave Leonard. I do not know what would have happened if Uncle Harlin had not spoken up. Perhaps I would have gone home with Mom and only God knows how my life would have played out. However, Uncle Harlin spoke up and said he agreed with Glenda. He said, "Snooks, the boy has had enough. Glenda is right. In one of these rages, somebody will not survive."

Mom, of course, was crying. Glenda was begging her to leave Leonard so we could all be together and for safety's sake. I had said little, if anything. Mom finally stated she had two marriages which ended in divorce. She would not have a third. She decided to try to make a go of it with Leonard.

Unfortunately, today divorce is quite common. In southern Missouri during that era, divorce was so uncommon most other kids had never even heard of divorce. There was a social stigma associated with divorce. I experienced many instances of embarrassment because of my parents' divorce. Often, kids my age would ask why I had a different last name than my mom.

Mom had already lost the chance to raise her first daughter. Now she was leaving her only son.

I certainly looked up to Uncle Harlin as an authority figure in my life. I desperately did not want to go back to being under Leonard's authority. Of course, I did not want to leave my mom and two younger sisters at home. I debated whether to go back and assist with damage control as best I could.

I had to make a choice. I agreed with Uncle Harlin and settled it in my mind that I'd had enough. I had no idea where or how I would live, but the nightmare with Leonard would end for me that night.

I have only recorded a handful of the incidents with Leonard and the misery of living with an abusive drunk. Physically, I had survived fairly well—other than some brain cells being rearranged and whatever impact stress, fear, hatred, and bitterness brings on the human body and soul. My mom loved me, and I loved her, but this was my opportunity to leave Leonard. I would not pass it up.

I did not really understand my mom's position. To forsake two of her children and go back to a man who had nearly beaten her to death so many times certainly made no sense. Today I can appreciate her desire to save her third marriage. I am not implying that risking physical harm is wise, and no woman should put up with the physical abuse my mom did. However, she had a plan to give her third marriage one last chance. In response to Glenda's plea for her to leave Leonard, Mom replied once that wherever we would go, Leonard would find us and kill all of us. I am sure fear played a major role and was likely the major reason she had not left Leonard.

However, Mom would soon make a stand, and God was merciful, as I will explain.

Like a Bird Out of Prison

Until writing this story, I had only told a few people that I left home when fourteen years old. Now I am writing a book about leaving home. I certainly would not recommend such actions for the norm, and I have always felt perhaps I did something wrong. As I remember, my mom did not command me to come home. I believe she understood my decision and even supported it, although it hurt her deeply to lose another one of her children. The Bible is clear that, as a general rule, children are to obey their parents. The gray area comes with an abusive stepparent. Is a great-uncle sufficient authority?

My leaving home would lead to a major change in my mother's life, and it was for the better. While she made her choice to do all she could to save her third marriage, she drew a line in the sand. Mom laid the law down to Leonard. She told him I was not coming back, and that made two children she had lost because of his drunkenness and temper rages. She also informed him that enough people knew of his behavior that she would win custody of their two daughters in a court of law, if it came to that.

Leonard was a master at trying to generate the perception of being the perfect husband/parent, but Mom promised she would get a restraining order against him, and he would never see his daughters again. Leonard loved his daughters. However, I would have never believed in a million years that he would stop drinking and abusing Mom. Such was the case, though. That's not to say that he did not still have a short temper fuse: Mom's marriage was not always a bed of roses. However, the drunkenness and beatings stopped. Leonard became more responsible. He would eventually volunteer with the Cabool Auxiliary Police. He would serve as an alderman on the Cabool City Council. Leonard would become a respectable dad to his two daughters and a very good grandpa to grandchildren to come, including my children.

Leonard always seemed to have almost superhuman strength. Once again, he did the nearly impossible by simply stopping the drunken rages. If he drank any more, it must not have been much, as the drunken rages and beating Mom stopped.

My dad quit drinking because of his stroke. Glenda's dad was off the wagon more than he was on the wagon for most of his life. However, cold turkey and all, Leonard gave up the bottle. Mom told me that Tennie and Nita cried so much and for so long when they found out I was not coming home that their hurt really troubled Leonard. In fact, Mom said that Leonard even broke down and cried. The girl's crying made him suffer, and Mom thought it was wonderful. Apparently, he had some realization of the damage his drunkenness and temper rages had done to several lives.

Following is a brief statement from Glenda in her own words about life with Leonard and my leaving home.

I still feel in my heart and soul that Leonard's fits would have continued until lives were lost. In his rages, he was the devil reincarnated. You would feel his rages coming on days ahead, knowing he was going to blow! One bad rage that I was present at was when Tennie was a baby in 1960. Leonard had rented a house just off Highway 17 south of Houston. Mom had a huge glass bowl of beans and at least two gallons of milk in glass jugs in the refrigerator when Leonard emptied the entire fridge onto the floor. That time Leonard did not leave. He stayed and saw that Jimmy and I hand waxed the living room hardwood floor (milk had flowed onto it) with paste wax while maintaining his usual Marine Corps manner. Of course, the house was riddled and Mom beaten.

My life would still afford much uncertainty. However, not living in constant fear of death and of Leonard's ridiculous demands, I felt like a bird out of prison. I'll leave it to you to decide if you think my leaving home was wrong. Of course, I still had a heart full of hatred, which would need to be dealt with, but the provisioning hand of God would prove sufficient for that task.

Actually, my troubled childhood would leave many issues in my life to be worked out by God's grace. Despite that, Grandpa Luther showed me life could be enjoyable. More than anyone else, Grandma Tennie taught me a strong work ethic. I had learned a lot about what not to do in life, such as drunkenness, financial irresponsibility, etc. As my childhood left me with some negative issues, my childhood also left me with some advantages and skills as I started life on my own.

I had twenty to thirty dollars in my wallet and the clothes on my back. With a determination to prove Leonard wrong, I was ready to start anew.

I had no idea about the life challenges awaiting me—or the adventures I would find as I commenced my journey down this new road into the next season of my life.

Part II

The Summer of My Life

Summer continues the growth begun in spring. The summer of my life was a time of much growth, and overall, the weather patterns considerably improved for me during this season. Gardeners know plants planted in the springtime will need a lot of attention—cultivation, watering, and weeding. Such nurturing will be required throughout the heat of summer to bring the desired fruit to maturation for a fall harvest. Such was the case for me. God orchestrated many laborers and circumstances to continue my growth through the summer of my life.

8

Free at Last

I could have likely stayed at Uncle Harlin's and traded room and board for farm work, but his farm was in a different school district. Instead, I wound up staying with Aunt Laveta and Uncle Glenn in Mountain Grove, Missouri. Aunt Laveta had moved from Springfield to Mountain Grove, and Uncle Glenn worked at the same milk plant in Cabool that Leonard did. I would ride with Uncle Glenn to the milk plant and walk to school from there.

I had a few awkward encounters with Leonard while waiting for Uncle Glenn to finish work, though we did not really interact with each other when we met. Uncle Glenn was a soft-spoken fellow with a gentle spirit. He was a great comfort to a troubled teen, and we had time to talk as we traveled to and from Cabool. Aunt Laveta and Uncle Glenn did not charge me for staying with them, but there was ample opportunity for me to reward their generosity.

I have already mentioned that Grandma Tennie, Aunt Laveta's mother, was the hardest-working woman I have ever known. However, Aunt Laveta did not inherit her mother's ability to complete a job. While Aunt Laveta had a heart of gold and was always a lot of fun to be around, finishing a job was not her forte. She was a superb cook but left quite a mess behind her in the kitchen. During my stay, I washed a lot of dishes, folded lots of laundry, and helped with any other chores I could, both inside and outside.

We also found time to play the card game of canasta, so it wasn't all work! The truth is, I received enormous help from family and friends during this troubled time in my life. I always tried to do whatever I could to recompense any such generosity. My goal was to earn my room and board by work. The fact that I no longer lived with the uncertainty and dangerous behavior of a man with an alcohol-induced rage left me feeling liberated, as if someone had released me from a prison. Helping out where I could was easy, because my gratitude for the change was so deep. Life was definitely looking up.

$50+

I stayed with Aunt Laveta and Uncle Glenn until the school year was complete, and then another door opened—but I'll get to that in a moment. First, let me tell you a bit about how I earned money the summer after I stayed with Aunt Laveta and Uncle Glenn.

One guy on our football team had several younger brothers, and he had a square-bale hay-hauling business. He needed an extra helper, so I wound up hauling square bales of hay as my primary job for the summer.

The going rate for a hired hand was two cents a bale. When working with the three youngest brothers, I received three cents per bale for additional heavy lifting. However, one hot summer day I wound up in a large field with only the two youngest brothers. Doing most of the heavy lifting would earn me five cents per bale. Fortunately, the bales were not extremely heavy and there were a lot of them.

The youngest brother could drive the flatbed truck. He was short enough he had to peep over the steering wheel, and then he would lose sight as he lowered his body to press the gas pedal. The other brother could drag the bales some, but he could not lift them very much. I'd toss each bale onto the truck bed and run to the next one. The bales would go into a large barn loft, where I would throw the bales from the truck bed into the barn loft and then climb into the loft to stack them. The two brothers could drag the bales around some for me. We began in the morning as soon as possible and worked until almost dark to complete the job. The total bale count for the day was just over a thousand bales, which resulted in what seemed like a giant payday of just over fifty dollars. I thought I had hit the big time.

Hauling hay was hard and dirty work, not to mention the inside of my arms being nearly raw from all the hay scrapes. There was an upside, though, besides making decent money for the time: the hard work was excellent conditioning for playing football.

Of course, baking my brain in many an old hay barn might have been another contributing factor to my failure of not becoming a rocket scientist. Such had always been a childhood dream.

I was even more convinced of the necessity of doing well in school after a hot summer of hauling hay. My goal was to have a high-paying job and prove Leonard wrong about me being a failure. In fact, I was obsessed with doing well in school and spent most of my time studying. I believe God used my studying obsession to keep me out of trouble. I did not want to run with others much as I felt I always needed to be studying. Math has always been my favorite subject, unlike others such as English (as you can likely tell). However, I worked hard on all subjects, as I knew they were all important for success. My mom, having taught in one-room country schools for several years, would annually get textbooks in the mail during the summer. The books were for her to evaluate in hopes she would purchase them for the coming school year. Back when I lived with her, as soon as the books came in and Leonard was not around, I would start doing the math books and then grade my work, as the answers also came with the books. I did not do so with any other subjects.

I have still maintained my love of math, but my obsession with proving Leonard wrong did not survive nearly as long—and we'll get to that in due time.

Sis and Bub

After living with Uncle Glenn and Aunt Laveta, I found refuge in the home of my sister.

Glenda and I had different dads, but both of us were born into troubled homes. We both weathered the fallout from divorce and the repercussions of a drunken father/stepfather. We entered the world in similar circumstances, and we could have easily exited this world together.

We both knew the social stigma of divorce during a time when that stigma was rare. We both partook in the refuge of country living with our mom's parents. Each of us recognizes how much we owe to that refuge. Without it, our lives would almost certainly not have played out for the better. We had been through a lot together. So, I guess it was appropriate for us to team up once again.

Glenda had met the man of her dreams, another Jim, about a year earlier, and they had married the previous fall. Her Jim has proven to be a gem of a catch, as he is an all-around good guy. Right after their marriage, the Marines drafted Jim and deployed him on a Mediterranean tour. After the tour, Jim and Glenda purchased a mobile home to park in Cabool before Jim left for Vietnam for a year. I moved in with Glenda when her Jim left for Vietnam.

Hopefully, living with me was better for my sister than living alone would have been. Not only were we not living alone, we were not living with an abusive drunk. Glenda is a character, thus we were never bored. Life was, once again, definitely looking up. Glenda worked at the hospital in Houston. I continued in high school, playing football and doing whatever work I could find to pay my own expenses.

But with Jim in Vietnam, underneath all the fun we had together, Glenda and I were living on pins and needles.

No Greater Love

Jim was not the only man in our family to get caught up in the maelstrom that was the conflict in Vietnam.

I mentioned earlier that Leonard had a son, Lyle Holloway, from a previous marriage. Lyle and I were stepbrothers. In the times I was around him, he always showed himself to be of good character, yet I never saw Leonard making any great effort to be much of a dad to his biological son. While writing this section, I checked with Mom to see if her perception was the same as mine, and she agreed totally with me.

Leonard and Lyle did not seem to have a lot in common. Lyle was quiet and well-mannered. I do not believe he had Leonard's extraordinary physical strength. In fact, Lyle seemed to be more like me than like Leonard. Lyle was eight years older than me. I did not see him a lot, but when he turned sixteen and got his driver's license, he would occasionally come to see us. I am guessing he was reaching out to his dad, as I believe most sons naturally desire such a relationship. He was my only big brother figure. I loved when we went to town and got sodas. While Lyle and I were not blood relatives, we had some common bonds. We were both trying to find our way through life without an earthly father figure. Leonard was a common denominator for both of us but was not fulfilling a father-figure role to either of us. We both knew the heartache of a broken home.

After high school, Lyle married, and eventually wound up in the army. In his first tour of duty, Lyle's station was at Fort Neely in Alaska, allowing his wife to go with him. He would complete his first tour of duty. Later, Lyle reenlisted, and the army sent him to Vietnam.

Thanks to a write-up by Army Sgt. Peter Brusyo Jr,[1] I learned something of what happened to Lyle there. Additionally, a special thanks to Peter Brusyo for his service and sacrifice in Vietnam and to his family for granting permission to share some of Peter's story.

Sgt. Brusyo was returning to base camp after a week in the jungle, when he and his fellow soldiers were fired upon by the Vietcong. Sgt. Brusyo was hit in the hip and in the back of the head. He was down for the count, when someone started crawling towards him to render aid, even though the fight was still raging.

The medic made it to Sgt. Brusyo, but as he began to try to help, the medic was almost immediately killed by Vietcong gunfire.

It took Sgt. Brusyo and his family some time to identify the man who died trying to help him.

It was Lyle Holloway.

Sgt. Brusyo quotes a Bible verse at the beginning of his account: John 15:13. I agree that it's an appropriate verse—it

---

[1] "Veteran's legacy: Vietnam Vet honors two soldiers who fell in Phu Loi Provence," VA News, U.S. Department of Veterans Affairs, August 17, 2017, https://www.blogs.va.gov/VAntage/40242/veterans-legacy-vietnam-vet-honors-two-soldiers-who-fell-in-phu-loi-provence/.

says that greater love has no man than he who lays down his life for his friends.

Lyle not only gave his life for his fallen soldiers and for his country, he laid it down for his family. While Lyle and his wife were at Fort Neely, they were exposed to radiation because the fort had a nuclear reactor. Note, nuclear power was a fairly new technology at the time and safety measures were sorely lacking. Lyle was told the radiation was most dangerous to a child within the womb. Sure enough, Lyle and his wife conceived a child while at Fort Neely, and after completing his first tour of duty, Lyle and his wife had a baby with a major medical condition. Their child's condition would require many surgeries and, of course, considerable expense. Lyle did not plan to reenlist in the army, but there were few good-paying jobs with medical insurance available in southern Missouri, where Lyle lived. Lyle reenlisted so his daughter would receive the needed medical care through military benefits.

Lyle knew that reenlisting would likely lead to a Vietnam tour. Perhaps the lack of a good father figure in Lyle's life planted in him the desire to be the father he never had and to give all for his daughter. Lyle was a great father, a great stepbrother, a great American, and, most of all, Lyle is a hero.

Receiving the Best Free Gift

I am going to back up a bit in my life story, as an important event in my life occurred prior to this time. However, that event ties in to Lyle's story of sacrifice—in fact, that event connected me to the story of the greatest sacrifice of all time.

Until I was about ten years old, I had not really spent any time with my dad or his family. However, when I was that age, Grandma Kissock started taking me to spend a couple of weeks with them during the summer. I usually had a good time as

Grandma Kissock liked to fish and we would go on a fishing trip or two.

While Grandma Kissock was a character, she also had some character flaws. Divorce has many ugly sides, and one is the tug-of-war in which one side of the marriage tries to win favor over the other side by berating the other party. Mom's side of my family never really berated my dad much other than to acknowledge he had a major drinking problem.

Such was not the case with Grandma Kissock: she always tried to justify my dad. Grandma Kissock made some subtle and often not-so-subtle insinuations that my mom was more to blame for their failed marriage than my dad was.

I was old enough to know that I had zero good memories of my dad. Even though my mom made some poor choices in life, I knew she had always tried to be a good mother to me. In fact, my dad and Leonard had beaten her up more than once while she tried to defend me. So, Grandma Kissock made no progress in winning my favoritism over to my dad. I did not hate my dad like I hated Leonard, but I certainly had no fondness for him either.

Grandma Kissock's widowhood forced her to make a living on her own at a fairly early age. In terms of working, she was of the same mold as Grandma Tennie. Specifically, she owned and operated several small cafés over many years. Despite not becoming rich, Grandma Kissock made a decent living through hard work and long hours. Her day started at 4 a.m., when she would arrive at her café to prepare for the early breakfast crowd and to make homemade pies. She usually closed by 6 p.m. but then had to get supplies for the next day. Her only day off was Sunday. When visiting, I would work in her café. I mainly waited tables and washed dishes. I really enjoyed the work. Grandma Kissock was quite a cutup and loved joking with her customers. She was outgoing, like Grandpa Luther.

One summer while visiting Grandma Kissock, I attended a revival meeting at her church, where I heard the gospel clearly preached. The gospel of Jesus Christ is declared in 1 Corinthians 15:1-4:

> Moreover, brethren, I declare unto you the gospel which I preached unto you, which also ye have received, and wherein ye stand; By which also ye are saved, if ye keep in memory what I preached unto you, unless ye have believed in vain. For I delivered unto you first of all that which I also received, how that Christ died for our sins according to the scriptures; And that he was buried, and that he rose again the third day, according to the scriptures.

Paul declares in the first verse that the Corinthians had received the gospel he had preached to them and that it was "wherein ye stand." We cannot receive the gospel by just mentally acknowledging it. Receiving the gospel requires a decision, a change of mind, a change of heart, a change of commitment from trusting anything else to trusting in Jesus to get to heaven. To receive the gospel is to stand firmly in the belief of what Jesus did in his death, burial, and resurrection as our only hope of eternal life.

The revival meeting lasted for several days. I did not make any decision in the first few services. The evangelist was preaching about the cross of Calvary and the blood the Son of God shed for mankind. The Scriptures declare, "For the preaching of the cross is to them that perish foolishness; but unto us which are saved it is the power of God" (1 Corinthians 1:18). Near the end of the week, I trusted in what Jesus did for me on that cross as payment for my sin debt and received the free gift of eternal life. I trusted his shed blood was sufficient for me to be forgiven of all my sins. I stand firmly in my belief that Jesus died on an old rugged cross for me and then arose from the grave and gives eternal life to all who will receive that free gift. As I said earlier, God is a Father to the fatherless, but God wants to be a Father to all.

The Bible declares we are all sinners and the wages of sin is eternal death. "For the wages of sin is death; but the gift of God is eternal life through Jesus Christ our Lord" (Romans 6:23). Eternal death is separation from God in the lake of fire, prepared for the devil and his followers. God declares how much he loves us in John 3:16: "For God so loved the world, that he gave his only begotten Son, that whosoever believeth in him should not perish, but have everlasting life." For all who receive by faith the good news of the gift of God will receive eternal life through Jesus Christ the Lord. "For by grace are ye saved through faith; and that not of yourselves: it is the gift of God: not of works, lest any man should boast" (Ephesians 2:8–9).

The key part is receiving what God has done for all mankind. If I had a free gift for you, the reader of this story, and you never received that gift, then it would be of no benefit to you. Jesus came to seek and to save the lost. We cannot receive salvation unless we recognize ourselves as sinners in need of forgiveness. Jesus is the way, the truth, and the life. We could trust in many things, but the only way to heaven is the way of Jesus. Many people seem good in the eyes of man. However, none of us are good enough in the eyes of God to make it to heaven without our sins being cleansed by the blood of Jesus. Likewise, many people seem bad in the eyes of man. Yet, none are too bad to make it to heaven if their sins are cleansed by the blood of Jesus. God's mercy is more boundless than the sea, and he will receive you by grace if you will receive him by faith. As the old hymn declares, "What can wash away my sin? Nothing but the blood of Jesus." Death is required for our sins, and Jesus died for us by the shedding of his blood. "In whom we have redemption through his blood, even the forgiveness of sins"

(Colossians 1:14). His death included the punishment and payment for all of man's sins, including yours and mine. There are no good works that can justify us. Getting to heaven is not based on what we can do but rather on what Jesus has done for us.

Let's suppose there is a free cure for cancer and you have terminal cancer. For whatever reason, you do not receive or use the free cure for cancer and die from that cancer. In this analogy, the cancer cure is only beneficial for those who receive the cure. Such is the case with Christ's shed blood or the message of the gospel. His shed blood is sufficient to forgive all of mankind's sins, but it is only of benefit to those who receive (by faith) God's free gift of eternal life.

As Lyle stepped into the fray, reaching out to save others out of love, Jesus reached out to save us. Only Jesus did not have to step into the world, into its grief and pain and violence. No one drafted him; no one forced him. Lyle's love, as great as it was, is only an echo of the great love of God, who poured himself out, suffering infinite pain, in order to redeem whosoever in faith shall call upon the name of the Lord.

After dying for us on the cross, in three days, Christ arose from the grave with victory over death and the grave. If we will receive by grace through faith what Jesus did for us on the cross, the Bible declares we shall receive the gift of God, which is eternal life through Jesus Christ our Lord. Salvation is of the Lord, as he has done everything for us. However, we have a part, which is the part of receiving or trusting Jesus as Lord and Savior. God's will is not for any to perish. Note, in order to receive eternal life, one must genuinely believe in their heart that Jesus died on the cross and shed his blood for their sins, and that he lives today, waiting for each soul to trust him as the only way to heaven. "That if thou shalt confess with thy mouth the Lord Jesus, and shalt believe in thine heart that God hath raised him from the dead, thou shalt be saved. For with the heart man believeth unto righteousness; and with the mouth confession is made unto salvation" (Romans 10:9–10).

If you, the reader of this story, have never received God's free gift of salvation, God is waiting for you to do so. God declares that today is the day of salvation. We have no promise of tomorrow. If you miss heaven, it will not be God's fault. God has done everything needed for a lost sinner to become a child of God. Receiving the free gift of eternal life is up to you. If you, the reader of my story, have not received the gift of eternal life, please do so right now! Receive and firmly stand in the gospel by turning from any other way than Jesus. "For whosoever shall call upon the name of the Lord shall be saved" (Romans 10:13). Call upon Jesus in prayer, confess your sins, ask for his forgiveness, and he will save you. Calling out is confessing what we believe in our heart about Jesus. Note, churches, religion, self-righteousness, baptism, good works, fame, fortune, or intellect cannot cleanse a sin-sick soul. There is no other way to receive eternal life than by trusting in what Jesus did for us on the cross. Commit yourself to following him.

After you have done this, I encourage you to find a good, Bible-believing church, so you can have company and help on this road of walking with God. We are meant to make this earthly journey with the brethren of God's children.

I will close this section with a song God gave me about Calvary, the place where Jesus was crucified. Spiritually speaking, Calvary is the place to receive the free gift of eternal life. If you, the reader, do not know the reality of Calvary, I trust you will make Calvary a reality right now.

The Reality of Calvary

Verse 1:
The reality of Calvary – Became so clear to me
When I found the remedy – For my sin-sick soul's need
His blood shed there so freely – Wrought so great a victory
All because of Calvary – Now in that cross I glory

Chorus:
The reality of Calvary – Is known by all who truly believe
For all whose sins – Have been cleansed
Know the Savior so sweet – Who was led like a sheep
To his slaughter on that tree – For mankind's iniquity
How I love that old, old story – And the reality of Calvary

Verse 2
For whosoever shall call upon – Jesus, the only one
Who has the power to forgive – And make the dead to live
The way, the truth, and the life – All other ways are a lie
For all must come through Christ's blood – Grace sufficient and enough

(Chorus Repeats)

9

From the Hayfield to the Factory

Glenda and I made it through the school year together, and my brother-in-law Jim made it through his tour in Vietnam. When he came back home, I moved to Springfield, Missouri, because Uncle Thurman lived there and he had offered to let me spend the summer with him. Thurman had completed his PhD in childhood education (he taught fifth grade) and had a house with a large yard and garden.

Jobs seemed to be plentiful in the area. That summer, I ended up working at a factory which made large oil filters. Part of my deal with Uncle Thurman was that I would help with house repairs, lawn, and garden work around his place, which I did—and enjoyed. I guess Grandma Tennie instilled in me the love of gardening, as I have gardened most of my life. While staying at Uncle Thurman's, I paid my own expenses, which was not a problem as I started my factory work at what was minimum wage at the time: $1.50/hour.

An elderly lady owned and operated the factory. She had taken over the company after her husband passed away. She soon found out I was a hard worker, and she rewarded me with lots of work. I enjoyed the hard work and learned a lot. Often on Saturdays, the owner paid me to do chores at her personal residence. I wound up working at this factory off and on for a couple of years and wore many hats. I was to open the factory up in the morning, monitor inventory, order supplies, receive supplies, ship products, make filters on the assembly line, clean the offices, burn the trash, and then lock the factory up. They appreciated my hard work. Most of the hires only did enough to avoid being fired. Of course, I had extra incentive as I was paying my own expenses.

I was also trying to save money for college and trying to prove to Leonard Holloway that I would not be a dismal failure.

The factory proved to be another environment which reinforced my commitment to school. Insulation was lacking in the metal Quonset hut building, causing it to be hot in the summer. Some products shipped in boxes that weighed over two hundred pounds. I could barely manhandle them onto the trucks—but once again, it was great conditioning for playing football.

Another Open Door

Though my brother-in-law Jim had safely returned from Vietnam, he still had another year to serve, and he would be stationed at Camp Pendleton in California, which meant that Glenda could go with him. Thus, their mobile home would be vacant. I wound up living there my junior year in high school.

The man who owned the trailer court was reluctant to have a sixteen-year-old renter, given the potential for partying. Glenda, who went to high school with him, convinced him I was a nerd and would probably study all the time. He reluctantly agreed. I had a lot of time to study and played my guitar a lot. Also, I paid my rent and utilities on time.

I continued to play football, which required a lot of time. Also, I worked at a grocery store, helped to haul milk, and took on any other work I could find. However, I had a rather limited income, so I had to live frugally. I would eat based upon how much money I had left over after paying other expenses, and most of the time, there was not much left over. Eggs were cheap, so I ate a lot of them. I remember around Christmas I splurged and bought a small, precooked meatloaf at the grocery store I worked at. Meatloaf is a favorite of mine. I stretched that small meatloaf out for quite a while and savored every morsel. I could not afford a car, so I walked everywhere I went.

'Enty-'ive

I had a tooth which had been aching for quite a while, so I decided to have it pulled. I was at school and went by the office to tell them I was going to the dentist during my lunch break. My goal was to be back in time for my next class. I walked to our town dentist, Dr. Dale. Fortunately, I got right in.

My dad's only brother, Alton Kissock, once had a toothache and pulled the tooth himself. He accomplished his objective but was drunk while performing the extraction. Since I was a teetotaler, that was not a viable option for me. At least that spared me from the obvious potential problem with inebriated tooth extraction: the distinct possibility of removing the wrong tooth. But it didn't solve the problem of money, which I didn't have much of.

I asked Dr. Dale if he would pull my tooth for twenty-five dollars, as that was all the money I had. He said yes, but the tooth X-ray and painkiller would come at an extra charge. I suggested skipping the X-ray and painkiller because I only had twenty-five dollars. He wanted to make sure I was certain about that. I confirmed I was, as I had no other option. We agreed the aching tooth would come out for twenty-five dollars.

Dr. Dale was a good-sized man. He certainly appeared to have plenty of strength to pull a tooth. Dr. Dale locked on to my tooth with his extraction tool and pulled for quite some time, to no avail. He indicated this might not go how we were both hoping it would. I kept reminding him of our agreement. He locked on my tooth again and pulled even harder.

Suddenly I heard a loud snap, profanity, and felt pain. My tooth had broken off. Dr. Dale said he would have to cut the tooth out and I would have to have a painkiller. He was poking around in my mouth while I was uttering "'enty-'ive" over and over. I was insistent on reminding him of our agreement. He conceded he would get it out and I would only pay for what we had agreed upon.

The tooth had a root that went down to my jawbone. He said with teeth like that, I should be a boxer. Maybe Leonard's direction for my life was right after all. After cutting the tooth out, Dr. Dale asked how I would get home. I told him I would walk. He said I could not walk as I might start bleeding, so the office phoned Uncle Herman. He now lived in Cabool. Once again, his wife, Aunt Jackie, came to my rescue and took care of me for the night.

In a Milk Shower

With rent, utilities, food, school, clothing, dental, and life expenses, I had to keep earning money any way I could. My brother-in-law Jim came from a large family. Johnny was his next youngest brother. Johnny hauled milk in cans for farmers and hired me to help him with his milk route on weekends. I am uncertain how much of his offer was prompted by a desire to help me or how much he was prompted by his actual need for help.

He had a large box truck to haul the heavy milk cans. As we would pick up the cans with milk, we would leave empty, clean cans for the next milking. The bottom of the box truck's bed was close to head height for me. It was a bit of a feat to get a ninety-pound can of milk into the truck. The milk can lid was just held in by friction but rarely came out. Milk would occasionally spill out when we tipped a can while loading the truck.

I have had the pleasure of working some jobs where I had someone to cut up with and have a good time with while working, and this job with Johnny was definitely one of those. We enjoyed making up silly songs and wisecracks while traveling between farms. However, we worked as fast as we could to get the milk picked up and the empty cans delivered. Yet another great football-conditioning activity! I needed the extra income, and I had a great time hauling milk, other than the occasional milk shower.

Yes, sometimes I got soaked in milk, but it was still better than the hours I spent cleaning up milk on my knees due to the alcohol-induced rage of my stepfather. That was needless suffering that I had no choice about going through; this was profitable labor that I chose for myself.

Sometimes I would go home with Johnny, which was always a real blast, as there was always a game going on with his large family. If not basketball or softball, there would likely be a game of Monopoly. Interacting with his family would impact a later decision I'll write more about. Johnny was one of many to lend a helping hand and be a positive influence in my life.

10

An Ever-So-Slim Chance

By all rights, I should not have been playing football, as it paid no money. Football practice and games took a lot of time that I could have spent working for money. Note, I had no other income or financial help other than what I earned. However, there was a big event that would take place during my junior year in high school: 1968 would be the first year Missouri high school teams would play for a state championship in football.

In my sophomore year, I played defensive end for most of the varsity games. I felt confident I would be the starting defensive end for my junior year for the varsity team, and that turned out to be the case. We had a good team, as most of the players were returning from the prior year with varsity experience.

Coach Seals had also done a good job the prior year of convincing us we could win the first Class 2A State Championship. The formula was quite simple: we just needed to win all of our games.

We began the season with great optimism. We were in good physical condition and knew how to execute the playbook. But then a not-so-funny event happened on our way to a state championship. We won our first game handily. Our second game was against Salem. They were a larger school than Cabool. However, that was of little concern, as Cabool seemed to always beat Salem in football. Of course, we had to play the game to see who would actually win … and that year Salem beat us in a close game.

Were we overconfident? Were we just not that good of a team? Was Salem just really good? After only two games, our team experienced disappointment as we realized our chance of a state championship was not good.

We were anxious about Coach's mood at the first practice after the loss. He had us all assemble for a meeting before the practice, and, to our surprise, Coach was all smiles. He said he had been running numbers and there was an ever-so-slim chance we could squeak into the playoffs. Each game would earn each team a certain number of points. If a smaller school beat a larger school, they would get more points than they would winning against a school of the same size or smaller. Winning with a greater point spread resulted in more points. Since we played some schools larger than us, Coach thought we had a slight chance of making the playoffs. We could not lose another game, and we would need to win some games with a large point spread. The odds were not good, but we were going to practice and play like we were going to win it all. After the regular season, the four teams with the most points from each class would play for the state championship for each class.

That season turned out to be a season to remember. I will share about a few games that stand out in my mind and about some lessons I learned from the old pigskin.

This Is It!

We thoroughly tested our resolve to win the very next week. We played West Plains, which was a larger school than ours. Their players were physically much larger than the players on our team.

The game became a defensive battle. They had little success moving the ball on us, and we had little success moving the ball on them. We were late in the fourth quarter and getting ready to receive a kickoff, as West Plains had just taken the lead 7-6. There was not much time on the clock, and we knew our odds of making an offensive drive were not good. We huddled to call a return play.

Normally, only the person calling the play would talk while in the huddle. However, in this huddle, everybody started talking at the same time, and we were all saying the same thing: "This is it!" We had to return the ball all the way as there was not enough time to make a drive. We had to win this game to have any hope of making the playoffs.

The return play which was called involved building a straight line of blockers in front of the returner. Being an end, I lined up on one side of the field. West Plains kicked the ball to the other side of the field. I was supposed to cross the field and make the first block in front of the returner. I was sprinting as fast as I could, and the other team had two speedsters running side by side to make the tackle.

Jumping into a body block, I took out the first two guys as the returner caught the ball. I wound up on the ground upside down and, from that angle, saw our team knocking the other team's players down like dominoes.

Our returner ran straight down the sideline all the way to the house for a game-winning touchdown.

Physical skills are a big part of football. The ability to execute plays is obviously required. However, sometimes the team who wants the win the most is going to win. I believe such was the case in this game. By all indications, the team we played may have been better than our team, but our resolve to win was the factor that made the difference.

The Slush Bowl!

We were playing Mountain Grove, which was just up the road from Cabool. This was our last regular-season game, and we had won all our games except for that early loss to Salem. The playoff points were too close to allow us to predict if we would make the top four. The only thing we knew was we had to beat Mountain Grove, or we had no chance at all.

However, the game was going to be difficult as the weather was terrible. We had heavy rain during the day. Before the game, the rain turned to sleet as the temperature was dropping fast. The football field was in terrible condition and had many large puddles of water, which were now an icy slush. Any ground contact was into freezing ice water. The wind was extremely strong and gusty. After the game started, the sleet turned to snow and eventually covered the ground except for the puddles of slush.

This was the coldest event in my life. I played both offense and defense in this game. I also made by far my worst play of the season. Our coach did not believe we should go into the locker room during halftime, as we could save time by staying outside to discuss halftime adjustments. I am guessing everybody on the team thought we would surely go in given the bitter cold. All the players were soaking wet with ice water, and the wintry wind gusts were literally freezing. However, Coach had us go to the far end of the field during the halftime, as opposed to going into the warm locker room.

During the second-half kickoff, I lined up on the far end of the field, opposite our team's side. As our kicker ran up to kick the ball, the football blew off the tee. He had to try again. This happened a couple more times. Someone had to hold the football down to get the kickoff made. Somehow, I had kind of gone into a frozen trance while waiting for the kickoff.

Suddenly, everyone was at the far end of the field and our defense was already lining up. I immediately sprinted down the field to get into position. I expected to be pulled for such a mess-up. However, I heard nothing about it. Perhaps the snow was heavy enough that our coach never noticed.

The good news was that we won the game.

The even better news is that after we won, we were allowed to get back onto the school bus and enjoy whatever heat we could soak up.

By the Skin of Our Teeth!

We took the fourth position of the Class 2A playoffs by the thinnest of margins. We were just a few hundredths of a point ahead of the fifth-place team, but we were in.

Since we were the number four seed, we played the number one seed. We were fairly confident, as we had played some schools larger than us and had made the playoffs despite one loss.

The number one seed was South Shelby, and they got the ball to start the game. Football is a game of momentum. South Shelby got the ball to start with, and they were marching right down the field. We were kind of flat-footed on defense and did not seem to be playing well at all.

Fortunately for us, South Shelby fumbled the football before scoring. I was the closest to the ball and pounced on it but could only get one hand on the ball. There were many other hands on the ball as well, but I was on top of it. Everyone was pulling for the ball, trying to be the owner.

It seemed like it took forever for the pile to clear, but finally I heard, "Number 80, get up, you have the ball."

I was number 80.

We played better after that and controlled most of the game after the turnover. However, South Shelby tied the game late and forced an overtime. We won in the overtime, and now we were down to one game left.

For the Team and for Our Coach

The next week, we faced Seneca for the state championship. We had started this journey back in August. Now we were in late November. We had survived the heat of summer and the freezing of winter. Now we needed to complete our journey with one more win.

Everyone on the team, I hope, had learned a major lesson about not giving up. Our championship prospects appeared bleak after the second-game defeat early in the season. However, Coach Seals never gave up, and he convinced us to fight on. He often told our team that when your back is against the wall, that's when you should fight all the harder. That lesson has carried on in my life, as I have a tenacity that makes me not want to concede on anything. I have met failure many times in life, but never without a good fight.

As a defensive end, I typically had blockers trying to keep me from making a tackle, but I learned to never give up on making a play. Many times, I made ankle or even shoestring tackles, as I'd learned to fight adversity and never give up.

I mentioned earlier that football is a team sport, and that lesson has been an enormous blessing in my life. I was not a big fan of everyone on our team, but when we were on the field, I was 100 percent behind every player. Coach always said we were all for one and one for all. The goal of the team was more important than my personal preferences.

I would later join the United States Air Force; much of military training is about being a team. Most of my adult working life has been in the corporate world, and I found trying to be a good team member was still important there. In fact, I had a boss who once told me I needed to promote myself more in order to get ahead. Note, my boss was trying to be helpful. I told him I was a believer in our team and had no problem promoting others in our team before promoting myself. From family life to church life, it all works better with a team approach. If you find a problem, tackle it as best you can, but having a good team around you is never a bad thing.

The Saturday of the big game came, and it was slightly cool, but not freezing. The game turned out to be a defensive battle. Both teams had turnovers and penalties. Both teams made some hard defensive hits. At halftime, neither team had scored. Our coach had always told us no one was a superstar on our team.

Everyone is important on a team—that's true—but, in reality, the quarterback on our team was a better athlete than anyone else. In the third quarter, he ran through a left side hole. Cutting sharply to the right, he scored a touchdown in an open field. We missed the extra point, but six points were all we needed. We went on to win the game 6-0. Both teams played a hard-fought defensive battle, but we were the ones who came out on top.

Coach was right about keeping up the fight and never giving up.

Life Lessons from Football

The state championship possibly held greater value to me than to some team members. Through it, I saw that a scrawny kid from a dysfunctional family could be part of something successful.

I learned many lessons from Coach Seals. He had many sayings, such as, "Winning without honor is not winning at all."

He coached us to play by the rules. We always had team prayer before every game and prayed for an injury-free game. Coach instructed us to hit hard as long as it was legal. In fact, Coach's last words after his pregame talk were usually something like this: "I saw the other team get off the bus. They looked big and strong, but you guys are a lot faster and a lot uglier, so get out there and knock somebody on their butt!" We often heard, "The bigger they are, the harder they fall." I am uncertain how true that is, but it seemed most of the time we were playing teams who were physically a lot bigger than our team.

Earlier, I mentioned my secret weapon when playing football. Football is such a unique sport; it is hard to quantify all the various aspects of the game. Much of my enthusiasm for success was to prove Leonard wrong about me being a dismal failure and not being tough. My heart was full of hatred for the man who had beaten my mother so many times and made my life so miserable. I had little trouble psyching myself up, as every ball carrier in my mind's eye became Leonard Holloway to me. I had the good pleasure of knocking the "you know what" out of them. That gave me an extra edge when fighting off blockers and putting a hit on someone.

After the season was over, we had a banquet for the football team and every member got a small trophy. Coach told a story about everyone as he gave them their trophy.

Coach told my story from the time we beat Houston, our biggest rival. Coach said after the game, the Houston coach was slow making it to midfield for the traditional handshake, but he finally arrived. With a smile, our coach stretched out his hand and told the Houston coach his team played a good game, and that we were fortunate to win. Houston's coach only responded with, "Number 80 killed us tonight. We double-teamed and triple-teamed him, and he still made tackles. Standing, falling down, or on the ground, he still stopped us."

I had an extra motivator not everyone on the field had. Additionally, I really bought into the concept of not quitting or giving up on a play. Even when on the ground, I was looking for an ankle or shoestring to get ahold of. If I did, the ball carrier was not going far. Milking cows and other hard work had given me a really good grip.

Eternal Lessons from Coach

Coach knew some about my personal life and that I was living on my own. He referred many odd job calls, such as raking leaves, to me. However, Coach was concerned with more than my physical life. I went to church with him several times. He would invite me to go to church with him by catching me after a Friday or Saturday night game and then extend an invitation with a rather gruff voice: "9 a.m.—be ready!" I knew what the invitation was about.

He attended a little country church that was in the middle of the sticks. The preacher was old. Several country folk attended that small church. The church did not have many to sing special music, and so Coach would often sing. He was a better coach than a singer, but his specials were as touching as any I have ever heard. He often sang the old hymn "I Need No Mansion Here Below." While sometimes just slightly off-key, he would sing from his heart and tears would flow down his big cheeks. Coach was a great encouragement and example in my life.

Years later, I was married with several children when I got a phone call about Coach Seals. Cabool was having a get-together for our football team, and Coach Seals would be there. I learned Coach Seals had cancer. He was not expected to live long. At the get-together, I expressed my gratitude to Coach for being a blessing in my life. Of course, he didn't want any credit, but I gave credit where credit was due.

He did not live long after that. I believe Coach is now singing with a glorified voice before the throne of grace.

Football and Coach Seals were such an important part of my life that God gave me a song about the experience:

That Old Pigskin

Verse 1:

I was just a teenage boy – When the football coach talked to me
Son, of course it's your choice – Why don't you try out for the team
Life had been a rocky road – So much I did not know
But I'd learn so much more – Than the sport I tried out for
Now I can see Coach's game plan – Was to help me to be a Christian man

Chorus:

Winning without honor – Is not winning at all
The bigger they are – The harder they fall
This team has no star – We're all for one and one for all
Fight all the harder – When your back's against the wall
I learned many a lesson – From that old pigskin
But what I learned the most – Was from a godly coach
From the playbook of life – Coach called John three sixteen
Believing on Jesus Christ – Put me on the winning team

Verse 2:

Now looking back through the years – I still think of that football field
Through all the blood, sweat, and tears – The lessons learned still are real
Coach has gone on to heaven – I'm sure there's other men
Who owe so much to him – For lessons from that pigskin
The witness of a godly coach – Whose life for Jesus Christ taught me the most

(Chorus Repeats)

——∞——

11

Back to the Factory

I completed my junior year in high school in Cabool about the time Glenda and Jim returned from California. Jim had honorably completed his service to our country. I returned to Springfield, staying with Uncle Thurman, and went back to work at the filter factory, where they welcomed me back. Additionally, I worked most Saturdays for the owner, doing odd jobs at her residence. Of course, I was the general groundskeeper at my uncle's house as well, so there was not a lot of free time. I spent what little free time I had playing my guitar or studying. I always tried to find books on classes that I would take the next semester to get a head start on those classes.

No Way

When August arrived, I had to make a decision. I would have loved to have gone back to Cabool and played football my senior year. Glenda and Jim had moved to Springfield, so I would have had to find another place to live, which would have been more expensive.

I knew in my heart there was no way I could afford to play football and pay my own expenses. That was a hard decision to accept, because they granted football scholarships for college during the senior year. I did not know if they would offer me one, but my goal was to attend the University of Missouri at Rolla, which is an engineering school. They had a football program, and they were not a Division I school. Based on my grades and football background, I thought I might have a better shot at a scholarship. During my sophomore year and my junior year, I started as a defensive end. I was also the starting offensive end for most of my junior year.

However, the reality of finances simply spelled "no way." Most of the time I played varsity football, I was facing upperclassmen. It would have been nice to play those in my same grade.

On the other hand, football is a rough sport, and even back then, I realized my body might be better off avoiding the physical toll football takes.

Still "No Way"

Since I could not afford to go back to Cabool and play football, I decided I would transfer to Springfield to complete high school. Better-paying work in Springfield was more available than it was in Cabool. I had also concluded that small towns were not for me anyway, as they afforded very few well-paying jobs, and my goal was to make a good income.

I did some checking: I only needed three classes to graduate from high school, and I could take all three classes in the morning. At my job, shipping was my responsibility. Since shipping ran late most days, I asked the factory owner if I could work from noon to 8 p.m. The owner was quite pleased with my suggestion. I would work full-time my senior year in high school. My goal was to make enough money for college. I was hoping for a scholarship, but Rolla was a highly ranked engineering school, and I knew there was no guarantee of a free ride. I had ruled out football, even though I thought football might increase my odds of getting a scholarship.

A coach intercepted me in the hallway after my first class on my first day. He introduced himself and wanted to verify I was Jim Kissock. I told him I was. He asked if I played on Cabool's championship team last year. I confirmed I had. He said if I would join the school's football team, I would be a starting defensive end for the game on Friday night.

What an offer! I would get out of all the grueling preseason practices. I was still in football shape, as I was still running and doing calisthenics, not to mention the strenuous work I was doing.

However, I still had to pay my own expenses. As I said earlier, reality was still spelling, "no way." I had to tell the coach that I had gone to a lot of effort to only take three classes, and all of them at the start of my school day. I had obligated myself to work from noon until 8 p.m. There was nothing I could do but thank him for the offer and refuse. He said if I changed my mind to let him know before game time.

The offer was tempting, but I knew reality dictated that I needed to work for income. I was fortunate to have played on a championship team. I would still vigorously pursue my studies and try to save as much as I could for college expenses.

Burning the Midnight Oil

English Literature II was my first class in my senior year, which wasn't my favorite, but things improved afterward. Next, I had Physics, which was followed by Pre-Calculus. On Sunday nights, I would make up enough bologna sandwiches for the entire week. Then I would put them in my uncle's freezer. I was quite the bologna-sandwich aficionado. I certainly don't claim such a diet to have been a wise choice. However, at that point in my life, a good diet was not a top priority.

I would grab a couple of frozen sandwiches to take with me to eat during my commute from school to work at noon. After working until 8 p.m., I would come back to my uncle's house and likely eat another bologna sandwich or a fried-egg sandwich. I would clean up and then study for the next day. Once done studying, I would sleep some and do it all again. My schedule afforded me little sleep.

I completed the school year and graduated. I had almost no interaction with my mom and Leonard after leaving home. However, they attended my high school graduation. Uncle Thurman had invited them.

I had heard Leonard was doing much better, but I was still skeptical and still hated the man. However, seeing them at my graduation helped to break the ice, and they invited me to see the house they'd bought just outside of Cabool. Eventually, I visited some, but not a lot. Leonard seemed to be different, but I was still distrustful. The wounds in my life of his abuse to my mom and me were still open sores. He had made no attempt at apologizing, and I was in no mood for forgiveness.

Too Much Drama for Me

As the school year ended, I would find out about my scholarship results. I was not thrilled, as I received a full scholarship to Drury College in Springfield. My coveted hopes for a Rolla scholarship did not come to fruition. My childhood dream was to be an astronaut—a dream influenced by the space-race era. If not that, then I wanted to be a fighter jet pilot. If not that, then to work for NASA. Being an aerospace engineer would be my next choice, so that I could work with the space program, or at least with aircraft. I am guessing many guys of my age in that era had similar dreams.

Drury was not a bad college. It was known for having an outstanding drama department. I'd experienced a childhood filled with drama. I was definitely not in pursuit of more drama. Of course, I could have chosen one of their other degree options, but Drury had no aerospace engineering degree. I quickly dismissed Drury as an option for me.

Even though they didn't offer me a scholarship, Rolla accepted my application. I expected that I'd have sufficient funds for my freshman year but nothing beyond that. Still, I resolved to pursue my dream of being an aerospace engineer.

Once again, life has so many forks in the road. Had I taken the scholarship in hand for Drury, my life would have likely played out totally differently. I never actualized my dreams of working in the space program, but pursuing my goal of fulfilling that dream would lead to a career that I have no major complaints about.

More Burning the Midnight Oil

I attended church with Uncle Thurman and met a couple, Clarence and Nancy, who would become lifelong friends. Clarence is a character. We hit it off, joking with one another.

Clarence is quite the entrepreneur and exemplifies one of the many reasons I love this country. Clarence came into this world in a family with little wealth. He was born with a hearing problem, which made grade school difficult for him, as he could not clearly hear instruction. Fortunately, his hearing problem was correctable as a child. After correcting his hearing problem, Clarence was behind most of his peers in the public school system. Clarence wasn't an honor student, but he still graduated. However, Clarence had a quality that schools can't teach: God gifted him with the courage to not be afraid to undertake a major challenge and then do the work to be successful.

Clarence took full advantage of America being the land of opportunity. He would start several businesses and was quite successful in all his endeavors. As I finished up my senior year in high school, I was planning on working at the filter factory until I began school at Rolla for the fall semester. However, Clarence was getting his heating and air-conditioning business off the ground. He asked if I could assist him for the summer, as he expected to be very busy and needed help. He offered more money than I was making at the factory. I told him I would talk to my current employer and get back to him. The factory owner didn't want to lose me but couldn't match Clarence's offer. She said she could not risk paying anyone that much, as others in the factory would expect the same. I wound up giving my two weeks' notice and began working with Clarence.

Clarence would be another force in my life for the better. I learned many labor skills from Clarence. He clearly showed how success is achievable for those willing to make the expenditure of simply working diligently. Working with Clarence was a great experience because we had a good time despite the long hours. We both liked to joke and were constantly making wisecracks to one another. His business was booming, as many houses were upgrading to central air-conditioning.

We were swamped with work. Our day began quite early and ended late at night, or maybe early the next day. We did service calls and upgrades to central air-conditioning during the day. We installed systems in houses under construction at nighttime since there was no occupancy. I installed a lot of ductwork during my time with Clarence. The return air duct for a central air-conditioning system often runs through the attic. One of my jobs was to insulate that duct. In the heat of a Missouri summer, those attics were like an oven—possibly yet another reason I never became a rocket scientist. I also spent a lot of time in crawl spaces underneath houses installing duct work.

I learned a lot, which is good, but even better, I had a great time working with Clarence. God was still providing positive influences to build my life. Clarence was more living proof that hard work and diligence were contributing factors to being successful—a lesson I would need as I moved into college and beyond.

12

You're a Miner Now!

Finally, my school days at Rolla arrived. Rolla's mascot is "the Miners," because originally, the school was called the School of Mines and Metallurgy. Currently, the school is the Missouri University of Science and Technology.

I enrolled in aerospace engineering. The dream seemed to be taking shape, but now I had the daunting task of completing the program. The school announced a high percentage of my freshman class would fail by the end of the first and second semesters. I guess that's the way it is at a highly ranked engineering school—graduation is not a participation trophy.

I did not flunk out my freshman year, but some classes were challenging. My grades were not straight As, as I had hoped for, but I was thankful to complete the school year with good grades. Likely, many who flunked out did more partying than studying. Since I was still a staunch teetotaler, there was no partying for me. My aim in studying hard since grade school was to get an education that would allow me to earn a living that wouldn't leave me waking up with snow on the floor beside my bed. I doubt many of the students at Rolla had as intense of a focus as I did. My life had been a mess as I was growing up, and my goal was for my life not to be that same mess now that I was an adult.

Additionally, I was going to prove Leonard wrong as to my competency.

I got into a work-study program to be a machinist assistant for the college. They applied the money I earned to my tuition charges. I made little money but enjoyed the work and learned some about being a machinist.

However, when I was not working, I was studying. I took chemistry. The professor commented that he had handed out a blank periodic table before and had given extra credit for all the blanks filled in correctly with the atomic symbol, name, and weight. So, I spent hours memorizing the periodic table. Unfortunately, he never handed out the blank table in my class.

Still, my attitude was to do everything possible to make my grades as good as possible. Or perhaps I should say I would do everything short of cheating—and I would eventually find out cheating was rampant. All the fraternities and dorms had files of all the old tests. Most instructors gave out the same tests from year to year, so many studied the tests before taking them. I lived off campus and did not have such access. As Coach Seals said, "Winning without honor is not winning at all." I earned my GPA the old-fashioned way: by lots and lots of studying. Eventually, I would also learn the frat and dorm students paid the janitors to pass on all mimeograph master copies of tests from the trash. So, many had the actual test to study before taking the test. I am guessing such is the case in many schools.

I will discuss more about school at Rolla. However, my time at Rolla would soon be interrupted for a few years.

Back in the Attic

I completed my freshman year and returned to Springfield to stay with Uncle Thurman. However, this time was different, as his house had become somewhat of a boardinghouse. Thurman and his first wife had divorced. Uncle Herman and his wife, Jackie, had divorced as well. Uncle Herman would stay some at

Thurman's. A cousin, Roxanne, was staying there while attending Southwest Missouri State College. Aunt Laveta and her first husband had divorced as well. Uncle Glenn was her second husband.

It was strange to watch such a spate of divorces take place. My mom was the first in the family to divorce, back when it was rare, but divorce became mainstream by my later teenage years. All I knew was that divorce seemed like a gigantic mess to me and I wanted nothing to do with it. I was skeptical of marriage, as I wondered how a person could marry and not wind up a divorce statistic. That question would loom even larger in my mind once I would meet a certain someone.

But that's getting ahead of myself.

I pursued education for a good job despite my family's issues. Hopefully, I would avoid the mess I had grown up in. Two school semesters had financially drained me, and I doubted I could make enough money in one summer for the fall semester ahead. However, Clarence hired me back, as his heating and air-conditioning business was still booming. So, once again, we worked many long, hard days. I still had a good time doing so. Once again, I was back in attics and under houses.

I just mentioned the divorce between Herman and Jackie. I will add that one regret (out of many) in my life is the fact that I never thanked Aunt Jackie for all she did for me. After she and Uncle Herman divorced, I never saw her again. I could have found out where she lived and paid proper respect, but I never got around to doing so before her passing away. I attended her funeral, but that was too late. That was how I learned the importance of paying respect when the opportunity exists. Besides having come to my rescue in life several times, Aunt Jackie was the best cook and kept the cleanest house of any person I have ever known. She was one of many who God used to get me through my childhood years.

If there is someone you have not thanked for helping you along your life's way, do it. Don't do like I did with Aunt Jackie.

I Won the Lottery!

As the time to start my second year of college drew closer, I was proven correct about not having enough money to complete two semesters. Grandma Tennie and Grandpa Luther had left me averse to debt, so I didn't consider student loans. I have no regrets today about not getting myself into a lot of student loan debt.

I worked through the fall semester and planned to resume college for the spring semester. However, I won the lottery, which interrupted my plans.

Not a money lottery, mind you, but the draft lottery for the Vietnam War.

In fact, all guys eligible for the draft and born on my birthday won the lottery as well. The draft board would draft me unless I had a deferment, such as college. I could not afford college, so I would likely be drafted.

I didn't have a choice about the draft, but I realized that I might have a choice about how I spent my service years. I had always wanted to be in the Air Force, and I knew the G.I. Bill would help pay for college. Of course, the Air Force would also afford me the opportunity to be around aircraft. So, I went to an Air Force recruiter in Springfield for testing. My scores were high, and the recruiter suggested I take a guaranteed career in electronics. While attending school in Cabool, I had taken an electricity/electronics class for a shop class. My Air Force test scores were high enough to receive the guarantee—and that was good, because without a guarantee, they could assign me to any duty whatsoever. I enlisted for a four-year commitment, with a guaranteed career in electronics.

Passing the training would secure an electronics career, per the recruiter. I admit, I was thinking of electronics relating to aircraft. That dream was still alive.

Even though I had the guarantee in hand, the recruiter was clear that if I flunked the training, then I was back to whatever duty they wanted to assign me—I know someone has to peel potatoes, but I did not want it to be me.

Note, I was not of the dope-smoking war protestor mentality. Fortunately, this great country and our constitution give folks the right to protest as protestors did. I want to preserve the rights of those who want to protest. I do not know why anyone would protest against freedom and liberty, but I will die for their right to do such. Now, I might suggest the Communist-sympathizing protestors go to their beloved Communist countries. Try protesting there and see how well that works.

Suffice it to say, I am totally against such totalitarian regimes as Marxism/socialism/Communism. I know the theory is they are all about redistribution, worker's rights, and supposed fairness. In reality, the people at the top live like royalty and everyone else becomes a slave to the state. Socialism is the promise of utopia for all, but in reality, it requires everyone to surrender their sovereignty (freedom) to the ruling elite. Ultimately, socialism gives total power to the state. No one owns anything (other than the ruling elite). Socialism is the carrot tied to a string that looks so good, but taking the carrot will spring a trap which enslaves.

One does not have to be a rocket scientist to see the failure of socialism/Communism. Just look up the numbers of the millions murdered by prominent socialists/Communists such as Stalin, Lenin, Mao, Pol Pot, etc. Observe the results of countries that destroyed opportunities for freedom and free enterprise.

Karl Marx, who is the founding father of Marxism (from which came socialism/Communism), "once explained that his object in life is 'to dethrone God and destroy capitalism.'"[2]

I appreciate that Karl Marx was honest about his life's goal. Karl's labors were in total opposition to biblical Christianity and free enterprise. Of course, God wins in the end. If Karl Marx didn't change his position before his death, he will eventually face being cast into the lake of fire. In the meantime, though, Marx's labors are still resulting in a multitude of calamities, deaths, and unmeasurable sufferings.

I believe the most prominent force in our midst to destroy the United States and Christianity is Communism. I give Communists credit for being dedicated and strategic. They have taken over much of our country's education, entertainment, courts, news reporting, and political positions. Communists have engineered much of the divisive agenda occurring in our country to divide and destroy the United States and, eventually, Bible-preaching churches, in my opinion. The agenda fits nicely into the hands of those who seek tyrannical power and wealth. If the Communists ever take total control of my country, these words might be my death warrant. If so, so be it, as I would rather be dead than red.

Perhaps you have detected my anti-Communist position. Back when I was facing the possibility of being drafted, I was also 100 percent for fighting against Communism. I still have no problem laying down my life fighting for Old Glory and for the rights of life, liberty, and the pursuit of happiness.

---

[2] Bill Connor, "The Marxist dream of dethroning God must fail," Voices, The Christian Post, June 25, 2022, https://www.christianpost.com/voices/the-marxist-dream-of-dethroning-god-must-fail.html.

Politicians and the mainstream media did substantial damage to our military efforts and cost the lives of many of our soldiers in the Vietnam War. I am not indicating there were no problems with the Vietnam War. Instead, I am saying I have no problem fighting against Communist/totalitarian regimes. Wars should be fought to be won or not fought at all. Also, wars should not be controlled by the aforementioned politicians and media, as I believe the Vietnam War was.

The United States Air Force accepted me, and I joined up near the end of 1971.

In the song below, I declare you can count me among those who love freedom.

Among Those Who Love Freedom

Verse 1:
For the affairs of men – God ordained government
From judges to kings – Often with evil rulings
Our founding fathers sought – a union endowed by God
With certain unalienable rights – And they paid the price
That America might be – The land of the free

Chorus:
Just count me among – Those who love freedom
Those willing to die – For the Stars and the Stripes
For one nation under God – With justice for all
For life and liberty – Free from tyranny
Just count me among – Those who love freedom
Just count me among – Those who love freedom

Verse 2:
So many enemies – Who hate our liberties
Who want to destroy – Freedoms that we enjoy
Government that will not – Impede the worship of God
A land of opportunity – and with private property
God let America be – The land of the free

(Chorus Repeats)

13

You're an Airman Now!

They transported me from Springfield to Kansas City for processing before boot camp. About thirty guys took the oath alongside me. We spent one night in Kansas City before flying to San Antonio, Texas, as the Air Force boot camp was nearby, at Lackland Air Force Base. This was my first time to fly, and I enjoyed the flight. Unfortunately, the trip was after dark, but it was still exciting.

Upon arrival in San Antonio, we picked up some other future airmen. Next, they bussed us to Lackland Air Force Base.

I thought our arrival was one of the more interesting times of my Air Force experiences. Our bus arrived around midnight. We lined up around the bus, with our legs spread and leaning forward with arms up on the bus to be frisked. I was next to several guys who, I am guessing, were gang related. They all had at least one pistol and several knives. They might have been armed for combat, but their weapons were all confiscated.

Next, we moved inside our barracks, and they assigned us each a bed on the top or bottom of a bunk bed. We each had a footlocker. The next big event was rather amusing looking back, but not so much at the time. They gave us a less-than-congenial introduction to military life: one training instructor was quite good at shouting, and each airman got a personal greeting, as in nose to nose. I guess he thought we were all hard of hearing and with poor vision, hence the shouting and closeness.

We had been told some basic information and how to respond to our questions. Of course, some were so bumfuzzled they could not even get their name right, let alone the other information. I was near the end of the line and did fairly well with my personal greeting. After all, I had similar experiences with Leonard. At least this time, I wasn't a marine—I was an airman. Despite everything, I have to say it was an improvement.

We were finally told we could go to bed. Our brief sleep was in our civilian clothes.

The next day, we got our military-issued clothing. Apparently, those issuing the clothing also thought we were hard of hearing, as we heard a lot more shouting and experienced an ordeal that was similar to that of the day before. The next day, we wore our uniforms and had our hair buzzed off. We left our barracks in formation and marched to where we would get our free haircut. There were dozens of other training flights, each with about forty-five airmen. We were told which building to line up in front of to get our haircut. There were several buildings—and that turned out to matter more than I expected.

We entered one end of the military barbershop, got buzzed, and exited the other end of the building. They had given us explicit orders to return immediately to the location where our flight had been in formation. However, following the order turned out not to be so simple. There were hundreds, or more likely over a thousand, airmen with peeled heads and identical-looking uniforms. Everyone looked just alike.

Before that, I'd never known how much clothes and hair identify a person. Many were just like me, wandering around, trying to recognize somebody in their flight. I finally found my flight, but I have often thought about how surprised I was to discover the difficulty of identifying anyone in that state.

The rest of basic training was not really difficult for me. They kept us up pretty late and then got us up early. High school football was a lot more challenging physically than the Air Force basic training, and Leonard had definitely taught me the basics of military life. In particular, the concept of following orders. Football had taught me the concept of teamwork, which was much of what basic training was all about. We had to all be out in formation early with beds made, shaved, etc. Those who could wake up and move had the responsibility of helping those who struggled with such a task.

I am guessing everyone who has served in the military remembers the stark reality of being under total control of the military chain of command. Nonconformity to that command leaves no good options. Leonard had conditioned me well, but nonetheless, such limited freedom is a rather solemn reality.

Decisions, Decisions

I took additional testing while in basic training, which provided more forks in my life's road. My test results showed I had a good aptitude for learning foreign languages. Of course, I had the guaranteed career field of electronics, but I could cancel that agreement if I chose. I had taken French in high school and enjoyed the class. The Air Force training for foreign language specialists consisted of attending one of three major universities for four years. All training would be at the expense of the Air Force. I would have no military activity while obtaining my foreign language degree, but I would have to enlist for at least six to eight more years of service. I might have signed up if I could have known the language I'd learn. However, the Air Force was honest with me and said if I was a foreign language specialist, they would pick my language. I told them if they would guarantee me Russian, I would gladly sign up. Russia/Communism/Marxism/socialism has always fascinated me. I didn't admire it, but I wanted to better understand the evil system to better combat it. Since the Vietnam War was going on, my assumption was I would learn Vietnamese. I was not sure how good of a long-term career choice that would be, so I turned down the language specialist offer. I have wondered several times what language they would have assigned me had I traversed that fork in my life's road.

I was left with my guaranteed career in electronics. As I stated earlier, I had hoped to work with electronics relating to aircraft, but the Air Force told me they needed computer support personnel, and they assigned me to be a computer repairman. They also informed me the Air Force had a lot of computers in Vietnam. However, when I got my orders, I was sent to work for the Strategic Air Command, or SAC. I would work as an electronic technician/computer repairman at one of three SAC headquarters in the US. I would remain at my assigned base for the rest of my four-year commitment. No world travel for me.

I was not disappointed with my assignment, as I perceived learning computers would likely be a valuable skill.

I did not know that I was just beginning the journey of a lifetime career in computer work.

Back to College

My technical training would be at Keesler Air Force Base near Biloxi, MS, and they were bussing me from San Antonio to Keesler. They informed me the evening of my last day at basic training that I was to be at my pickup location at 0300 hours. If I missed the bus, I would have to go through basic training again. I arose early to make sure I would make my early departure time. A few other airmen showed up, but there was no bus to board. Finally, someone came by and told us the bus would arrive at 0800 hours. The 0300 time was a little farewell gift from basic training. Oh, for the good old days of military life. After being picked up, we were off to Biloxi.

Only a highway separated Keesler Air Force Base from the ocean. Unfortunately, I was busy enough that I did not have much time to enjoy the beach.

I immediately began my electronics training. Classes were at least eight hours per day and were quite intense. They were also very good. The instructors were excellent, and the equipment we used was also good. I believe we had eight guys in our class to learn about the SAC computer system. As students, we picked nicknames for each other. Mine was the "strong, silent one." I was in good physical shape and was quite introverted. I was not much of a conversationalist. I was focused on acquiring a skill that would be of benefit to me down the road. I was determined not to squander this opportunity. I was also serving my country and would be one small cog in the Cold War against Communism—and I was passionately opposed to Communism.

Being cooped up with a handful of guys for almost a year for intense instruction was an experience. I learned a lot about electronics and the computer system that I would work with. The Air Force equated their training to college courses called the Community College of the Air Force. I would later use many of these credits towards a bachelor of science degree.

Honestly, my life was pretty similar to how it had been at school at Rolla. I was in class all day and studied most of the evening. Now that I was through basic training, it didn't seem like my life had changed much.

Change was coming, though, and soon I wouldn't be just a student sitting in a classroom—I would be part of a team that was responsible for our national defense against a possible nuclear attack. The Cold War era was a time of concern about the possibility of a nuclear attack on our soil and about our response if such an event ever happened. Many born in my time were trained in "duck and cover" in public schools in the case of a nuclear attack from Russia. Fortunately, the anticipated nuclear holocaust never materialized.

14

Top Secret

I wound up in Louisiana for the rest of my Air Force duty, at Barksdale Air Force Base. My extensive world travels in the Air Force were to Texas, Mississippi, and Louisiana. Actually, I enjoyed my time in Louisiana. Of course, it gets hot there in the summer. One good thing about computer work is that I was in a heavily air-conditioned environment to keep the computer equipment from overheating, so I stayed cool while at work. My time at Barksdale would be a time of making many decisions in my life and bringing direction to my life as well.

I was trained on a data communications computer system for processing military intelligence. The intelligence could come from the Cold War with the Russians and any other military actions, such as Vietnam. SAC had three headquarters, which were all duplicates; thus, we could lose two sites and still offer communications.

Each site had a red phone to the POTUS, who could provide the nuclear codes required to launch a nuclear action if so needed. Generals and admirals were at these sites to process the data collected and presented to them. The computer system was located several stories below ground level to protect the equipment in case of an attack from Russia. Just above the computer equipment floor was the presentation area in which the military leaders would view the intelligence data. Several large theater-type screens displayed the military intelligence in the viewing area.

To be in the viewing area and to work on the equipment, I was required to have a top secret security clearance. Normally, technicians like myself were not in the viewing area, unless there was an equipment problem which required maintenance. Design for this computer system began in the late 50s. They installed the system in the early to mid-60s. Basically, the system was a precursor to mainframe computers in use today. The system was quite state-of-the-art at the time. However, any smartwatch today offers many times the computer power of that system.

The design of the system was created before integrated circuits or computer chips were available. The system was built with discrete components on large circuit boards. The result was a large room with rows and rows of cabinets containing all the circuit boards. Each cabinet had a high-speed fan blowing cold air to keep the equipment from overheating. We had two systems, so one could always be online while the other was offline for maintenance or just on standby. The system had a whopping 32K of main memory storage, which was called core memory, as tiny ferrite donuts were used to store a positive (1) or a negative (0) charge. We actually had a plane of core memory fail while I was there. I was involved in replacing it, which required a lot of very tedious soldering. The system had traditional disk and tape storage.

Since the creation of the SAC system, technology has advanced considerably. However, where there is a will, there is a way. Technology did not really exist to present the digital data on the movie screens for the military leaders to view. The problem was solved by exposing digital data to film. Next, the exposed film would be automatically run through the chemical processes to develop the film. They dried the film and fed it into a movie projector to display the data. The data viewed on the movie screens were from movie video reels, just like a Hollywood movie. The process was not simple, but it worked.

Something Really Weird

My Air Force training was very good. I enjoyed getting my hands on the actual computer system I had trained for. The system required twenty-four-hour support, so I was working different shifts but enjoyed the work. When we were not performing preventative maintenance or fixing a problem, we had time to play cards, read, etc. One guy was a chess whiz and could find no one to play with him, so I volunteered, as I had always wanted to play. He had to instruct me, but we played a lot. However, my wins were very few, as he was quite good at the game. Since I was on call twenty-four hours a day, I got out of duties such as KP, cleaning the base, and regular formations. My work was basically like a civilian job, except that I had to wear a uniform and follow basic military rules.

One thing seemed really weird in my life at this time. For the first time, I had some extra money and the time to do something besides work or study. Air Force life was not nearly as demanding on my time as life with Leonard had been. By the time I reached Barksdale, I was making close to $500/month. The amount wasn't huge, but I had no expenses since I lived and ate for free on base. I had more spending money than I'd ever had before. I would save quite a bit, but I spent some of it. I bought a 35mm camera and got into photography. The base provided a facility and equipment to develop black-and-white film. All I had to buy was the photo paper. I started playing tennis with a guy I worked with. Tennis was a lot of fun. I tried to play ping-pong some, but the Asian contingent on base were basically unbeatable by us non-Asians.

A coworker and I both wanted to learn more about computer programming, so he and I started working with the offline system at work when we had time. We got approval to do so. We wrote a lot of utilities that could be helpful in supporting the system. However, the only language available to write in was the machine assembler language, which was rather tedious coding. So, we coded a FORTRAN compiler to simplify our programming by using a higher level, or a simpler language. Neither one of us had coded a compiler before, but once again, where there is a will, there is a way. It took a lot of hours, including some all-nighters, but we accomplished our objective.

A branch of Louisiana State University (LSU) had just opened near Barksdale. My programming friend and I took some classes there. We met the retired Air Force officer who was in charge of the computer department. However, he did not really know a lot about the school's mainframe computer. Computers were so new, there were few who knew much about them. My friend and I did a lot of work on the college's IBM mainframe. This was great for us, as IBM was the big name in data processing back then. My friend and I became student instructors for teaching assembler language for the IBM mainframe for evening classes. IBM did not have a FORTRAN compiler for the school's mainframe. So, my friend and I coded a FORTRAN compiler for the school and taught FORTRAN for evening classes. No pay, but free computer room access for our labor. We were able to learn a lot about their IBM mainframe.

I think I used the word *nerd* before, and I am guessing I was a full-fledged computer nerd by this time. However, I could see this computer stuff appeared to have a good potential for future jobs.

I believe God ordered this event in my life for plans that I did not know about at the time. I do not believe a kid from a dysfunctional family without connections or money accidentally got in on the ground floor of a coming computer revolution—a revolution which would afford many well-paying jobs. Additionally, the computers I have worked with were based on logic, like mathematics is, and I like logic. I have joked that I like computers, as they don't bleed. Of course, the future of computers with AI will likely be considerably different from my computer experiences.

God had plans for my life that I could best achieve by having a good income. Computers would not be an end in themselves but rather the means to an end.

Thumbs-Up or Thumbs-Down?

I continued working as a repairman for the SAC computer for several months. However, we had another group near our work area called Module Repair. Even on our SAC computer, we would troubleshoot down to the failing board and then just replace that board to fix the computer. The Module Repair group would fix the printed circuit board and about any other piece of electronic equipment on the base.

Chief Master Sergeant Black was in charge of Module Repair. I inquired about joining his group. He said he would find out from my direct report if that was okay, and they actually had an opening at the moment. He also informed me I would have several months of training. Then my trainer would give me a thumbs-up or thumbs-down to determine whether I could work in module repair. If I could not do the work, they would not take me.

I almost immediately began my training, and I soon received a thumbs-up to join the group. Module repair only worked dayshift, which was nice, but they were very busy. There was rarely any free time. However, the work was very interesting. We basically would get printed circuit boards, and we could generate all necessary inputs, such as power and signals to the board. Next, we could trace those signals with a piece of test equipment called an oscilloscope. We called ourselves oscope jockeys, as we spent most of our time tracing electrical signals to determine a failing component to be replaced. The human eye cannot see electricity or electrons flowing. However, the oscilloscope shows what the electrical signals would look like if you could see them and how electronic devices affect electrical signals.

I found the work very interesting and really enjoyed my job. Much like hard physical work was excellent conditioning for playing football, tracing electrical signals gave me a much better understanding of electronic components.

Do You Know What Flows Downhill?

I continued to work in module repair, and it was mostly all good, but I got myself in a bit of a pickle in making one particular repair.

I mentioned earlier the viewing or presentation area where the generals and admirals were. I also mentioned that in that area was a red phone through which the POTUS could pass on the codes to activate a nuclear action. The equipment which had that capability was called the Alert Transmit Console. There were two of them, so one could always be online while the other was on standby or being worked on if needed. Each console had a red phone, many buttons, lights, and a keyboard. The console included a display monitor or a CRT.

On the day in question, the CRT had burned out in one console. Chief Master Sergeant Black assigned me to take a new

CRT and replace the defective one. The CRT was heavy, so he sent Don, a civil service employee, to help me. We had procedures, and we followed them. First, we verified the failing unit was offline and the working unit was online. Since the unit we were working on was offline, we could power the Alert Transmit Console off. We should not have been able to cause anything unusual—at least, in theory, that should have been true. We followed the procedure to remove the failing CRT and to install the new one. Once we had the console back together, we powered the unit back on.

Not long after powering the unit on, all hell seemed to break loose. Sirens were going off. Red lights were flashing. Buzzers were buzzing and beepers were beeping. Officers were running around screaming as if something major was happening.

Don and I had no clue what was going on, so we decided to verify the new CRT was working and then get out of the area. However, before we left the console area, a full-bird colonel came running up to us. He addressed me, as civil service employees are not totally under military control, but I was. Rather frantically, he asked me if I knew what flows downhill. I did not know what was going on, but I could surmise the gravity of the situation was significant. I was quite certain he did not want a flippant answer from me, so I gave him a hearty "Yes sir." Just like I had done many times for Leonard.

Immediately, he stated, "Airman, you are the lowest ranking man in this area, and you are in it deep." He commanded me not to move and assured me he would be back to take care of me. As he was leaving, he commented, "Airman, you have just activated every B-52 bomber in the United States Air Force for a military attack. I have to cancel this activation, then I will be back."

Each console also had a printer associated with it, to log activities. The associated printer showed the Alert Transmit

Console we had worked on had generated the activation. Don and I were in total bewilderment as there was nothing we had done which should have caused such an event. Even if we had wanted to do it, there was no way we *could* have done it.

Somehow, Chief Master Sergeant Black heard about the situation and showed up to find out what had happened. He wanted to know if there was anything we did that could have caused the activation. We assured him the unit had been offline and still was. All we did was power the unit off, replace the CRT, and then power the unit back on. We had followed the procedure in detail. I had always gotten along well with Chief Master Sergeant Black, and he seemed to believe me and Don. He said he would do what he could to defend us, but he was also low ranking in this area, as most of the personnel present in the viewing area were officers.

The colonel returned and set up an interrogation. We reviewed the procedure for removing the CRT and installing the new one. We showed how we powered on the console while in an offline state and did nothing more.

I was quite fortunate that I was not doing this alone. Don assured everyone we had only followed standard procedures. Chief Master Sergeant Black vouched for our integrity and competency. He also argued that there was no way we could know the codes to generate an activation. They decided to further investigate the matter. Neither Don nor I was to be in the viewing area while this matter was being investigated. They eventually brought the vendor on-site who manufactured the equipment. Their engineers reviewed the Alert Transmit Console design. They eventually concluded there was a possibility of a phantom activation when powering a unit on. The engineers would make equipment modifications to prevent another false activation. They cleared Don and me of any wrongdoing.

A few weeks after the incident, Chief Master Sergeant Black let me know the results of the accidental activation had been excellent. Everyone was glad we had the exercise. SAC had never executed a totally unplanned test. The B-52 birds got off the ground quickly, and the system worked as designed. Most importantly, the cancellation of the activation worked as well.

I did not get any commendation for my contribution to this highly successful test.

$24,000

Overall, I enjoyed my work and my time in the Air Force. I felt I served my country but still learned a lot. I even contributed to the Cold War opposing evil Communism. As I said earlier, for the first time in my life, I had some money and time to do a few things besides work or study. The Air Force invested a lot in me, and they had an incentive program to retain their investment. The incentive program was called the Variable Reenlistment Bonus (VRB). My training afforded the max VRB for an enlisted airman. If I would sign on the dotted line for another four to six years, I would receive $24,000 as a bonus above my regular pay. I could buy a nice new car in the $3,000 to $4,000 range. I could have purchased a nice house with the VRB amount.

Even so, the military is still the military. I grew up in a military-style environment with Leonard, and I decided I'd had all the military I really cared for. So, I turned down the VRB pay, but it was tempting.

One facet of military life that I did not care for was the booze which flowed so freely. Marijuana usage was rampant as well. A person can be in the military and not drink alcohol, but you will be in a distinct minority—perhaps even all alone. In fact, immorality was quite abundant.

I sometimes shudder to hear of a young person going into the military. I believe serving our country is honorable to do. Yet, I wonder if that young person has a strong enough moral compass to resist being absorbed by the immorality which permeates the rank and file. From what I have heard, the situation is only worse today. I am not trying to pretend to be holier-than-thou, but once again, my life has been a learning process. My childhood left me programmed to stay away from booze. One thing my dad, Glenda's dad, and Leonard had in common was they all came out of the military with a drinking problem. That problem caused great difficulties in their lives and for others in their lives. I do not believe they are unique in that situation. Of course, they served in combat and I did not, but I would not duplicate their problem with alcohol.

I took no chances with booze, and I have zero regrets about that decision. Exiting the Air Force, I had valuable skills and no alcohol problems. I credit the grace of God for not being trapped by a liquor bottle. All my experiences involving alcohol were negative, except for using empty bottles as targets.

Leaving the military was a big change in my life, but unbeknownst to me, an even bigger change was on the horizon.

15

Thy Will Be Done

At this point of time in the military, I had some time to reflect on my life and my relationship with the Lord. I had learned a lot from a good church near my base, but my childhood had left me somewhat perplexed about several issues.

Marriage was certainly a major area of confusion. I was interested in marriage, but I was also fearful of a marriage disaster like those I had witnessed during my childhood and like those many others in my family had experienced. A good marriage seemed like a dream, but I did not want a bad marriage nightmare.

What was the answer? I concluded to put the matter into God's hands after reading my Bible and praying. I simply prayed for God's will to be done. As best I could, I told God if he wanted me to have a good marriage, then it was up to him to arrange it. If not, then I would trust that God's will for me to be single would be the best for my life. I certainly would rather be single than live through the marriage mess I'd witnessed as a child.

I think this decision was one of the best decisions I ever made, as God would soon answer my prayer. However, the key was coming to the point of surrendering to God's will.

Life is full of many troubling issues. Whether the dilemma is marriage, childbearing, jobs, finances, health, making a purchase, where to live, etc., the most important decision a

Christian can make is to place the matter into God's hands and then joyfully be willing to accept God's will. God certainly knows what is best for us.

Such was the case in my life, as within a matter of days, God would commence directing his will for my life regarding marriage.

Love is Simple as A, B, C, Dee

Shortly after putting the matter of marriage into God's hands, I got a letter from Cousin Paul letting me know that when I was in on leave, he had a young lady friend by the name of Sherry he wanted me to meet. Paul thought we would be a good match. He had a farmer friend, Gary, who he was trying to match up with another young lady, this one by the name of Dee. Sherry and Dee were both schoolteachers in the area and were friends with Paul's fiancée, Reta.

Soon I took leave for Christmas and headed back to Missouri. When I saw Paul, he tried to arrange my meeting with Sherry, but she had already left the area to go back to her hometown for Christmas. Since Gary and Dee had not met yet, Paul arranged for me to meet Dee instead.

I wound up taking Dee bowling. She beat me at bowling, but I claim a physical handicap: I had just had an ingrown toenail removed. That likely had no effect on my score, but at least I have an excuse.

Cousin Paul was partially correct in his matchups, as he had the right players, just not the correct pairing. Gary and Sherry would eventually meet and marry. Dee and I would do so as well. By the way, both marriages have withstood the test of time. Paul and Reta also married, and that, too, was a successful pairing.

Smitten

Dee was a slender, attractive, young Christian lady, with whom I was soon smitten. Reciprocity from Dee was not as quick, but fortunately for me, her interest in me developed reasonably soon as well. The state of Arkansas separated us, but I managed several weekend trips back to Missouri. Our communication also involved expensive phone calls and letters.

There was a new stretch of very straight road in Arkansas. The speed limit was at least eighty. Yet I still got a speeding ticket on one of my whirlwind weekend visits to Missouri. The highway patrolman shared with me, "Son, it's not like the speed limit is real low right here." Love is not cheap!

Soon Dee and I would begin pondering the subject of marriage.

Let's Make a Deal

As stated earlier, I was smitten, but I was still concerned about having a good marriage versus a disaster. I believed God had arranged our meeting—or was I just stricken over this sweet young chick my cousin had introduced me to? I had no problem tying the knot, so to speak, if marriage was God's will and our vows would last till death do us part, but because of all the failed marriages in my family, I was certain that love could be blinding.

I don't really believe many get married with the expectation of divorce. I decided we needed to be certain we would be compatible for a lifetime together. So, I laid the gauntlet down. We needed to have an agreement on anything which would be a nonnegotiable issue in our marriage.

I began with the subject of divorce. I had not really shared any of my childhood stories with Dee. Perhaps I should have, but I was still in a mode of denial and really did not talk about it to anyone. She knew I was from a divorced family. Her family had little or no divorce.

My first requirement was that if we married, we would not divorce. I suggested living on different floors or ends of the house if we couldn't get along. The bottom line was we were going to vow before God that only death would end our marriage. We would not turn from those vows and divorce. Note, I am acutely aware divorce happens in the real world and is sometimes unavoidable, especially in the case of abuse or for physical safety. I was just clarifying that we were going into this venture with the commitment that we might as well make our marriage work. We had agreed to not end it with divorce. If such commitment does not exist before marrying, then don't get married. Additionally, death by murder would not be a viable option for ending our marriage! I'm not sure if Dee thought I was crazy or not, but she agreed to my argument about divorce.

My second petition, which was totally nonnegotiable, was booze. I emphatically declared we would have an alcohol-free marriage and home. Once again, Dee did not really know about my terrible experiences with liquor. I told Dee no one would bring booze into our home. Whether it was my family or hers, it would not happen. I was nonnegotiable on this point, and it would be best to go our separate ways if she could not live with a no-booze policy.

Dee had grown up in a good home without alcohol. She had also not seen the ugly side of liquor I grew up with. To clarify, I promised Dee that I would do everything, except work in the liquor industry, to provide and care for her. If the only work I could find involved liquor, she had better be prepared to meet her Lord because of starvation.

You might say that seems rather extreme. Well, for one, it was the truth. Second, I wanted to be sure she understood that my position was that we would build our marriage without booze. Dee did not drink liquor, or we would have never gotten to this point. I wanted to make certain she had no problem being a teetotaler for all her married days with me. Fortunately for me, she had no problem with my second demand.

I had one last petition. As I have already stated, love can be blinding. I believe my first two requests should be a requirement for every marriage. Probably, this last request for marriage would not always need to be carried to the extreme I took it to. However, I was still concerned about making a mistake in marriage. I told Dee we were going to seek a blessing from all of those important in our life about us marrying. We would include my dad, whose mind was not good from all of his strokes.

We would also ask Leonard. I still hated Leonard, but he had been an authority figure in my life. Leonard had stopped drinking and abusing Mom, so at this point, I visited with them some. I did not know how he would respond, but I trusted God would direct his response.

We would start with parents and grandparents. Next, we would ask other family members, friends, and clergy. The agreement was that if anyone had any concern about us marrying, we would go our separate ways. If God was in our marriage, I believed he would direct everyone to be supportive. Note, Dee was teaching school near several of my family members and had spent some time with them while I was in the military. Dee agreed, and once again, fortunately for me, everyone was supportive.

Years later, I joked I was even asking strangers on the street, trying to find someone to tell me to not marry this woman, but

I just couldn't find anyone. Actually, I felt totally at peace, as every person we talked to thought we should get married.

A young couple might not go to the extreme we did, but they should definitely seek honest counsel from others. I will repeat once again, love can be blinding. I have often thought the couple getting married maybe the two least likely to know if they should do so. Especially in brief engagements such as Dee and I had.

Next, Dee had her turn, and she only had one nonnegotiable demand. She wanted children or no marriage. She knew I had been uncomfortable with the subject, but she did not know why. I certainly did not want to put a child through a bad marriage, and that was my concern. I was not really against children but just scared of a mess. Tennie and Nita had been a highlight in my life at home. They were a lot of fun. I believed our marriage was God's will, and I agreed we would have children. Dee was a schoolteacher, so our conclusion was we would have two children. When our children were of school age, Dee would return to teaching in the public schools with our future children.

Note, this was *our* plan, but God had a different plan and would direct our life accordingly.

My sister Glenda went through a similar process with the Jim she married. When Jim proposed to her, she gave him two nonnegotiable demands. One was no alcohol, and the other was no infidelity, as her father had a major problem with both. Jim said he could live with those requests, and such has been the case in their lifelong marriage.

Before concluding this season of my life, I want to emphasize the gravity of a marriage commitment. The time to negotiate is before getting married—though perhaps *negotiating* is not the proper word. *Agreeing* on important issues might be a better goal. There are foundational issues where your agreement should be based on God's Word, and God can build a marriage on your obedience to his Word.

Of course, marriage will present a multitude of other issues, but having a foundation set will be the key for everything else to come.

Elbow Macaroni

After Dee and I had cleared the above-mentioned hurdles, I proposed to her. Once again, fortunately for me, she accepted my proposal. I have always been a jokester and have an alternative reality story to explain why I married the woman: when she asked me if we could partake in holy matrimony, I said yes, because I thought she asked if we could make elbow macaroni.

All jokes aside, we would soon tie the knot and enter a new season of my life—full of challenges I couldn't have seen coming but full of the most amazing blessings too.

Part III

The Autumn of My Life

Fall has always been my favorite season of the year. The autumn of my life is also the favorite season of my life. Of course, fall is harvesttime. Fall is the time to reap the rewards of the labors from the springtime and the summer. Of course, harvesting is work, but it's good, rewarding work. Nature's beauty can be spectacular in the fall, and the autumn of my life has been beautiful too. The Lord of the Harvest granted us a bountiful harvest of seedlings, which have provided a multitude of precious memories. Of course, with each passing day of fall, the reality of a likely harsh winter draws closer. Thus, there is a strategic importance of enjoying the bounty of the fall harvest and the beauty of autumn before the coming winter season.

16

I Do

The completion date for my four-year commitment with the Air Force was in November. The Vietnam War had just ended, and I could get out early for a significant life event such as marriage or going to college. Since I planned on both events, I applied for and received an early out—lessening my expected time in the military by about four months. Shortly after getting out of the Air Force, I joined the ranks of the married.

'Twas a hot Missouri summer day when Dee and I tied the knot in the country church Dee was attending, which was also close to where I had grown up. After exchanging "I do," we took off to Florida for our honeymoon. I had allocated enough money for a decent honeymoon, but we had a decision to make on practicality right out of the chute in our marriage. We could do a shorter trip of one week and splurge on more expensive hotels and eating out, or we could go more economically and do a two-week trip to Florida.

Both of us agreed on the longer stay. We traveled down the Gulf-coast side and came back up the Atlantic-coast side. Budget motels and several meals of Vienna sausages stretched our honeymoon money. (Note, we both really like Vienna sausages.) We explored the many attractions of Florida during the day and regularly visited the beaches in the evenings.

The honeymoon was a good start to what has been a good marriage. Financial practicality has continued on from our honeymoon until the current day.

Prior to our marriage, we purchased a used mobile home in Cabool and had it moved to Licking, MO. I had the money saved to pay cash for our mobile home, and we liked that option better than the option of losing money to rent. (Yes, we had to pay rent on the lot itself, but that wasn't much.) We hoped to recoup our investment when we bought our first house.

I also had cash saved for us to live on while I was in college. The plan was that I would commute to Rolla for college and Dee would still teach in Raymondville.

Of course, we had to move and set up the mobile home. Leonard assisted with that and was a big help.

I should say that, at this point, in order to see Mom and my sisters, I recognized I had to get along with Leonard, and he did seem to have changed a lot. A no-liquor life had definitely improved his bedside manner, but I still had a lot of emotions stored up towards him—and those emotions would not go away for some time.

The Lord still had some work to do in my heart.

More Practicality

I had one year towards an aerospace engineering degree at Rolla, but I had just spent almost four years working with computers. Plus, I had at least another year of transferrable college credits from the Air Force and LSU that would apply towards a computer science degree. So, I changed my major to computer science. I certainly see nothing wrong with having dreams as a child, and I've shared my dreams about working with rockets, but sometimes practicality dictates direction.

Even if it wasn't my childhood dream, getting in on the ground floor of the computer revolution was a blessing. I still believe God blessed my life with an avenue to make a decent living. I have seen the sign, "To err is human, but to really foul things up takes a computer." Computers can be rather exasperating, but I have no consternation with the career choice I made. God gives each of us a bent in life, and technical skills seemed to be natural for me, so I would pursue that course for my life's work.

You Are Crazy

When I left home at fourteen and studied like crazy for years, one of my goals was to generate a large income. The reason for my goal of significant wealth was twofold. First, I wanted to prove Leonard wrong about my competency. Second, I did not want to be as poor as we were when I was growing up. Back then, we often had black-eyed pea soup, which was mostly water, for our meal. After leaving home, I did not eat black-eyed peas for years, as I was sick of them (though eventually I did resume eating them again).

However, now I found myself married, and we were planning on having two children. God was still working in my life to help me be more like him. God had changed my thinking a lot, and being very rich was no longer my primary obsession. Plus, I knew in my heart that I was a country boy and not cut out for big-city life. When career days or a job fair came to Rolla during my senior year, my advisor asked me which companies I was going to meet with. I had good grades, four years' experience in the Air Force, and he thought I could command a premium salary. When I told him I was not meeting with anyone, he said, "You are crazy." My decision to look for a job in a small town did not impress him. The large corporations like Boeing, IBM, McDonald Douglas, etc. were certainly going to provide their employees with more income, better benefits, and more future opportunities. However, I made a life decision that I would rather live and raise a family in more of a small-town, rural environment. Once, I'd planned on going to the big city in pursuit of the big bucks, but now God had completely changed my direction.

Looking back, I can certainly say I don't regret not having to deal with the major traffic issues a large city brings. But even more than missing out on the big city hassles, country living affords many other blessings. We would eventually own two small farms, which would not likely have happened in a large city.

The college had a physical bulletin board for posted jobs. One day I saw a small ad for a job in Jefferson City, MO. I applied for the job, and they hired me.

We had moved our used mobile home up Hwy 63N to Licking for my first year of school. We would move our mobile home again from Licking to Rolla via Hwy 63N for my second and last year of school. Finally, we would move our mobile home one more time up 63N to the Jefferson City area in Central Missouri. It was a good thing our dwelling was fit for highway travel!

I graduated summa cum laude, which I thought was pretty good considering I had no dubiously obtained tests to study from, like most students did. We bought a three-acre lot to put our mobile home on. Before finishing college, we found out our first child was on the way. A lot of big events took place in a short period of time. I finished my duty in the Air Force, married, completed college, and had my first non-military job as a computer professional. Now we were expecting our first child. Sometimes life comes fast.

In fact, life has always seemed to come fast to me.

Much of the autumn of my life would be the experience of raising a family and watching how God directed us in that endeavor. Money and debt are important factors in life, and maybe never more so than when you have a family to raise, so I'd like to talk about them both a bit here. I want to share how God helped us to be financially responsible.

Dee and I began our marriage debt free. We have remained debt free except for our first house and two vehicles while raising a good sized family and purchasing two farms. I am certainly not boasting in us, but I believe God Almighty has blessed us as we tried to follow biblical financial principles. I have seen financial problems listed as the number one reason for divorce. As my story goes on, I will share some of how God has led us in the area of finances throughout our lives.

Our First House

We lived in our mobile home on three acres for about six months before we found a house on four acres that we liked. We listed our mobile home and property in a local paper and found a buyer. We made little profit, but we got all the equity back from the purchase of the mobile home and land. We basically had near rent-free living for about two and a half years. We borrowed money for our first house, but we had almost a 50 percent down payment. The bank gave us a twenty-year loan, but I made my monthly payments in an amount that would pay it off in fifteen years—and then we actually ended up paying the loan off even earlier than that.

The house was a fairly new brick rancher. We moved into the house just before our first child was born. Indeed, we were living the dream. Note, Dee and I both lived frugally to pay off that loan as soon as possible. For example, the house was all electric with baseboard heat. We moved in January, which was cold. When we got our first electric bill, I decided we could heat much more economically. The house had a flue for a wood stove in the unfinished part of the basement, so we soon bought a wood furnace. I used my heating and air-conditioning experience to run ductwork in the basement to the upstairs. Thus began many years of cutting firewood, which has been an enjoyable pastime. Cutting firewood has also been my primary exercise program, which continues up to the time of this writing.

Blessing #1

Having grown up on a farm and having been around cattle a lot, I relate a lot of life to cows. Having children is certainly different from raising cattle, but if there were no difference, I would have likely gotten rid of Dee after our first child. With cattle, farmers usually ship cows that are not good calvers. Well, I did not ship Dee despite her not being an easy calver. She was in hard labor for what seemed like a week but was only over twenty-four hours. However, we had lost most of two nights' sleep or rest. We were both exhausted. While still in labor, Dee seriously asked me to just take her home, as she was going to forget the whole thing. I assured her that was not a viable option, and eventually God blessed us with a healthy baby boy we named Aaron.

Dee feels blessed that she never was very sick with any of her pregnancies, but none of her deliveries were easy. This was our first time through the process, and I was uncertain about having future children, given the ordeal we had just been through. However, some of Dee's first words after Aaron's appearance were, "I hope our next delivery is easier than this one." While I may have been unsure, Dee was not. In fact, I would hear that same sentiment several more times, with more deliveries to come.

God would bless Aaron with a musical talent for singing and playing instruments. In fact, God blessed him with perfect pitch, or the ability to identify any note on the piano just by hearing it. He would be the oldest brother of more siblings to come.

California, Here I Come ... Again

While we settled in a fairly small town, I wound up working in San Jose, CA, for a few months to oversee the development of a customized computer system. We loaded up and left for California. We were fortunate to find a nice apartment we could rent by the month. While I did not want to live permanently in a big city, I did not mind a few months. Aaron was just a few months old when we left on this journey. He logged a lot of miles with us on this trip and was a pretty good baby. When I was not working, we did a lot of sightseeing. The spectacular beauty and the majesty of the giant redwood trees were clearly the highlight of our California sightseeing. Once my work project was complete, we returned home via the Rocky Mountains to enjoy even more sightseeing. In fact, I was so impressed with the redwood trees, God allowed me to write a song by that title:

Giant Redwood Trees

Verse 1:
Giant redwood trees – A gentle ocean breeze
Rocky Mountains steep – Grand Canyon so deep
Hazy Smokey Mountains – Golden fruited plain
Roaring Niagara Falls – God's handiwork in it all

Chorus:
God has given this land so much – Midst the many church steeples
So great has been his touch – Upon this land and people
But as America turns from – The God who's blessed this nation
How my heart breaks – To see our foundation shake
Will we return to the God who made – America great

Verse 2:
The land of the free – The Statue of Liberty
Our constitution – One sovereign nation
The American dream – Bastion of freedom
Religious liberty – God has blessed so mightily

(Chorus Repeats)

Blessing #2

God soon blessed our household with a little girl, Elizabeth. As she grew older, sometimes we would call her Goldilocks, as she was a cute blondie. She was a very good-natured baby and child. Elizabeth showed musical talent as well and would eventually play several instruments and sing too. We practiced the disciplinary act of spanking with our children. However, Elizabeth was so well behaved that she got very few spankings— possibly more than a couple, but really very few. Her efforts to keep family life peaceful made her known as a peacemaker.

Now we had what we considered at the time to be the perfect family. We had one boy and one girl. We would support the goal of zero population growth. In time, Dee would go back to teaching in the public schools, and we would have a double income.

At least … that was what we expected. After all, our plan was to only have two children. When Elizabeth outgrew her baby bed, we sold it and all of our baby equipment.

However, neither Dee nor I wanted to do anything to ensure no more children. We really enjoyed the two we had. So, we changed our original plan and decided to have three children. Two just didn't seem like quite enough. We assumed three children would be our new perfect family.

Surely, three would be enough.

After all, it wasn't like we'd been wrong before.

17

Forgiveness

While I finished up college, we faithfully attended a church in Rolla. After moving near Jefferson City, we joined a small country church which was close to where we moved our mobile home and was also close to our first house. Our church had a revival meeting, and I do not remember the evangelist at all, but I remember one of his sermons. One evening, he preached on forgiveness. The evangelist described how our Savior was beaten, spit upon, mocked, and crucified. Yet before Jesus died on the cross, he spoke the amazing words, "Father, forgive them." The evangelist pointed out that to be like Christ requires forgiving those who have offended us.

As I heard his words, I found myself under conviction and knew exactly what was troubling my soul. Many years of anger, hatred, and bitterness towards Leonard were like a dam in my heart that needed to be broken and drained. The evangelist gave an altar call to come forward and make things right with God, but I did not move. I was uncertain I could let God break that dam or that I even wanted him to.

After the service, Dee remained inside the church while I stepped outside. It was a pleasant evening, and I walked around the church grounds. I was still under conviction. I had not walked far before I knew I needed to do business with God. Soon, I bowed on my knees in the damp, dewy grass and asked God to help me forgive Leonard. I wanted to be more like

Christ than I wanted to continue the anger, hatred, and bitterness. God was gracious and broke that dam.

What had happened in the past was now really in the past rather than filling up a reservoir in my heart. Tears could now flow freely down my cheeks rather than being held back by a great dam of bitterness.

I considered saying something to Leonard about my forgiving him—and maybe I should have, but I did not. I basically expected he would have felt insulted that I thought he had done anything wrong. Much of the time when he had acted so vilely, he had been drunk, and often drunks don't even remember what they've done. I chose to not tell Leonard what God had done in my heart.

I'll skip ahead several years and break the chronological order of the story.

I previously mentioned Leonard had smoked most of his life, which would eventually take a toll. Leonard's smoking eventually caught up with him, leading to a diagnosis of lung cancer. He underwent surgery to remove part of one lung to halt the progression of the disease. He had a few years of reasonable health after the surgery, but the cancer eventually came back and spread throughout his body. Mom called to let us know that if we wanted to see Leonard at their home, we needed to come down, as they would soon leave to Springfield for his hospice time.

We loaded up all of our kids and traveled for our last visit with Leonard. He was feeble and sometimes needed assistance to move around, yet it pleased him to see us. After lunch, I went into the living room. Leonard made his way into the living room by himself and said he needed to talk with me. I supposed he might have some instruction for me, for after his passing. However, to my surprise, Leonard told me he wanted to apologize for the way he treated me when I was at home, and he asked for my forgiveness.

I could not believe my ears, but what a gift it was to be able to tell him truly that God had dealt with me many years ago and that I had already forgiven him!

There is more to this part of my story. Leonard knew he was terminal. He did not attend church and had no profession of faith. Many were praying for his salvation, including me. Mom was faithful to church and asked her pastor to come by their house and visit with Leonard. Her pastor shared the gospel with Leonard, and by faith he accepted Christ as his Savior. Thus, I believe it was God who convicted Leonard to make things right with me. I don't believe the old Leonard would have done such.

After asking me for forgiveness, Leonard shared that he had once been trapped in a foxhole under heavy fire in the Philippines during the war. He promised to live for God if he survived the foxhole. He confessed that God had completed his part of the bargain, but Leonard had not done his part. Leonard told me he had always been strong, and it seemed he could just do whatever he wanted in life and get away with it. He had lived his life that way. He confessed he made a lot of mistakes in his life. The way he had treated me was one of them, and he just wanted to make one of those mistakes right while he had time. I assured him all was well between the two of us.

God is definitely in the healing business. When I forgave Leonard, the wounds of my childhood finally began to heal. My wounds were still open sores at that point, and considerable time would be required before all that was left would just be a scar.

It's important to me to note that all the positive moves Leonard and I made were all the result of God working. God had to bring major conviction into my heart for the process of healing to commence. He also knew the right time to give

Leonard a chance for redemption for his spiritual healing. Since Leonard and I both responded in God's will to his grace and mercy towards each of us, I am able to record a good ending to a bad story of domestic abuse.

My friend, if you have wounds in your life that seem to be more than you can bear, bring them to the Great Physician. Jesus knows how to begin the healing process, if we will surrender to his will.

Below is a song God gave me about bitterness. The biblical character Joseph, who was mistreated by his family, said God worked the evil deeds of his brothers for good. Joseph could give glory to God for his life and even his sufferings. While I was a child, Leonard's influence was not good, but those sufferings worked for good in my life. Joseph endured a lot of suffering, including being sold into slavery and falsely imprisoned for years, but he was rewarded by becoming second in command in all of Egypt. Such has been the case in my life—not being rewarded with heights of prominence but with a wonderful wife, children, and labors.

This song has a lighthearted melody, but the message is very serious. We can either get bitter or we can get better. If bitterness has been an issue in your life, I trust you, the reader of this story, will choose to get better by God's grace rather than becoming more bitter.

Bitter or Better

Verse 1:
No doubt Joseph was done wrong – His brothers thought they'd gotten rid of him
So many years had gone on – And great in the land was famine
But Joseph was not bitter when – His brothers came begging food from him

Chorus:
You can get bitter – Or you can get better
Might as well be gladder – Or you're gonna get madder
You'll hurt nobody else – More than yourself
So if you think you've been done wrong – Listen to the message of this song
You need to be bigger – Than the bitter
And let God's Spirit help forgive it and forget it – Or you're gonna let it
Make you more bitter- And you'll never get better

Verse 2:
This man never once did sin – Yet he was despised and rejected
The crowd cried crucify him – For us bitter gall he tasted
But he did not get bitter then – Rather he cried, Father forgive them

(Chorus Repeats)

Blessing #3

Sarah arrived and completed what we thought would be our perfect family. She was another cute blondie. She grew into a high-spirited child who always had a bounce in her step. Sarah turned out to like music as well and would eventually join right in on the family singing. Since I played guitar, all our children sang Christian children's songs as they grew up. The best time to get started with music is from birth on. Actually, all our children listened to gospel music in the womb as they grew.

After Sarah started walking, when I would get home from work, each girl would put their feet on one of mine and wrap their arms around a leg. I would walk around for several minutes with a girl attached to each leg.

I have to say, Sarah contributed absolutely *nothing* to our plan of just having three children. As soon as we had her, we realized that without her, we would have missed a giant blessing. If we'd been wrong about two being enough (three was clearly better), were we wrong about three being enough?

Our perfect plans seemed to show signs of poor planning—and we couldn't help but notice.

Is Three Enough?

We were going to have just two children, but now we had three. Once again, neither Dee nor I wanted to do anything that would permanently prevent the possibility of having more children. We had read some Christian material which pointed out the fact that God calls children a blessing. If children are a blessing, then why would we want to limit his blessings? All of God's blessings are very good. We wondered why we sought God's will for many areas of our life but had not really done so with something as important as how many children we should have. Our family planning up to this point had been pretty much what we wanted within the confines of social normalcy. We had given minor consideration for what God wanted. Bottom line, we decided we would just let God give us however many children he wanted to. If we had no more, that would be fine, or if he gave us a dozen more, that would be fine. Dee and I both had reasonably good health. I had a decent income. We entrusted childbearing to God, who knows best and gives life.

Note, we have many friends who have not been able to have any children or maybe have just had one or two and would love to have more. I know that can be difficult, but I still believe we should turn this area over to God and accept his will. He makes no mistakes. We have friends who have medical issues that present a problem for childbearing. I am not referring to such a situation, and I acknowledge there could be other extenuating circumstances in relation to childbearing. However, I am referring to those who choose to limit God's will related to childbearing when there is no basic reason to do such. I believe Christianity has lost much by not encouraging large families, which would further enlarge the kingdom of God.

Dee was in her early thirties when Sarah was born, which the medical world considered old for childbearing. So, we got no support from the medical world for our decision to have more children if it was God's will. We had some family members and friends who thought we were crazy for having more children. Of course, the medical world kept warning us of the increased probability of having a child with a disability, which may be true. However, that possibility is there in any pregnancy, and we would have loved such a child no more or less than any of our other children.

In the end, Dee was forty-six when our last child was born. I am not saying everyone should follow our exact path, but I believe every Christian should seek God's will in childbearing. I fear the world has had an enormous influence in this area. Now I am not a proponent of the zero-population growth objective. God gives life, and he knows what he is doing. He also controls the universe and knows how many people this earth can sustain. Creating life is beyond our power, but we can impede God's desire for life—life that perhaps God has plans to use for his glory and for the benefit of mankind. In the big picture, birth control in its current form is a fairly new invention. The goal of marriage for most of humanity's time on this planet was to have a good number of children. The latter half of the twentieth century changed the process. Dee and I chose to let God determine the number of children we would have. God would do our family planning.

Additionally, I always had a blast when visiting all the siblings of my brother-in-law, Jim, who had a large family. If God was willing, we would have our own blast with our own large family—I admit, my visits with Jim's family did color my outlook in a favorable way.

The Desires of Thine Heart

As a wedding gift, we had received a wall plaque engraved with Psalm 37:4: "Delight thyself also in the Lord: and he shall give thee the desires of thine heart." Dee hung that plaque in our bedroom.

One day, that verse caught my eye. I thought I should likely have some desires of my heart that would please God as we were trying to delight ourselves in God. Thus, I asked God to bless our family with musical talent, which we could use for his glory, as a response to that verse of promise. I did not ask for fame or fortune. I believe God answered my simple petition, as all our children either play instruments or enjoy singing for the glory of God. My mom's family sang a lot together, which was a blessing to her family, as I believe it has been to our family.

Blessing #4

In time, God blessed us with our fourth child, Lydia Faith. She was our first girl with darker hair. We gave Lydia the middle name of Faith. We chose to have our first three children, but now we were having children by faith in God and in submission to his perfect will.

Lydia was full of life and another great blessing. My fondest memory of Lydia was of her swinging in the backyard. I would guess she was about two years old. She had taken to singing early and was usually singing a gospel song, which was the case on this day while she was swinging. However, as young children often do, she did not sing the words exactly as the songwriter had penned them. The correct lyrics to the song are, "Living by faith in Jesus above, trusting, confiding in his great love." Her version of the song was like this: "Lydia Faith in Jesus above, trusting, confiding in his great love."

Dee and I were working in the garden and heard her revised version but found no need to correct her, as her version was our desire for her life.

Lydia was our third girl in a row, and she and her older sisters formed what we called the girl pack. The three of them got along well and spent a lot of time living life together. They also sang harmony together as a trio growing up. They are all still personally close even today.

Lydia would be our last little girl to hold and watch grow up. Several years later, God gave me the following song, which is dedicated to my three daughters, daddy's little girls.

Daddy's Little Girl

Verse 1:
Seems like just yesterday – God brought you our way
On top of the world – With our pretty little girl
God had entrusted us – With life so precious
You were dedicated to – The God who made you
So that in all your days – You might walk in God's ways

Chorus:
Child, in my mind's eye you'll always be – Daddy's little girl to me
Even tho' now I see you're a young lady – Still in my mind's eye you'll always be
Daddy's little girl to me you'll always be – Daddy's little girl to me

Verse 2:
From those little girl days – To little girl ways
Right from the start – You had your daddy's heart
Lots of hugs and kisses – Daddy's little princess
With lots of homemade mud pies – Scraped knees and a few cries
The years have passed so quickly – As now you're a young lady

(Chorus Repeats)

Verse 3:
My child, look at you now – In your wedding gown
Such a pretty lady – Arrayed in great beauty
On the day you dreamed of – The man of your love
Leaving Father and Mother – To cleave to another
Before I give you away – I've just one thing to say

(Chorus Repeats)

Blessing #5

We had one boy and three girls, so it looked like the majority of our children would be of the female gender. However, number five turned out to be a boy, and we named him Elijah, after Elijah in the Bible. We have always felt we named him correctly, as he has always been a character—just like Elijah in the Bible.

He was quite the daredevil as a child. We had friends we shared the Fourth of July with. They always got a kick out of Elijah setting off children's fireworks, as he would not even blink an eye even during fairly loud fireworks. Elijah was not a big talker, but he was quite a cutup. He was probably ten years old or so when one day he came walking into the living room where the rest of the family was. That is not really unusual—what was unusual was that he had three legs. He had cut a leg off an old pair of pants, stuffed it, attached a shoe to it, and then attached the third leg to the pants he was wearing. He made the third leg move like it was walking too. Needless to say, he got quite the laugh from all the rest of the family. He also became daddy's helper on our farms. Even when he was young, he was always a big help.

Childbearing Is Rough on Us Husbands

During our childbearing years, I performed a comedy routine which went something like this:

Upon arrival at the hospital, they greeted my wife with a wheelchair. The husband has to do all the administrative work, and then he has the chore of trying to find his wife. Of course, the wife gets an adjustable bed with a swarm of attention from the hospital staff, while the husband has to stand for hours on end. After standing for hours and hours, I would get such comforting comments from nurses as, "Don't pass out and bust your head on the floor, as we don't have time to mess with you." They waited on my wife hand and foot and gave her all the attention. As the action is heating up, I'm holding my wife's hand while she is crushing my fingers. I tell you, having children is not easy on us husbands!

These were beautiful years, and our growing family was a delight to us. We were together, we were following the Lord, and we were living in the country the way we had planned. The one thing missing was our dream farm. Surely that would be the next thing!

Our dreams, though, are not always God's dreams.

One thing I can tell you: God's plan is always better than ours.

18

The Dream Farm

We had five children and believed God would give us more. Dee and I had both grown up on farms. Our four acres of ground were very rough and not really suitable for doing much with. We had brought in a dump truck load of soil for our garden spot so we could raise some food. We had our house paid off and some money saved to buy a farm. I had gotten a second job teaching computer classes in the evening at a nearby university to add to our savings. Once again, frugal living was required to pursue our objectives.

What was our objective? We had decided to purchase an actual farm. Dee and I both wanted our children to enjoy farm living, playing, and working.

Sometime before looking for our farm, Dee and I got rid of our TV. Our hope was for a large family from God—a family who would experience life, not just view it on TV.

Farm living definitely affords the opportunity to experience life, and to stay busy.

We began looking and soon found what I thought was the dream farm. The farm had an almost new large earth contact home and a year-round spring which fed a beautiful stream that flowed through the property. The ninety acres of land was hilly and was about half open pasture and half woods. Rock cliffs adorned the stream. Deer and turkey were plentiful, making it a hunting paradise. There was even an old one-room schoolhouse on the property that we were going to fix up.

We put our property on the market and signed a contract on the dream farm, contingent on selling our house. We could have just purchased the property as we had no mortgage. However, we believed God's will for us was to use our property's equity and the savings we had to buy a farm, thus staying debt free.

The real estate market was slow due to high interest rates. We signed for a six-month listing with a real estate agent and had almost no one even look at our house. We signed up for another six months. Still no lookers or buyers. One day, we got a call from our real estate agent to inform us that the farm we wanted to buy had another contract. We had three days to either agree to buy with a loan or let the property go. I really wanted that property. However, our prayer had been that if it was God's will for us to own the dream farm, our current property would sell and we would pay cash for the farm. So, we let the dream farm go. While I still look back fondly on what I called the dream farm, I trust that was not God's will. He had a farm planned for us, as we would soon see. The owners of the dream farm had mentioned to be careful in the woods as the farm had a lot of snakes on the property. Perhaps God spared us potential dangers there.

God's Farm for Us

We had missed being able to buy the dream farm and only had a couple of weeks left with our real estate listing. We still had no one even looking at our property, so we were going to let the real estate listing expire and wait a while before trying again. However, I noticed a listing in our local newspaper for an eighty-acre farm in the nearby community of Tebbetts. I called the number in the newspaper, and the owner said we were welcome to come out and look. We loaded up all five children and went to look at the eighty-acre farm. I had asked about the price, and it was significantly more than we could afford, but we were just looking. The owners were an elderly couple who had never had children. They had been on the farm for all of their married life. They were retiring and moving into Jefferson City.

Our kids took off running all over the farm. The farm had two lakes, each several acres in size, a large barn, a granary bin, lots of sheds, and a large garden spot. The house was an older two-story house with an unfinished basement. While the house was old, it still looked quite nice. It had four bedrooms but was none too big for our family of seven. The biggest attraction for me was that the land was in the Missouri River bottom—it was all black river-bottom dirt. Gardening would be like paradise in that soil.

We looked around and thanked the owners for their time and explained that we were just looking, as we had to sell our house before we could do anything. Also, we explained we believed God's will for us was to not go into debt; we had a fixed limit on how much we could spend, but we appreciated their time. This was on a Saturday.

As we left the farm in our full-size van, Dee was rather quiet. I was guessing she was not quite as enthused about the river-bottom farm as I was. I finally asked her what she thought about the farm. She responded, "The house is not as large as we need." I replied to her, "I'm in love with the dirt." Dee responded to me, "If our house sells this week, then I will move to this farm with you."

Of course, neither one of us expected anything to happen, as we had to sell our house and did not have enough money anyway to buy the Tebbetts farm.

The next day Vance, who owned the Tebbetts farm, called me. He told me the previous and original owners of his farm had never had children. He and his wife could not have children. They loved their farm and decided their farm should have children running, playing, and working on it, so they wanted us to buy their farm. They had watched our children running around their farm and decided that was what their farm needed. I thanked him but reiterated that we had listed our house for almost a year with minimal interest. Vance told me to let them know when our property sold. I promised him I would but doubted such would happen. Also, note that Vance already had offers from others to buy his farm at his asking price, but Vance and his wife, Opal, decided they would rather sell to us.

On Monday, the next day, we got a call from our real estate agent, saying that they wanted to show our house. Dee loaded up the kids and left for town so the prospective buyers could look at our house. Sure enough, the next day we had a contract on our house for a price reasonably close to what we were asking. Now we had our house sold, but we did not have a farm that we could afford. I called Vance and told him to our surprise we had a contract on our house and needed to buy a farm. I assured him I thought he had his farm reasonably priced, but it was more than we could afford without going into debt. He wanted to know what we could pay, so I told him the amount, which was significantly less than he was asking. He said he would have to talk to his wife about that but would get back to me.

In a few minutes, he called back and said they would sell for what we could pay cash for. Talk about a whirlwind! We had gone close to a year trying for the farm we wanted and had not gotten it. However, during that time, we were constantly praying we would only get it if it was God's will. Now we gawked at a farm we thought there was no way we could buy, and in a matter of hours, we had our farm.

I believe the difference is praying for God's will. We trusted God to get us a farm we could pay cash for. Note, it delighted the sellers that their farm would have a bunch of children running all over it. I have wondered if we had only had two children if that would have been enough children to move their hearts to sell to us.

I have found that doing things God's way is always the best. There was no doubt in our minds that this was God's doing.

Farm Livin'

The real estate deals all completed successfully, and we moved to our eighty-acre farm. I had not worked on a farm since I was fourteen and quickly realized I had a lot to learn. At the time we bought the farm, we had an area farmer who wrote editorials and entertaining stories about farming, and he used the moniker of "The World's Worst Farmer." I am uncertain, but I might have given him a run for his money when it came to his title.

However, my primary goal was not really raising cattle or crops but children. Don't get me wrong, I enjoyed farming. Of course, I had to work my computer job or jobs, but farming was a lot of fun.

The town of Tebbetts was in the Missouri River bottom and was basically a grain town with little else other than a general store, post office and granaries. More than a town, Tebbetts was and still is a community in which the folks are friendly and willing to help one another. Our house was located in the small town. Many people in the area would soon get to know and become friends with our kids. Our older kids would find odd jobs with many of the older folks around town. The elderly lady who owned the general store feared storms and would hire Elizabeth to stay the night with her if the weather was stormy. Elizabeth made pretty good money to just sleep. The town is also a high spot in the Missouri River bottom and had not flooded that anyone could remember, so we were not concerned about flooding—but I will write more about that later.

Another farmer in the area, who had Simmental beef cattle, was renting our pasture. I did not have money to go out and buy a lot of cattle, so we worked out a deal that I would buy some of his herd over time. I was not very familiar with Simmental cattle, but they are a large breed; they're hardy and give a lot of milk, as they have dairy production in their lineage. Simmental cattle are a good breed, but mine had a nasty disposition. They were like mules. They were not flighty but fighty. However, they produced nice calves. We would eventually work up to having a herd size of about twenty to thirty cows and a bull.

Since we had a lot of kids, we could use a lot of milk. So, we purchased a milk cow. We found and bought a large Guernsey milk cow. She had the body of a large Holstein cow but had the orange color spots of a Guernsey. Her name was Miss Daisy, and she was a near perfect milk cow. I taught everyone how to milk. Dee and the kids did the morning milking. The kids and I would be responsible for the evening milking. Years ago, most country homes had at least one milk cow, and I fully understand why. One good milk cow produces a lot of food. After calving, Miss Daisy would easily give six to eight gallons of milk a day and feed the calf she had, which was even more than we could use. I usually bought two to three calves for her to raise, plus the calf she had. Additionally, we took all the milk we wanted. We would usually butcher a couple of steers every year that were raised by Miss Daisy. Thus, we had plenty of beef. We had steak so often the kids would sometimes complain, "Not steak again."

We had a hand crank butter churn to make our own butter and plenty of cream to make homemade ice cream. Of course, a cow has to be milked twice every day. It is no trivial undertaking, but I believe milking was an excellent learning experience for all our children. Miss Daisy was almost like a part of the family. She definitely contributed to the family welfare.

Of course we could not farm without chickens. I'm not sure our children loved the chickens greatly, but they did feed the chickens and gather the eggs. We had to keep the chickens secured in a pen or varmints would get them. I don't think we ever lost any chickens in Tebbetts to varmints. Since we lived in a granary town, we had rats that would try to eat the chicken feed. We had traps, and I would pay the kids a quarter for every rat they could catch. We also had a cat that was a great rat catcher.

Chickens are rather interesting creatures to watch. Dee always enjoyed the chickens. We did not butcher many for eating, as neither Dee nor I particularly cared for the butchering process.

While in Tebbetts, we started eating homemade bread. Dee and the girls were the bread makers. We would buy wheat berries, and we had an electric grinder to make fresh flour from the entire wheat berry. Manufacturers can label store-bought bread as 100 percent wheat bread, but they are not using the entire wheat berry. It's not technically false advertising since they still use wheat, but bread manufacturers typically remove the wheat germ and other nutritional parts to extend the shelf life of the bread. The benefit of using the entire wheat berry is gaining all of its nutrition. We usually made five to six loaves of bread at a time, and we would give at least one loaf to someone in our community. Often, we would visit older folks. I would take my guitar and play for the kids to sing gospel songs. We would give them a loaf of freshly made bread and a gospel tract.

(This simple act would have a major impact on our lives down the road.)

Then there was the gardening! Or perhaps more properly, I should call it "the dream gardening." Don't think that we needed a green thumb with such black dirt! It was almost impossible *not* to grow food in dirt like that.

We raised a lot of food. The previous owners had a large garden behind the house, but I decided we needed another garden just for sweet corn and potatoes. We grew about every kind of vegetable we could think of. We have pictures of sweet potatoes not much smaller than a bowling ball. One year, we raised over two hundred pounds of sweet potatoes. We had okra and corn so tall we had to use a stepladder to pick it. Like I said, soil makes a difference. My love of the dirt was justified. Dee would usually can at least one hundred quarts of green beans and many other items. We never raised a lot of strawberries, as we had a place nearby where we could pick our own at a reasonable price. With all the kids helping, we would pick over one hundred pounds of strawberries. What we didn't eat fresh, Dee would freeze.

Our house was an older, two-story house with a full unfinished basement. Our house was in view of many other houses in the town of Tebbetts. We had not lived there long before others in the community pointed out that Vance and Opal never had many lights on after dark. After our arrival, the house was lit up like a Christmas tree. How else could it be with a house full of children?

Bottom line is we really enjoyed our new community, and the farm kept us busy, which is a good thing. Not having children do meaningful work is a great disservice to them, in my opinion. All work and no play may make Jack a dull boy, but all play and no work will make Jack worthless.

Not Enough Oxygen?

I wound up working with IBM mainframe computers. I was a system programmer, which meant I was basically in charge of the technical support of the overall system, which included installing the operating system and hardware configuration. A system programmer is at the top of the food chain to get a problem resolved if no one else could. Being on call 24/7 and working irregular hours is part of a system programmer's life.

I enjoyed the work. New hardware and software required constant training. System programmers were a scarce resource, and I got a lot of calls from headhunters offering great pay and benefits if I were willing to move. However, most of the jobs were in big cities, so I had little interest in them.

I was working for a manufacturing plant which made pad mount residential transformers. Our business depended on residential construction. Thus, when construction was low, the company would often have layoffs. System programmers were a necessary, hard-to-find commodity, so I wasn't worried about losing my job. However, it turned out I almost *did* lose my job—but not due to my job performance.

The company had an engineer who wanted to get into management, and they made him the manager of my work group. I reported directly to this manager as my boss. This should have been fine, except that my new boss was a big liberal and did not like conservatives at all.

One day I was at my desk, and my boss phoned me to come into his office as he needed to discuss something with me. I went to his office to find out what the issue was. He asked me to close his office door. I was guessing the need for privacy was not a good thing. My boss began by verifying I had a large family. I told him I had five children, but I did not consider that a really large family. He informed me that since people like me have over two children, people like him and his wife could not have any children. The reason he could not have children was because there would not be enough oxygen for everyone.

Unfortunately, he was quite serious. He had totally bought into the zero-population growth propaganda (more on that later). All I could tell him was he would just have to trust me on this one: there would indeed be enough oxygen for him and his wife to have a child or two.

He did not heed my counsel, as they never had children. However, he did try to lay me off. Other managers could veto a layoff if they felt the person ordering it was making the wrong call.

A majority of other managers vetoed my boss's decision to lay me off. Eventually, the company removed him from management, and the company was once again no longer concerned with my family size.

I have never regretted the size of our family—not even when it came close to costing me my job. Soon, though, we would learn that while nothing can make God's blessings less than blessings, sometimes sorrows can still be found amidst the blessings of God. Such would be the case on the road just ahead in our lives. Yet God promises in Romans 8:28, "And we know that *all things work* together for good to them that love God, to them who are the called according to his purpose" (emphasis added).

19

———∞———

Blessings #6 and #7

I have combined the next two blessings. Other than Dee not being an easy calver and, of course, not being a spring chicken, we seemed to be in a groove of good fortune in growing a large family. Dee had not had many problems with her pregnancies and was now pregnant with blessing #6.

One day while I was at work, the neighbor's cows got out, and Dee and the kids went to help get them back in. While doing so, Dee stepped in a pothole and fell down. We were still fairly new in the area. Our neighbor whose cows got out was concerned that if we had any problems with Dee's pregnancy, we might be upset with them over their cows getting out. We assured them that was not an issue, as cows get out and that was no one's fault.

Unfortunately, Dee miscarried not long after that. I wouldn't say having children was easy as falling off a log. However, after five successful pregnancies, our expectation was that we would just keep on having children without major issues.

Now we faced the reality that God may have determined our quiver would be full with five. As we faced that possibility, we acknowledged that God was sovereign over all of these matters, and yet we did not see any good or biblical reason to stop seeking the blessings that we hoped for. Dee and I both desired more children, and reasonably soon we would be expecting again.

However, blessing #7 ended in miscarriage as well.

Dee was in her early forties. Doctors strongly opposed us having more children. Many of our family and friends were of the same opinion. However, Dee and I both desired to have more children. We had resolved to not do anything to block or prevent a future baby that God might bless us with. Of course, we were content with God's will, but we saw nothing wrong with praying for more children if that would be in God's will.

I want to note that we believe our children lost in miscarriage are still a blessing. We believe these two children are awaiting us in heaven. King David lost an infant, and he declared he could not bring the child back to life, but someday he would see his child in heaven. We look forward to meeting blessings #6 and #7 in heaven.

Blessing #8

We were attending a country church near our farm, and it had a revival meeting going on. We had just found out Dee was expecting again. Of course, her last two pregnancies had ended in miscarriage. Dee was forty-two. One evening after the service, Dee and I noticed our pastor, his wife, the evangelist, and his wife were in the auditorium. We told the four of them we had just found out Dee was expecting again and asked if they would pray with us that God would give us a healthy child. All six of us knelt and prayed for our new child. I prayed specifically that God would give us a child to be used for his glory.

In the spring of the next year, God gave us a boy we named Benjamin. Ben was a delightful baby and child. He was a hoot too. At one year of age, he could talk in full sentences. I had a training class in Florida and told Dee she should come with me. She said she couldn't leave Ben. I said his airfare would be free and he wouldn't be any problem. Such was the case: he went with us and kept us entertained by his constant talking.

The bottom front louvered grill on our refrigerator would occasionally fall off. The grill was metal and about the width of a guitar neck. Being louvered, it even looked somewhat like a guitar neck. Ben learned how to remove that grill when he was about two years old. Just about any time our family was playing musical instruments, Ben would go get that louvered refrigerator grill and join right in while strumming it like a rock guitar. We were pretty sure he was going to like music and play instruments. Such was the case as God blessed Ben with musical talent. He plays several instruments and sings as well. He has just recently started writing gospel songs. I believe he will produce many excellent songs. Whatever Ben's musical future may be, he got his start on our refrigerator's louvered vent grill. Ben is an assistant pastor and music minister. No doubt in my mind, God answered our prayers at church that evening.

Note, in prayer, we had given all our children to God, as he is the one who made them and knows best. We use the term "our children," but they are really God's children. We were only stewards over them for a short while. One more additional note: after Dee's delivery of Ben, I would hear once again, "I hope my next delivery goes well."

Dee didn't think we were done yet, and I didn't either, but we would have to wait a little while to find out the fulfillment of God's plan for our childbearing.

Homeschooling

Meanwhile, we still had to raise and educate the children we had. We decided early in our marriage that we wanted our children to have a Christian worldview. It wasn't enough just to welcome into our family the children who God had graciously granted to us. We wanted to make sure we were also raising them, to the best of our ability, in the way God wanted them to be raised.

That intention led us into some new adventures—including politics!

My mom, Uncle Thurman, and Dee were all public-school teachers. The one-room schoolhouse that was friendly to Christian principles was now a thing of the past, which meant we couldn't offer our children the same experience we'd had as kids. Public schools were becoming secular and couldn't offer much Christian influence. So, when Aaron reached school age, we enrolled him in a local Christian school. We were not really pleased with our first years' experience at the school, so we tried to help the school some for the coming year. Dee taught art, and I taught a computer class at the school.

However, at the end of the year, we decided we were going to do something different. We were uncertain if there were any parochial schools in our area that we would like better. We faced a dilemma for the upcoming school year, when Aaron would be in the second grade and Elizabeth would start kindergarten.

One day while driving in Jefferson City, I was trying to listen to a Christian radio station that was in Arkansas. I usually got a decent reception of that station, but that day it was mostly static. However, one word that came over the airwaves was crystal clear: *homeschooling*. Unfortunately, I did not get any other information about that word from the broadcast. This would have been in the mid-80s. I had never heard that term before. The concept of teaching our children at home seemed totally foreign. After getting home, I told Dee about the unfamiliar word I heard on the radio. The concept was just as foreign to her.

I am uncertain we would have done much with our newly learned word had I not mentioned homeschooling to a coworker. When I did, he said he knew two families who were planning on homeschooling their children the next year. We soon met those two families. They did not know of anyone else doing such a thing, and *we* did not know if it was even legal! I am sure there were other family's homeschooling across the nation at that time, but we did not know of any. After praying and looking into God's Word, we found that the concept seemed in line with God's will, as his Word commands parents to train their children. What better way to do that than to do all the children's schooling at home? We quickly joined with the other two families in homeschool planning.

Homeschooling was indeed a foreign concept. Our church, some friends, and some family did not receive our decision well. In all fairness, I can see why, as it was something that was simply an unknown. Most who heard of what we were going to do were concerned about the legality of our plan. Despite our uncertainty regarding its legality, studying homeschooling convinced us it was God's will for our family. We took a position of not really advertising what we were doing, as we were not looking for trouble. However, word spread quickly. Soon we had the local TV station calling and wanting to video us homeschooling for the evening news. We agreed, as we did not believe we were doing anything wrong. In fact, the TV station wound up making two visits.

We didn't know it when we started doing it, but homeschooling was about to take off like a rocket. Many families across the nation started teaching their children at home. Almost all the states were busy determining what to do about homeschooling. Some states quickly stated homeschooling was legal. A few states initially declared homeschooling to be illegal. A judge in the St. Louis area told our state legislature to address homeschooling or he would rule on the matter. We heard the judge was liberal and would likely rule against homeschooling. On the second TV interview at our house, they asked me what we would do if the judge in the St. Louis area ruled against homeschooling in the state of Missouri. I already knew the answer and quickly responded that we would move to a state in which we could legally teach our children at home.

We wound up with some good folks from the St. Louis area who wanted to homeschool and who did a lot of lobbying with our state legislature to make homeschooling legal. Living in Jefferson City, our state capital, I lobbied as well. Some legislators opposed the concept. I am uncertain of the exact sequence of events, but there was a fair amount of shenanigans which took place in getting a good homeschool law passed. The law passed as the last act of the session for the year. I was present at the vote.

At first, there were signs that it hadn't gone our way. Some legislators seemed relieved to have made homeschooling illegal in our state. A local radio station in St. Louis announced the next morning that homeschooling was officially illegal in Missouri.

However, when the dust settled, it turned out that the law passed was a very favorable homeschool bill. Once again, God was merciful to us and many others who would pursue homeschooling for their children.

Satan wants to destroy families. From our experience, homeschooling is a wonderful way to build strong families. Strong families build strong churches, which in turn build a strong nation.

Blessings #9 and #10

Returning to the subject of building a family: we had left the building of our family in God's hands, and after the arrival of Benjamin, time would tell if God had more building plans for our family or not. Based upon age alone, we were running out of time.

We were definitely going against the norm, as Dee was now near her mid-forties. However, we still wanted at least one more baby to hold and raise. We enjoyed our children, and they were indeed a blessing. Based on age alone, the odds were not in our favor, but we were trusting in God, not statistics. We did nothing to prevent more blessings. The Bible says we see through a glass darkly in this old world. There is so much we do not understand. God gave us two more pregnancies that ended in miscarriages. We don't know why this happened, but we still believe there will come a day when we will meet our four children from miscarriages. That will be a glad reunion!

For several years, I wanted to write a song in dedication to the four children we never got to raise. Below is the song God gave me for those four children, and for all miscarried children.

Child, You're Not Forgotten

Verse 1:

We were so busy getting ready for – Our new gift from the Lord
So great was our joy – Wondering if a girl or a boy
But happiness would be so brief – Just a few precious weeks
With no child left to hold – Seems emptiness can fill a soul
Child, I know you're gone – But you're not forgotten
And I'm not certain how we'll meet – But let me share what I believe

Chorus:

King David lost an infant son – With a heart so broken
He could not bring the child back again – But he could say, "I shall
go to him"
And I believe by God's grace – Child, we will have our day
You abide in innocence – I'll come through the blood that cleanses
I just can't wait to see – If you look just a little like me
We'll have time to get to know one another – Together forever with
the Savior

Verse 2:

I never played peek-a-boo, peek-a-boo – Or patty-cake with you
Nor this little piggy – Went to market, one went wee, wee, wee
Never sang you a lullaby – Or woke to hear your cry
Never rocked you to sleep – No time for precious memories
Tho' time has moved on – Child, you're not forgotten
And I'm not certain how we'll meet – But let me share what I believe

(Chorus Repeats)

Blessing #11

Dee was now forty-five, and our prayer was still that God might give us another bundle of joy if that would be in his will. We certainly would not block any blessings. Of course, our last two pregnancies did not end as we wanted, but our prayer was still that God might give us our seventh child to hold and cherish. Dee would soon carry that seventh child. She was forty-six when our last child, David, was born. David had a prolapsed cord and thus was delivered by an emergency C-section, but all ended well. We had the same event with Elijah.

David was another character. He was our biggest night roamer. If we heard a bump in the night, it was not a burglar, but David up playing with his toys. He figured out how to get out of bed at an early age. David played some music and enjoys singing, but his bent seemed to be more towards working with his hands, especially on anything mechanical.

When Dee awoke from the anesthesia after David's delivery, unlike so many times before, she made no mention of another baby. We both knew in our hearts that God had blessed us far greater than we deserved with the wealth of children.

Our Multiroom Country School

Now we had our quiver full with seven children, and, as I said, since we couldn't give them the one-room public schoolhouse of our youth, we had to build something new for them on our own. Dee and I are both convinced that homeschooling has been a giant blessing to our family. We feel blessed to have been part of a significant alternative to public-school education from the beginning. I certainly make no apologies for being a homeschooling cheerleader. Humans can do homeschooling badly, just like anything else they're involved with. Of course, public schools can do schooling badly as well. I believe most homeschoolers dedicate themselves to excellence.

The bottom line is that it is not the government's or the church's responsibility to train children, but the parents'. The greatest benefit of homeschooling is that it makes families close. Our children are like that. In most traditional schools, children go their separate ways to be with peers and sometimes are not really close to their siblings. Not so with homeschooling, as they grow up together. They play together. They learn together.

When we started homeschooling, the most common question we received was about socialization. *What will you do about socialization?* Socialization is not a problem. Our children socialized mostly at church, which we call fellowship. We visited and sang for a lot of shut-ins. Our children felt comfortable socializing with people of all ages. Most homeschooled children do not have a peer-oriented world like many children in public schools do.

Not all families can or will homeschool. However, parents are still responsible for training their children. Parents should stay involved with their children's education, whichever route they choose to go. Parents should refute those areas of education which totally oppose biblical concepts.

Another giant benefit of homeschooling is that children can move at their own pace and excel with their interests. A gifted child can explore independently, not having to stay at the slower pace of the group. If school is challenging to a child, they can move at whatever their pace is—once again, they are not forced to move at the pace of their public-school peers. There's less chance of ridicule or embarrassment in a home school than in a peer setting.

The benefits of homeschooling continue with the opportunity homeschooling gives you to specialize in areas that are of particular interest to the family. Our children worked a lot on music. Thus, when not doing the three Rs, they were often practicing instruments or singing.

I previously mentioned teamwork. Teamwork is essential for homeschooling. Homeschooling is an opportunity for an exciting adventure. Homeschooling does not have peer pressure like you will find in a traditional school setting. Of course, homeschooling will not likely have the facilities and equipment of public schools. However, homeschooling still offers many other benefits. We believe God is the creator of everything and education is remiss if there is no mention of him in the education process. Public schools offer a secular education void of the very creator God.

Homeschool parents are the primary influence for their children. Homeschooling allows siblings to have a greater influence on their siblings than peer pressure or cultural pressures. Homeschool children can move at different grade levels for different subjects. Older kids learn by helping teach younger kids.

All of our homeschooled children who have children are homeschooling or plan on homeschooling their children. They recognize the value of this biblical education approach. God has blessed homeschooling, as it has grown from what we once knew to be only three families to a giant phenomenon in our nation.

No, we couldn't give our children the one-room schoolhouse of our youth, but I believe that we ended up giving them something even better. Instead of a *one-room* country schoolhouse, our whole house was available as a *multiroom* country schoolhouse.

The education our kids received has helped them to handle, with God's help, the trials that life has thrown at them.

The trials in life can overwhelm us like floods.

Sometimes, as I'll show you in the next chapter, those floods are very, very literal.

20

———∞———

When Trials Come Like a Flood

I am going to back up in time a bit. After Ben was born, we would find out how high Tebbetts was in the Missouri River bottom. The spring of '93 would be extremely wet. However, the local rain was not the problem—the problem was that the Missouri River basin to the north of us was getting inordinate rain amounts. They often received several inches of rain in a day during that spring and early summer. Flooding of the Missouri River was fairly common, but the rains of '93 would lead to a five-hundred-year flood and break flood levels all along the Missouri River basin.

Our area would be no exception.

We were living in the Missouri River bottom, and the manufacturing plant I worked at was also in the same river bottom. I had to fight the flood at home and at work as well. As the river literally surrounded our facility at work, production was shut down in favor of devoting all our effort into sandbagging. We did everything possible to save the plant and hence our jobs.

However, I faced complications in my job at work because we had the responsibility of providing mainframe computing to our sister plant in Athens, Georgia. Of course, they were not flooding, but our mainframe needed to be fully operable for Athens to continue their business operations. Without our mainframe working, they would have to shut down as well. Our plant was having electrical power problems. Also, our data communication lines to Athens were experiencing major issues, as they were under water. We barged in a large diesel generator and powered our mainframe from it. The data communication lines eventually failed, so we set up a microwave tower on top of our building for data communications to the top of a building in Jefferson City. The microwave afforded us less capacity, but it was enough to keep Athens operable. We risked wiping out our entire facility if our sandbagging failed. Initially, the thought was that we should be able to sandbag enough to prevent a disaster. But as the water kept rising, it became more evident that we might lose the facility. If we lost our facility, the Athens business would be dramatically impacted.

We had a bank in Jefferson City that we had an agreement with to back each other up in case of a disaster. We contacted them, asking if we could set up our Athens system on their mainframe, to which they readily agreed. Once the Athens system was operable at the bank, we would just need the phone company to switch all our data communication lines for Athens to the bank. Then Athens would be back in business. On July 31, my boss called me at home to inform me that if the river rose any higher, we would lose our facility. He said they wanted to bring the Athens system up at the bank. I drove to an access point, and they boated me in to our plant. I would take backups and everything I would need to bring the Athens system up at the bank.

The main roads into Jefferson City were impassable, but there was a route that would take over two hours of driving to get to the bank. The normal drive time would have been less than ten minutes. They gave me a large Jon boat and a driver who would transport me across the river to just below the Missouri State Capitol. Then, a driver would take me to the bank. My boss and the plant manager assured me I did not have to cross via boat, as there was obviously some danger. I assumed the danger would be less than the many times I rode with a drunk driver as a child, so I loaded the boat. Unfortunately, I did not have a cell phone or camera, but the sights were spectacular. Floating in the turbulent, raging floodwaters was everything from dead animal carcasses to household furniture. We would go over power lines. Fortunately, the top foot or so of power poles were sticking out of the water. The Jon boat driver would shut off the engine and tilt the engine up to ensure not getting the propeller into the actual power line. We crossed below the Missouri River Bridge into Jefferson City. The bridge piers caused the water on the other side to form an immense wall of spraying water.

Mark, an IBM employee and good friend, assisted me in getting the Athens system up at the bank. However, on that very day, the river crested. The water was literally a few inches from going over the sandbags around our plant. Breaching the sandbags would have caused the facility to be flooded and would have meant an end to our employment. Was that a coincidence or was God merciful to all the employees there? We never had to actually use the setup at the bank for Athens.

Back at home, the old-timers around Tebbetts were confident our area would not flood in '93. However, there were several houses closer to the river than our house. The river forecast raised concerns about potential flooding, including our house. I called the county and had them dump sand at our farm with sandbags so we could begin sandbagging for our community. One patriarch in the community told me I was getting a little carried away, as no one would flood in the Tebbetts area. However, we started sandbagging and put some around our house. Those with homes closer to the river started taking sandbags as well for their houses. The river would eventually surround some of those, but the sandbags kept their houses from flooding. They were quite thankful we had sandbagged. The town patriarch changed his mind and acknowledged that sandbagging was the right choice.

I previously mentioned having a lot to learn about farming. We attended church with friends, Bill and Sue. They had become our mentors and did much to help us with our farming adventure. As the river approached our property, I realized I needed to move my cows. Bill came to our rescue and said he had a lot of grass, so we could move them to his farm. The Simmental cattle were not really cooperative in loading. One cow, Miss Ami, would not go into Bill's cattle trailer. We had her roped and up to the trailer, but she refused to go in. I had an electric cattle prod, but she would just shake from the electrical shock and not move at all. Bill had worked cattle a lot and, with some forceful persuasion, Ami finally jumped in the trailer. With all my herd loaded, Bill relocated them to higher ground.

I had already moved my large, round hay bales to higher ground. The river was not on my property yet. However, soon the river would cover my pastureland where my cattle would have been. My neighbor did not move his cattle, and they had to drive them out of the river water to relocate them. The only thing we lost in the flooding was our honeybees. We only had them a few years, and we had three hives. I could have moved them but just ran out of time. The river did not get into our chicken house, so they were fine. Note, our house and chickens were on the parts of our property farthest from the river. We had a standalone garage close to our house. The river would rise to within a few inches of the garage and thus probably twenty feet from our house. When I would back out of our garage, I would back into the river just a bit. Our garden did not flood. Note, we were not supposed to flood, so we had no flood insurance. We were concerned that our house was so old that the basement might collapse if the water got in our house. I faced the reality of possibly losing both my job and house. However, the water came up next to our garage and stopped right there. Another coincidence, or perhaps divine intervention?

I have one more story about the flood. Our farm was all in the river bottom. The previous owner had sharecropped about thirty acres for row crops. This land was also the furthest from the river, as our house was. I used the same guy, Butch, to sharecrop the land. With such a small acreage, we did not make big money, but it was still income that I had to do very little for.

We prioritize Sunday as the Lord's Day and a day of rest as much as possible. I believe the biblical principle is that God made the universe in six days and rested on the seventh. Since we are made in the image of God, I'd say one day a week for rest is a good idea for mankind. Of course, livestock has to be fed and milk cows have to be milked, etc. If the ox is in the ditch, get it out. However, there are a lot of activities we try to avoid on Sundays, such as mowing our yard, planting the garden, etc. So, when I met Butch to discuss my small row-crop acreage, I asked him if he would mind not planting or harvesting our small acreage on Sundays. I told him I had no problem with whatever he did on Sundays, but I would appreciate him working his schedule around our property. Butch said that would be no problem at all. He row-cropped several hundred acres in total and could easily do as I requested. Butch had planted soybeans on our small acreage the year of the flood, and the rows were perpendicular to the river. Pretty much any plant the flood waters touched would die. Despite the river cresting, we were on the dry side as the flooding came from upstream. As the river flooded our property, it came to the exact height necessary to irrigate down the rows of our beans yet not high enough to touch the actual plants. Come harvest time, I had a very good yield. Butch stated that my request to not plant or harvest on Sundays might be valid, given the only acreage he harvested that year was mine. In fact, there were few crops harvested in the entire Missouri River bottom that year. Once again, the river rose to my favor, or as I believe, the river rose as directed by a higher power. The town of Tebbetts was further from the river than our house and did not flood at all.

We would survive the flood of '93. God was merciful to us. Our house was intact, as was my place of employment. Even our row crop was safe and watered. I can't say I would want to do it all again, but it was an experience. Aaron was old enough to help a lot with sandbagging for our neighbors, including delivering sandbags via boat. I believe we witnessed the faithful and powerful hand of a caring God.

The Lady of My Love

A songwriter who is a husband would not be worth his salt if he did not write a love song for his wife. I'm not implying I am much of a songwriter. However, the following song is my love song for my lovely wife. I obviously wrote this song after the flood of '93, as I refer to that flood in the song. As I thought about what to write, the words came easily. The thought came to me: I could never thank God enough for the lady of my love. This one is for my lovely gift from God, the lady of my love.

The Lady of My Love

Verse 1:
I prayed as a young man – Lord, choose my lady's hand
Help me to wait until – I know your perfect will
I still remember the day – You brought her my way
I knew she was the one – Chosen in heaven

Chorus:
I could never thank God enough – For the lady of my love
She's been more than just a wife – She's God's gift to my life
She's the answer to my prayer – She's given me her loving care
I could never thank God enough – For the lady of my love

Verse 2:
Now when I stop and look – Into our life's picture book
The many joys I see – The precious memories
God's blessings through the years – Sure, there's been some tears
When trials came like a flood – In God we trusted

(Chorus Repeats)

Verse 3:
The years have come and gone – Someday there will be just one
Death will do us part – I believe in my heart
We'll join hands in heaven – Tho' in marriage not given
Still she will always be – Special to me

(Chorus Repeats)

River Bottom Livin'

My lady and I really enjoyed our time in the Missouri River bottom. Also, we really enjoyed the many good folks we met there. Of course, many of those folks were the hardworking farmer type, my favorite type of people. As already stated, we loved how everything grew so fast and big in the river bottom. Dee loves flowers, and we had several kinds, including her favorite, roses. Most of our land was cleared for pasture and row cropping. We had several enormous trees in our yard, in fence rows and around the lakes. We had some large pecan trees for picking up pecans in the fall. The river bottom afforded many blessings, such as growing gardens, flowers, trees, cattle, row crops, and children.

Of course, with the good usually comes some not-so-good, and such was our experience of living in the river bottom, like the flood of '93. The river bottom offered more bugs in the summer (think mosquitoes). In the winter, the wind really glides down a river bottom. The wind chill was the important number to check before going outside in the winter, not the temperature.

We had an evangelist who once preached a series on looking for the beauty in the valley. Many songwriters have written about the valleys of life. Having lived in a valley for several years gave me special appreciation for living in a valley. Usually, beauty is easy to behold from the mountaintop. However, despite all the trials of the valley, the valley's great beauty remains, and it is most vividly observed from up close while inside the valley. Following is a short song God gave me about looking for the beauty in the valley.

Look for the Beauty

Verse:
From the mountaintop it seems you can see – The valley just traveled
so clearly
The trials and the fears found there – No longer seem to hold such
scare
In the mountaintop's bright sunlight – Life seems easier walking by
sight
But there's another valley to cross – Another time to trust in God
For in the valley below – What lies ahead only God knows
'Midst trial and difficulty – Through the shadows in the valley
God's blessings still abound – His beauty can be found

Chorus:
Look for the beauty – God's prepared in the valley
It's only up close – You see each petal of the rose
Tho' thorns may pierce the flesh – God's blessings still refresh
In between the mountaintops – Don't forget to stop
And look for the beauty – God's prepared in the valley

(Chorus Repeats)

21

Honor Thy Father ...

As I showed in the last chapter, life was good for our family around this time—fruitful and good. The floods and farm life brought physical challenges, but those were times which brought our immediate family closer together. As if life was not busy enough, we would soon have another family issue that would require considerable time. This time, my dad's family would demand some of our family's resources. Of course, this was somewhat ironic in that my dad's family had not played a major role in my life, but Dee and I believed God expected us to honor them by doing what we could for them.

We spent time with my dad's family while living in our first house and in Tebbetts. Except for brief summer and Christmas visits, I'd spent little time with my dad's family as a child. Of course, I still have no quality memories of my dad. My dad and I weren't close, but I didn't harbor any animosity towards him. Once married, Dee and I visited with him and his family some as they were physically close to where we lived in Licking and Rolla. As we started having children, they wanted to see the grandkids, so we would visit fairly regularly. My dad stayed with his mom, my grandma Kissock, unless his health was too bad. Then he stayed in the Soldier's Home in St. James.

I was not really close to the Kissock side like I was my mom's family. However, I was the only person left in the family. My dad only had one brother, Alton, and he had no children from his marriage. As they all aged, it was apparent someone was going to have to help, and I was the only choice. Despite not being close to them, I felt obligated to honor my dad and his family. I will share a little about helping my dad, Grandma Kissock, and Uncle Alton.

My Dad

As I've stated, I never got to know my dad very much personally because of his problem with alcohol and his severe strokes. My dad seemingly could have had the world by the tail. Instead, he lived the last half of his life in a wheelchair, unable to do much of anything and owning almost nothing.

Pearl Harbor launched our country into WWII soon after my dad graduated from high school. My dad joined the army and passed the tests required to join the Army Air Corps. He trained as an airplane mechanic for the Flying Fortress B-17 bomber. He also completed aerial gunner school and trained to be a flight engineer. A flight engineer in those times would know basically everything about the B-17. He'd assist the pilot and copilot with fuel and damage monitoring during bombing missions. The flight engineer would man the 50-caliber machine gun in the top turret. My dad also flew some missions as a tail gunner.

My dad received his crew wings to be a member of a B-17 bomber crew. He flew out of the Great Ashfield Airdrome, which was about one hundred miles northeast of London. I have many letters he wrote to his family back home during the war. Of course, he could not really say anything about the active war, so they are not really interesting; but when the war was over, he still flew a few missions and could share some stories. I will copy a couple of segments from his letters. The first is about a mission in which the United States dropped food into

Holland, as those still alive were starving from the German occupation:

> I sure had a swell trip over Holland the other day as I went along with a load of food we were dropping over there. We were flying real low and you could see the country well. The flowers were in bloom and the houses and the windmills were just like the pictures you see of the place. The people would wave at the planes as they went over. It sure was really something to see.

This excerpt is about picking up prisoners of war in Austria:

> I went to Austria and up to Ireland the other day. We sure had a swell trip down to Austria. We picked up a load of French PWs. I had a little engine trouble over France and we had to spend the night as I could not get parts that night. We tried to make it to Paris but couldn't. We flew over Paris the next day.
>
> I guess you remember when the buzz bomb blitz was on. Well, we had a few to come over here and one went right over our barracks. They really make some racket, but things are pretty dead around here right now. No excitement of any kind.

The following excerpt was sent during the war. Apparently, he could express his political viewpoint in the mail going back home. His opinion of Roosevelt seemed to be the same as that of my mom's family:

> I'm sitting down to write you as it seems you worry yourself to death if you don't hear from me every other day. Well, there is no use for you worrying about me, as that doesn't help anyone. I'm in the Army now and the best I can do is play ball and take what comes my way with a smile, as the war wouldn't be fun for you if it was lost. I wish I could do more than what I am as I'm not like those yellow rats that voted for Roosevelt and then are afraid of the Army. If I could, I would do more. Guess I am unlucky to be in a world war, but maybe I can help someone else.

My dad stated there was no use in his family worrying about him, but in reality, the bomber group missions were extremely dangerous. The Germans had excellent fighter pilots, and their planes shot down many of our bombers. German antiaircraft would shoot flak at the approaching bombers that exploded and sent shrapnel flying. We had many airmen killed in air or in plane crashes. The Germans usually captured those who parachuted, and they became POWs.

The mental stress of flying missions or even just mentally processing the substantial loss of planes and fellow soldiers was simply staggering. My dad returned from the war alive but with a drinking problem. I am certain many others returned in the same condition. My dad had a friend who told me my dad met a young woman in England and they were going to marry. However, the German bombing of England killed her. I certainly cannot process the turmoil of what my dad and so many others endured in WWII. However, the end result was my dad came back a drunk and was not a father to me. The ill effects of alcohol would cause his life to spiral out of control. He would have several car wrecks from drunkenness and eventually many strokes.

I mentioned my dad could have had the world by the tail. He was quite skilled in aviation after the war. He flew with a friend after being back home and could have done well in aviation alone. My dad had a rich aunt who had no children and left my dad considerable wealth, including cash and a farm in Oklahoma. Another friend of my dad told me he saw the paperwork on a banana plantation in Brazil my dad inherited. I do not know if that is factual. I have paperwork on the cash and the Oklahoma farm. Drinking prevented my dad from graduating with an engineering degree from the School of Mines and Metallurgy. Instead, my dad drank all of his inheritance up and wound up in a wheelchair.

I never really knew anything about my dad until I pieced his life together from papers I found after his death and from a few of my dad's friends. I am presuming my dad drank some alcohol before going into the Air Corps, but he came out drinking a lot. Instead of him having the world by the tail, the liquor bottle had a firm grip on my dad.

Growing up, I wanted to be involved with aviation, but I didn't know that my dad was heavily involved with it. I grew up with a love of math, never knowing my dad's favorite subject was math.

The truth is, the booze separated us. As I've said before, I've experienced no positive results from alcohol. The best advice regarding alcohol I've ever found is simply to stay away from the stuff.

If my dad had done that, perhaps I could have shared some of the loves of my life with him.

Uncle Alton

My dad's alcohol-abusing habit separated him from those he loved, but it didn't have quite the same effect on his brother, my uncle Alton (though its effect on Alton was still not good). To say Uncle Alton was country would be a gigantic understatement. Besides that, he was quite a character. Thus, I will share a few stories about Uncle Alton.

Alton was a good-sized fellow with large hands and a kind heart. He tried to farm, but I'm not sure he was a great farmer. However, he was a good welder, as he repaired farm equipment for other farmers for miles around his place. In his old shack of a shop, he had a large metal lathe and could make just about any part for farm equipment. Usually, he charged little or nothing, as he always tried to help others. He baled a lot of hay in the summer, but the work he loved was logging. He once told me that for him, logging in the woods on a bitter-cold winter day was more fun than any kid could have on a Christmas morning.

Alton and his wife, Letha, had no children, leaving just the two of them and frequent visitors. Their house was basically a tiny shack. They were tiny house people before tiny houses were cool. It was hard to get rich on a small farm. Alton did not charge much for all he did to help neighbors, so they learned to live country simple. However, they were both quite content in life. They lived near the small community of Maples, which was not really a town. At one time Maples had a general store and a post office, both of which are now gone. Alton and Letha's tiny house was the grand central station of Maples, MO. Often, neighbors came so Alton could do mechanical work for them. Other times, people just came to visit. Even without Letha and Alton being home, people would visit and sit in lawn chairs in their yard. Alton was a fiddle player, which was quite amazing, as his fingers were about the size of a fiddle neck. Others in the community would bring instruments, and they would play music late into the night while sitting in lawn chairs outside.

For years, Alton had a drinking problem, but he was a happy drunk and was never violent, unlike his brother, my dad. I remember Alton's friends saying that once when Alton was drunk and in a boat on a river, he lost his paddles. Since he had his fiddle with him, he used it as a paddle. The fiddle seemed no worse for the wear.

Alton stopped drinking and even eventually quit smoking, but when he was in his sixties, they diagnosed him with bladder cancer. He had his bladder removed at the University Hospital in Columbia, MO. Alton begged the doctors to give him a spinal block and prop him up so he could watch the surgery via the mirror. The doctors did not fulfill Alton's request, which he said would have been a highlight of his life. This is the uncle who once pulled a tooth of his own while inebriated. Some in his community could not afford official funeral services, so they would bring the deceased to Alton to prepare the body for burial. Apparently, blood and guts did not bother him.

Alton and Letha were a testament to the fact that wealth is not required to live a fulfilled life. They were country to the core. They had few worldly possessions but were rich in friendships.

Alton did not survive his bladder cancer. I have never been to a funeral with as large of an attendance as his had. I like to think that the size of his funeral was a tribute to his generosity, giving him the same sort of kindness that he had bestowed on so many others. He was another good country farmer type.

Grandma Kissock

Grandma Kissock, the mother of both my father and Uncle Alton, was another character in my life. I have already mentioned she was quite a workhorse for most of her life. She helped care for and support my dad through his drinking problems and the severe strokes he had. I believe my dad might have been more functional after his strokes if Grandma had not babied him so much. My mom mentioned several times to me that she told my dad if he would try to get help with his drinking problem, she would stay with him. He never sought help. I do not believe Grandma Kissock really helped him when she tried to blame everything else for his problems, thus enabling him to keep drinking.

Uncle Alton was the first to pass away, and then my dad. Grandma Kissock said watching her children being buried were the hardest events in her life. She would live into her late nineties. No other family was available to care for Grandma Kissock, so we accepted our responsibility. Eventually, we moved her into our first house, but she did not like the arrangement. We didn't really care for it either. We got her an apartment in Jefferson City for a while, but finally decided she was too old to be safely living by herself. Fortunately, we found a lady close to where we lived who had a boardinghouse for older ladies. This worked well for several years. The owner of the house cooked the meals and did her laundry.

We often took Grandma and another boardinghouse resident shopping on Saturday mornings. Grandma was hard of hearing. Our last stop was usually at a grocery store so the boarders could buy some snacks. Grandma liked pears. I was following behind Grandma in the store's produce section when she passed by the pears. I asked her if she wanted a pear. She stopped in her tracks and let me know she did not want a beer. I should know she didn't drink beer, and she did not appreciate me trying to get her to buy beer. She was loud enough that everyone around us was looking at me like, *What in the world is that man trying to do?* This was one of many somewhat humorous episodes with Grandma Kissock.

Grandma Kissock had some health issues, and several times she would decide I needed to take her to the emergency room. Usually this happened late at night, but this one time was earlier on a Saturday afternoon. Due to our late departure from the emergency room, Grandma missed her meal at the boardinghouse. So, we swung by McDonald's. We went through the drive-through, where I ordered her regular meal, which was a soda and a plain hamburger with nothing on it but ketchup. She did not like pickles. I got her order and gave her the hamburger and drink. She unwrapped her hamburger, opened it up, and picked up her hamburger patty. Her vision was not good, and she was holding her hamburger patty just a few inches from her eyes. I finally asked her, "What in the world are you doing, Grandma?" She said she was trying to figure out what was on her hamburger. I told her it was her hamburger patty. She looked at me and said, "I thought it was a pickle." I assured her it was her hamburger patty and told her to put it back on the bun and eat it. This was when McDonald's and Burger King were having commercial wars. I have always thought Burger King would have loved a video of Grandma's difficulty in visually distinguishing the size of her hamburger patty from the size of a pickle.

We definitely got a taste of taking care of older adults in dealing with Grandma Kissock. Once, I took her for a regular doctor's visit. We were in the waiting room, as were several other people. Grandma's gaze suddenly shifted to the floor. She slowly leaned forward like something caught her attention on the floor. Everyone else in the room watched, trying to figure out what she was doing. Once she was stooped way over, she picked up the hem of her dress and blew her nose on it. I immediately said, "Grandma, what are you doing? You know better than that." She whispered back to me, "Yeah, I know it, but when you're my age, people think you're crazy, so you can do anything you think of."

That might be so, but I kindly requested her to never do that again.

Indeed, Grandma Kissock was quite a jokester. When she was around ninety and someone offered her coffee, she would usually say, "Well, I guess not. My mama told me not to drink coffee until I was old, so I better wait." Then she would laugh and have her coffee.

Grandma, in her mid-nineties, fell and broke her hip. She resumed walking after the first fall but broke her other hip in a subsequent fall. She never walked again but used her wheelchair well and lived to be ninety-eight.

Like all of us, she had some faults, but she left little doubt about whether or not she was a character.

22

Back on the Farm

The interactions with my father's side of the family happened over many years. Such life events are often not convenient, but that is how life works. Now it's time to return to our life-on-the-farm narrative. After the flood, a neighbor replanted grass on my hayfield for me. The river-bottom soil did not take long to produce new grass, and so we were able to bring our cows back by fall.

We had a great spot for a bonfire, and we had them often. Our land was all flat, which made for great bike riding and four wheeling for our children. We fished in the lakes and had a flat-bottom boat with a trolling motor so we could cruise our lakes.

We had one old barn, which was not connected to any of the pastures, which had a large loft in it that was in pretty good shape. I did not need the barn for farming, so the kids took that for a large playhouse. They spent a lot of hours up there playing. Fortunately, no one fell out of the loft, as it was quite high. They had one other smaller shed for another playhouse.

We had lots of mowing, but enough of us to keep up with it. However, with mowing, milking, gardening, keeping fences up, feeding the beef cows and chickens, cooking, laundry, homeschooling, church, etc., we stayed pretty busy. Of course, we always had a new baby to take care of, but our babies were mostly pretty good. The children were learning musical instruments, including piano, guitar, mandolin, accordion, violin, etc. So, inside the house, we usually had some kind of music going on. If not kids playing or practicing, we had Southern gospel music playing. I would say our biggest entertainment activity was going to Southern gospel quartet concerts. Any concert within a three-to-four-hour drive was fair game for us to attend. Indeed, we were living our dream of a large family and farm livin', with a lot of gospel music thrown in.

How to Hypnotize a Cow

The previous owner of our farm had rented out our pastureland. I would eventually buy some cows from the guy who had it rented, Glen. The grass was so rich in the river bottom that some cows had problems with their toenails growing too long. I had never heard of such a thing growing up in southern Missouri in rocky red clay soil. One cow I bought, Emily, needed her toenails trimmed, and Glen said he would help me do that. One day Glen was over, and Emily was lying under a tree chewing her cud. Glen told me this would be a good time to trim her nails, but it would take two people. Glen approached her first with a cattle prod. Once he got close enough, he started rubbing her with the tip of the prod from just below her front leg, down the side of her belly, to just in front of her back leg. He would then go back the way he came and just kept repeating. It seemed to put her in a trance. Glen had me take the prod and instructed me to push firmly but avoid pushing too hard. I did as instructed. Glen then moved her feet around as needed to trim her nails. I had never seen this before. I have asked others about it and have yet to find anyone else who has heard of this, but it worked.

Still, I'd love to know more about where Glen picked up this trick. If you happen to know, I hope you'll reach out and tell me about it.

Farm #2

We had our seventh child while in Tebbetts. The house we were in had four bedrooms, but none of them were large. In fact, none of the rooms were really large in the house. We fit much better when our children were smaller, but now our family was growing in number and in size. We needed to do something. Humongous maple trees surrounded the house. Cutting any of them down was something we didn't want to do and finding an affordable way to add to the house was challenging. We had a minimal budget for the building project, and we chose to continue our policy of not going into debt. Of course, buying another farm with a bigger house was an option. We still had memories of the flood and did not really want to do that again. Our long-term plan (a few years down the road) was to buy another farm with a larger house. In the meantime, we needed to fix our place up for selling.

About this same time, our older kids were supposed to go to our town mall and sing at a music store on a Saturday. The store called and had to cancel, but the kids still wanted to go somewhere. I had noticed in our local paper that an eighty-acre farm was for sale in New Bloomfield, so I made arrangements with a realtor to meet at the property. We went to the property and did not see a realtor's car, but we were not sure, so I knocked on the door of the house. The door was answered by Virginia, the elderly woman who owned the property with her husband. I told her my family was supposed to meet a realtor here. She informed me the realtor had not notified her. Later we found out that the realtor had agreed to the time but then forgot about it.

Since we were already there, Virginia said we could still look around. She showed us through the house. It was much larger than our current house. The farm had even more barns and sheds than our current farm. Virginia's husband, Jim, had a green thumb and had turned the yard into a parklike setting with lots of flower beds and fruit trees all over the property. A small lake sat behind the house and was viewable from a nice sunroom in the back of the house. The land was rolling and, of course, was not a river bottom but still looked like good dirt. They had a large garden as well.

Like the prior owners of our current property, the owners of this new property had decided they were too old to take care of the farm. They were building a new house to retire in. We visited with Virginia for a while, and she found out we were from Tebbetts. Upon leaving, we expressed gratitude to Virginia for her time and complimented the house and farm but clarified that we were just looking. We told her we were just trying to get a feel for what other farms were like, as sometime down the road we planned on buying another farm, but that we would have to sell our property before we did that, as we believed God wanted us to stay out of debt. We returned home with no thoughts of doing anything with the property we had just seen. Virginia had told us they already had contract offers for the full list price. Of course, we were not even close to selling and buying—or so we thought.

On the next Monday, the realtor called Dee and apologized for missing our meeting. However, the main reason she called was to inform us that Virginia wanted us to buy their property. Dee called me at work to share Virginia's request. I informed Dee that we couldn't proceed with buying since our house wasn't yet for sale. I told Dee to share our appreciation to

Virginia and also to explain we weren't serious about purchasing at the moment. You just don't sell a farm overnight (well, at least that is what I was thinking).

The realtor passed our message on, but then got back to us to say that Virginia wanted us to let her know as soon as our property sold. Keep in mind that we had done nothing in preparation to sell. We were not even close to being ready to sell our property. This was still on the Monday after the Saturday when we'd seen the property.

After getting home from work, I told Dee that a neighbor, Steve, who owned land between me and the river, might be interested in our property. Once at a feed store, I had asked Steve if he would be interested in our property if we ever sold. He had indicated he might. Since Virginia was eager to sell us their farm, I called Steve. He said he was interested and would stop by the next evening. He came by and looked at our house and farm. When done looking, he rather frankly asked, "What do you want for this place?" I did not have a number clearly defined in my mind, so I shot him what I thought was a fairly high price. He replied he would take it. Immediately I thought, "I should have asked for more." Of course I couldn't do that, but I added that the price I gave was for the property in "as is" condition. We would not be responsible for fixing anything. He agreed. Then I made one more stipulation. We needed to go back and look at the other farm one more time to make certain we wanted to move there. Steve agreed to that too.

Eventually, we found out why Virginia wanted to sell to us. Virginia's best friend was a widow in the Tebbetts area. She was one of the elderly ladies we had taken the kids to sing for, and we had given her a loaf of homemade bread. Virginia's friend gave us the best of recommendations, and Virginia decided she wanted to sell to us. The next Saturday, we returned and looked at the New Bloomfield farm to complete the deal. Once again, we did another whirlwind selling/buying deal. If the realtor had arrived on time, we wouldn't have talked to Virginia and wouldn't have pursued the property. Once again, we knew this was God's doing. We would still stay out of debt.

The New Bloomfield house was not new, but it wasn't as old as the Tebbetts house, and it had considerably more square footage. We needed the space and soon occupied it with all nine of us. Dee made the statement that you have not lived until you have packed up twenty-two-plus years of marriage, seven kids' worth of stuff, forty-plus head of cattle, farm equipment, dogs, cats, chickens, etc., etc., etc. However, with the help of family and friends, we completed the move.

Big Bull Mischief

I would like to convey what I consider a funny story from life on the farm. We had a large hay barn fairly close to the house, where I would water and feed grain to the beef cattle. I had a large Black Angus bull. I watered the herd in a metal water tank, which was about two feet wide and six feet long, with rounded ends.

As the cattle finished up eating their grain, I leaned against a gate near the watering tank. A large steer, probably six hundred to seven hundred pounds, had wandered over to the tank for a drink. The bull lifted his head while eating and looked at the steer. He promptly pranced over to the water tank and immediately put his head under the belly of the steer that was drinking water. The bull hefted the steer upwards and sent it tumbling through the air, ultimately splashing it upside down into the water tank. The bull sneaked away, acting like he had pulled off quite a trick. This appeared to be a prank by a cow, which was new to me.

I did not find the bull's prank amusing, because this steer was worth a lot of money if kept alive. My three youngest sons were outside the barn throwing a football around. I called them to come and help. The steer was kicking and thrashing like crazy, trying to keep from drowning. I was going to try tipping the tank over with some long poles I had. Before we could get the poles in place, the steer got himself turned over and jumped out of the tank.

The young steer had likely been annoying the old bull and suffered the consequences. You never know what to expect on a farm.

Firewood

While we really liked our bigger house, it was not exactly energy efficient. However, it had two fireplaces and a wood furnace in the basement. We also had a propane furnace, but of course that cost money, so we heated mostly with wood. We kept three fires burning to warm the house, requiring a lot of firewood. The boys and I cut, hauled, split, and stacked a lot of firewood. We would eventually buy a wood-pellet stove, which cut our wood processing down a good bit. I helped with firewood cutting and splitting as a child. I have maintained that activity for most of my life, including the present, as I just cut a pickup load of wood before writing this paragraph.

Back on the New Farm

We have loved everywhere we have lived. We believe the primary reason for that is the fact that God ordered all our moves. Moving to the dream farm would have been out of God's will, as he never opened a door for it. We could have borrowed money and made it happen, but instead we waited upon the Lord. Our Tebbetts farm will always be special. Most of our children were young when we moved there. It was our first farm and holds a multitude of precious memories, including the beauty of living in a river valley. Tebbetts was not Mayberry, but it had some similarities to that fabled place.

When we arrived at our second farm, our older children were teenagers/driving/not young children/etc. We still had young children, but not all our children were young anymore. As the farms changed, so had our family. We would end up loving our second farm as well. The house and property seemed to fit our family very well, especially the larger house. We still had our milk cow. Still had a place to fish. Still had the beef cattle. We still had a large garden, but I would once again add another garden. We still had our chickens, dogs, and cats. Still had a lot of farm work and a good place to enjoy life. Of course, we still had lots of gospel music. Still had a great environment to finish raising our family and for homeschooling. Dee and I are thankful to God for such a blessing!

Speaking of Dee, none of these blessings would have been possible without her. A good wife and mother is one of the greatest blessings God can give a family—but being a good wife and mother is not easy. It takes dedication, love, and a focus on following the Lord.

You don't have to take my word for it, though. As you'll see a little way into the next chapter, you can take Dee's word for it as well.

23

The Hand that Rocks the Cradle

In reviewing my story, I see that I have seriously understated the role of my wife in whatever success I have had in life and, likewise, in whatever success our family has had. Once while Dee was in junior high school, the teacher asked what each student wanted to be when they grew up. The other students named many occupations. Dee simply stated she wanted to get married and have children. Her response drew some snickers from several in the class, but I believe that is a wonderful goal for a young lady. I still believe the adage that the hand that rocks the cradle rules the world. Certainly, in the life of our children, a loving mother's influence has been monumental. I know this goes against current social norms, but I still believe there is nothing wrong with the age-old model of Dad being the primary breadwinner and Mom being at the forefront of raising the children.

Of course, Dee's life was not just simply nurturing children. She homeschooled all of them, directed work activities, worked in the garden, canned garden produce, helped with milking our family cow, and many more tasks than I could list. She readily assisted with frugal living to allow us to purchase a farm and afford a large family. I have joked over the years that I had so many children and bought the farms so I could keep my wife busy enough to keep her from running the streets at nighttime. Obviously, my plan worked! We were not really the little house on the prairie, but we definitely had some similarities. Bottom line is God blessed me and our family greatly to have a godly wife and mom who did an excellent job of fulfilling those roles.

I want to share a devotion written by Dee. She prepared this message for a ladies' meeting at our church near 2005. Our childbearing days were over at this time, but we still had several children at home. The following are some thoughts Dee put together at that time pertaining to her experiences of being a wife and a mom to seven children.

Dee's Devotion

> But speak thou the things which become sound doctrine ... The aged women likewise, that they be in behaviour as becometh holiness, not false accusers, not given to much wine, teachers of good things; That they may teach the young women to be sober, to love their husbands, to love their children, To be discreet, chaste, keepers at home, good, obedient to their own husbands, that the word of God be not blasphemed. (Titus 2:1, 3-5)

Following Titus 2 will not take us to heaven, but because we are justified by God's mercy and grace, we should by all means want to do good works.

Whatever our station in life—aged women, young women, or mothers—we are called to be faithful—so faithful that the critics of our religion, be it neighbor, fellow worker, or family, will have nothing to say against us.

I thought I would start by giving a testimony of my life. Verse 3 talks of the aged women and many of you only know me as a poor old woman with seven kids. Well, I haven't always been old, but I guess you could say that I always wanted children.

I was raised in a church that preached the Word, and I gave my heart to Jesus before I was ten years old. There have been many ups and downs in my life, but I have never doubted God's saving love for me.

I can still remember that in junior high school, we were asked what we wanted to be when we grew up. I was laughed at when I said, "Be married and have children." By the time I was a senior in high school, it seemed God didn't have marriage in my near future, so I went to college and majored in elementary education with a minor in art and Christianity. God led me to teach in a rural K–8 school of two hundred students. My students became my kids. I spent more time with them than many of their parents did. God taught me much about loving children in those first teaching years.

During my third year of teaching, I finally surrendered to the Lord my desire to be married. I vowed to be the best old maid schoolteacher there ever was, if that is what God wanted for me.

I think what he really wanted was for me to surrender, because soon after that, I was introduced to this young man in the Air Force.

Seven months after we met and a couple of weeks after my twenty-fifth birthday, we were married—that was thirty years ago at the time of this writing.

As a young married couple, we adopted the mindset of our peers. You know—get a good education, good job, nice house, car, and clothes, and take some great vacations. Oh, and by the way, have a couple kids.

It wasn't until I was in my early thirties and after we had that perfect family—a son and a daughter—that God began to work in my life. The baby bed was sold, and we were talking about me going back to teaching as soon as we got both kids into school. You know—it was time to get on with *my* life.

Am I ever thankful that the Lord had other plans and changed our hearts! He helped me realize that being a wife and mother *is* my life. I'm so sad to say that I can remember no one pointing me in the direction of the Titus woman, as described in verses 3–5 of the second chapter of the epistle. Now that I am closer in age to the "older woman," I feel I need to encourage you younger women and mothers to follow the example of Titus 2:5: Be sober or wise, love and be obedient to your husband, be discreet, chaste, keepers at home, and love your children.

I would like to emphasize one of those thoughts from Titus: "that they may teach the young women … to love their children."

In God's divine plan, the family was established to provide the most secure and loving environment possible for the human child to grow up in. The family provides for the emotional, intellectual, physical, and spiritual growth of that child.

For most of mankind's history, the family has been the greatest influence on a child. Today, peers and even social media may be the greatest influence on a child. I still believe children should ideally be primarily influenced by their family's structure while being raised in the nurture and admonition of the Lord.

In John 10:11-15, Jesus tells us that he is the Good Shepherd. The hireling will never love the sheep like the Good Shepherd does. We can be like the Good Shepherd with our children or leave their training up to the hired hand. As mothers, we should know our children better than anyone and, most importantly, love them the most because God has loaned them to us.

I don't think many would question the fact that children need their parents, and need their mothers in particular. But while we can be physically present for our children, are we really *all* there? Are we busy with too many personal activities— wrapped up in a craft project, in the middle of a book or a TV show, or trying to prepare our house and yard for the "House

Beautiful" award? God holds us parents accountable for these children he has placed in our care. We should love children truly, unlike someone who is just hired to take care of them. Sometimes that means if we want to do what's best for our children, and make a permanent difference in their lives, we must pay a price. Are we guilty of giving our children everything but ourselves? I admit I've been there more than once.

I read a book about a missionary's wife. Unfortunately, I don't remember her name or the book title. She made a statement in her book which made a profound effect upon my life. The missionary wife was asked what she would have done differently if raising her family today. She said, "I would stay home more, see that my children were fed spiritually, and be kinder to my children."

When I look back on my own life, I'd say these are all very important. I have never regretted staying home with my children. I have not regretted spending the last twenty years homeschooling. I don't know how many times someone has said, "I could never do that—I couldn't stand to have my kids home all day." Actually, I think that is a little sad. I *like* my kids. (Well, most of the time.) Enjoy these years that happen only once and which, believe me, are too soon gone forever.

As good mothers, we see that our children have food so they can grow healthy and strong, but it is just as important that we use everyday experiences to feed them with truths from God's Word. Every child comes from God and ought to live for God's purposes.

Sometimes I think we often forget the awe and wonder of conception. Being rich or poor, educated or uneducated, godly or ungodly makes no difference regarding who has his children. We can easily forget the part God plays in "every" birth.

I can remember sometime after our third child, Sarah, was born, that we decided we would trust God for any future children. (My doctor had told me that I was approaching that age, thirty-five, when I should seriously rethink having any more children.) But how many times had we heard the preacher say, "Who knows what is best for you? God does—just trust him with your life"? So, we took the challenge and let the Lord decide on how many and when.

After having children #4, Lydia, and #5, Elijah, I thought, *Boy, this is easy.* That's when God really got ahold of my heart and made me realize that each child really comes from God and I and my husband are to see that they fulfill the purpose that God has for them.

I had a miscarriage when Elijah was two. It was the most heartbreaking thing that ever happened to me—ranking right up there with my dad's death several years earlier. But God got me through it and again we were back on track, leaving things to the Lord. Well, kind of. (I can still remember thinking that the next time I'd be more careful. I had taken a fall before my first miscarriage.) As much as I wanted to think I was trusting the Lord, I was still attributing the miscarriage to my actions apart from God's.

A year later, I was pregnant again and then, without any warning at the end of my first trimester, I miscarried again. That's when I could really say, "Lord, it's all in your hands." Perhaps this long wait of four and a half years was to help God lay a groundwork of prayer in my life. At forty-three years old, I gave birth to #6, Benjamin (by the way, he was one of my easiest pregnancies and deliveries). We can say his existence was bathed in prayer.

There were two more miscarriages after Ben was born. Several people told us that they thought six was enough and we should do something to ensure our family was complete.

Even through all those trials and difficulties, I never regretted letting God be in control. Three and half years later, when I was forty-six and a half years of age, David, #7, our last blessing, was born. God gave me a peace that only he can give. In my heart I knew that David completed our family.

I shared all that to say that each child must be thought of as a sacred charge—an assignment from God. God's will for your life may not include children, or may include only a child or two, or may include a dozen. We must be willing to accept God's will and trust him to know what is best for us.

The last point the missionary made was that she would have been kinder to her children. This is my weak point, I'm afraid. I've found that many times in the past, I've had to apologize for things I've said. Again, in really loving our children, we must be kind in word and deed. These children are a part of God's plan, as stated in Jeremiah 1:5: "Before I formed thee in the belly I knew thee; and before thou camest forth out of the womb I sanctified thee, and I ordained thee a prophet unto the nations."

God had a plan for Jeremiah's life even before his beginning. I think that God has plans for our children too—those born and unborn. I don't want to mess those plans up by resenting the interruptions children cause in my life's schedule.

Of course, being kinder still includes discipline. Proverbs 29:15 declares, "The rod and reproof give wisdom: but a child left to himself bringeth his mother to shame." As mothers, we should not leave our children to their own selves, but rather discipline them in love as opposed to disciplining them in anger.

Thank God that you can be involved in his plans for the children God has entrusted you with.

A Quiver Full

I hope you enjoyed that devotion by Dee. I know I am thankful to God to have had her as my companion all these years, and glad to have had her putting all of the above wisdom and love into practice as she mothered our children.

After David was born, we did nothing to prevent more children, but God had settled our quiver full with seven arrows down here on this old earth. Of course, we have four more in heaven. Dee and I are thankful God redirected our original plan of having two children. Through the autumn of our life, our job was to ensure the arrows in our quiver would be straight and true, so that each one would be fit for the Master's use. God gave me the following song to convey that message.

Little Arrow

Verse 1:
Like arrows in the hand – Of a mighty man
Children are a blessing – But each will need much training
That someday the Master might choose – Them for his own use
As he will know each one's worth – As their life is launched forth

Chorus:
Little arrow, it's so important how you grow
You see, the Master Archer will always know
How well you travel the straight and narrow
Someday to be worthy of the Master's bow
Little arrow, be careful how you grow

Verse 2:
Little arrow, you'll not miss – God's mark you will hit
If you'll grow straight and true – As God's Word instructs you to
So whatever God sends you through – Just fine you will do
You see the Master will know – If you are worthy of his bow

(Chorus Repeats)

I will not dwell long on child discipline other than to say a child that is out of control is no fun to be around. Thus, we began discipline very early. By the time a child crawls and is getting into things, the child should have some conceptual understanding of what the word "no" is all about. Obviously, I am not referring to abuse but to the commencement of understanding discipline. Early effort reduces childhood discipline problems in years to come. We enjoyed our little arrows because we tried to get them straight as possible at an early age.

A friend of mine in high school, Mike, told me that at a very young age he was misbehaving in a crowd and his dad gave him a gentle swat on his bottom. Mike said he was so embarrassed that he never wanted anything like that to happen again. From then on, he tried his best to walk the straight and narrow. Mike required very little discipline training. Most children are not quite that accommodating, but we believe in the old saying based on God's Word, "Spare the rod and spoil the child."

Raising children seems to be somewhat of a balancing act. I have emphasized what I believe about the importance of work, but childhood should still be fun. Amidst work activities, there should be time to enjoy life as well. Likewise, discipline is of absolute importance, but God warns of not provoking children to wrath. Certainly, discipline should not cross the boundary into abuse or cause a broken spirit. The Scriptures declare that a just weight and balance are the Lord's. Parents need to seek a godly balance in raising children.

The autumn of my life was the time of marriage, childbearing, and child rearing. Indeed, the best season of life for Dee and me. Our children are now adults and all of them are married, giving us the joy of grandchildren. With grandchildren, we still seem to always have a baby around, which we enjoy. As we enter the winter season of our lives, I thank God for his blessing of children and grandchildren in our lives.

Part IV

The Winter of My Life

Harvesting is over. The once hardy, producing plants will eventually succumb to the cold, hard winter ahead. Such is the reality for the winter season of life.

The old plants will eventually be gone, but results from their production can live on ad infinitum via seedlings passed on. Perhaps nourishment provided by the plants to others will help sustain many through the seasons of their lives. Additionally, seedlings generated from the former plants may continue the cycle of regeneration and be a blessing to many for many seasons to come. Winter certainly holds great beauty, but I also know there is a bleak forecast for this plant in the coming winter season of my life. I do not know when the storm will hit that this earthen shell will not survive.

This plant is thankful to the Lord of the Harvest for survival through the seasons of life. Eventually, the physical body of this plant will return as dust to the earth. However, I am eternally grateful for all the seasons of my life. I am especially thankful for the springtime storms, which hardened a young plant to withstand the heat of a summer season. I am eternally grateful for the many who tended to, helped cultivate, and nurtured this plant. The Lord of the Harvest blessed me mightily by mating me with a wonderful companion plant. Of course, the fall-time of my life has been the best, seeing a harvest after all the storms of spring and the heat of summer. New plants are being spawned from the plants spawned by this old plant and companion plant. When the winter season of this plant's life closes, this body will wait for a glorious resurrection into an eternal season with no storms and no ending.

24

Precious Memories

Looking back, I feel comfortable saying Dee and I chose a road less traveled, and it has made all the difference, as Robert Frost penned. Eleven children, farm, milk cow, sizeable gardens, stay-at-home mom, homeschooling, getting out of debt, staying out of debt, and a lot of homemade ice cream, with gospel music thrown in. Can't say the road we chose was best for my 401k or early retirement, but I have zero regrets. A multitude of precious memories are of far greater value than a larger 401k.

Dee and I have come to what I am calling the winter of our life. We feel blessed to have reached an old age. God has indeed been merciful to us. When first married, we had no idea what God had planned for our union. Once again, God was merciful to give us direction and understanding. God opened the windows in heaven and showered great blessings upon our family. I never had much of an enjoyable childhood, but God gave me a wonderful family in the autumn and winter of my life. Words cannot encapsulate the joy of a happy family. Not all was perfect, but it was a lot of fun watching all our children grow into adulthood. Of course, life is still a lot of fun when our family gets together (our seven children with their spouses, plus twenty-one grandchildren, with hopefully more grandchildren to come).

Dee and I are pushing fifty years of marriage. We get along pretty well, other than Dee's fatigue from my stupid jokes. We both agree the best time of our life and marriage was when all seven of our children were at home. Dee does scrapbooking basically to help preserve those precious memories. Having children is indeed a lot of work, but we found children to be a lot of fun, which God calls blessings. Dull moments have been rare in our married life. Recently, when we had all the clan at home (about thirty people at that time) and we were preparing a meal, I crossed paths with Dee and said, "It's a bit of a circus, isn't it?" She replied, "Yes, but it is our circus" (and that makes all the difference).

An Old Man

When I left home at fourteen, my focus was on financial fortune. I basically stowed away my childhood memories in a private room in my mind. I tried to keep that room locked as best as I could and just not visit there. After being married for a few years, I concluded that perhaps my wife might better understand some of my likely peculiar beliefs and behaviors (like no alcohol) if I let her peek into my private room and witness some artifacts I had suppressed there. I supposed she might better understand where I wanted to go in life if she better understood where I had come from.

So I shared my childhood memories with my wife.

Dee expressed surprise at some of the stories I shared with her, just as I have shared them in this book. In fact, she said the stories of Leonard were hard to believe, as he had been a wonderful grandpa to our children. In time, Mom and Glenda would confirm what the old Leonard was like. Dee would be my only soulmate to know what I had protected as secrets.

Here, at the end of this book, I will share a few more stories, but mostly I want to share what I've learned from my stories. It's the wise man who observes life and then learns something from it (Proverbs 24:32); our experiences are *meant* to teach us things.

I'd like to share some of what I've learned with you.

First, however, I want to close the loop on my childhood stories.

There was a lot of bad in my childhood such as being beaten, coldcocked, enduring ridiculous demands, fear, embarrassment, etc. Beyond bad lies ugly. Divorce is a great breeding ground for ugly. Certainly, abuse is fertile ground for ugly to flourish in. Fear is like a fertilizer to grant ugly great yields.

By the grace of God, I also had some good in my childhood. My mom loved me and did what she could for me. The reader may think my mom was a bad mother because of the mess and danger we were in. She certainly made some poor choices. However, I would counter that the reality of her fear that Leonard was capable of killing all of us gave her rather limited options. Armchair quarterbacking is easier without actual game experience. In my opinion, Mom did the best she could do, given the situation. I had three sisters, Grandma Tennie, Grandpa Luther, and Mom's family, all of whom have been good to me. I had many Mom #2s, including Grandma Tennie, Aunt Laveta, Aunt Jackie, and Glenda. Of course, the greatest support of all was an Almighty God who kept me alive and intervened more times than I am even aware of. I have often thought of the many times I rode with a drunk Leonard as he drove us at triple-digit speed on narrow, curvy blacktop or gravel roads. However, by the grace of God, I have arrived to be an old man.

While sci-fi movies and books have had time machines for a long time, we know that is just fiction. Life does not work like that. The song below asks rhetorically, "If you could go back for just one day, where would you go?" For me, the answer to that question is quite certain. I would want to go back to our Tebbetts farm with all seven of our children living at home. It would not have to be a special event but rather just to a day as ordinary as they got with our seven children, milk cow, beef cattle, chickens, gardens, lakes, dogs, and cats. Perhaps we could do a little fishing. Play some games. Make homemade ice cream. Have a bonfire in the evening with some good old homemade gospel music. That's where I would go.

Where would you go?

If You Could Go Back

Verse 1:
Sunday mornin' headin' out – To our little country church house
Our family all dressed up – Gettin' ready to worship
And I'll not forget the day when – The Lord forgave all my sin
Lookin' down my life's road – So many sights to behold

Chorus:
Life is like a one-way street – There's just no backin' up in time
So many precious memories – In the picture book of our mind
But what if there was a way – To go back for just one day
Now you and I know – Life don't work like that
But where would you go – If you could go back

Verse 2:
Oh how excited I was – Goin' to Grandma and Grandpa's
So many Fourth of Julys – Watching fireworks in the sky
I've loved ones gone on to heaven – How they're missed but not forgotten
Reflections of the past – Memories fleeting so fast

(Chorus Repeats)

A Tribute to Mom

Before I move on to the lessons that most of this last part of the book is going to be about, I want to close the loop on the story of my mother's life. It's a lasting memory, and so it probably belongs here, in the last part of this book. I mentioned early in this writing that I had to get into gear for writing this story. Apparently, I shifted into a granny low gear, as I have taken years, not months, to finish this effort. I also mentioned that my mother read all my childhood stories and fully supported my efforts and accuracy in writing this story. However, before completing the latter part of my story, my mother passed away nearing the age of ninety-two. She lived a long life.

After Leonard's passing, Mom told me and Glenda that she had wasted her whole life marrying bad men. As I have said before, my mother was a good woman. To my and Glenda's knowledge, she never drank alcohol, she never used foul language. She supported her parents and family as best she could. She tried to be the best mother she could be, given the mess we were in. Mom was always faithful to church and God. She was an excellent teacher. She was always concerned about the physical and spiritual needs of others. Mom would often take Thanksgiving meals and Christmas meals to shut-ins. She had a gentle spirit about her. She could have easily been bitter and mean from the many times a drunken husband beat and abused her, but that was not the case.

After Leonard's passing, Mom eventually moved into a very nice retirement home in Springfield. She loved the cafeteria there, the lovely facility, and made many friends there. In fact, Mom met a gentleman there, Gene, who had recently lost his wife. Mom and Gene became the best of friends. They were both fans of the St. Louis Cardinals and watched sports and old movies together. They considered marriage, but decided they were both too old. Yet, they remained very special friends. Gene gave my mother the love and respect she had always wanted, treating her like a queen. I believe Gene was a blessing from God to my mother as she had tried to live right in very difficult marital situations. Mom readily agreed the mess she was in was her fault because of her extremely poor life choices. We all make some bad choices, but the important part is how we live our life even when we have messed up.

Gene passed away before my mother. I think Mom lost a lot of her will to keep living after losing the good man she had always wanted.

Another blessing my mom received in her later years was the fact she overcame her colon problems. She took some herbal supplements which may have helped. However, the cure may have been the fact she was just simply enjoying life in her retirement home with Gene. Whatever the reason, Mom started eating about everything. Mom put on some weight and even found herself somewhat plump after being a beanpole for over seventy years. She especially enjoyed being able to eat hot dogs with no ill effects.

As I just said, I believe God blessed my mother in her later years. She grew old with grace and enjoyed her life. Mom would readily agree she made some bonehead decisions in life. Her mistakes and misfortunes could have easily defined her. Instead, she lived her best for God, her family, and friends. Mom's passing was relatively quick and without a great deal of suffering. All of her children had time to spend with her in her last weeks. In the race of life, Mom had a very shaky start but finished strong. Way to go, Mom.

Perhaps the reader of this story has made some poor choices or decisions in life. As long as you are alive here on earth, it is never too late to choose God and to do right. If life were a card game, some are dealt a terrible hand due to no fault of their

own, but the best way to play that hand is always to choose God and do what is right. We never know when God might open the windows in heaven and shower down blessings.

I just mentioned the phrase *the windows in heaven*. The book of 2 Kings in the Scriptures tells the story of God's children being in the midst of a horrible famine. Furthermore, the Syrian army had surrounded them. Indeed, there seemed to be no hope.

I can look back in my childhood at times I felt there was no hope.

In the midst of famine and siege, four leprous Israelites decided to surrender to the Syrian army, as they faced starvation if they did nothing. When these four men entered the Syrian camp, to their great surprise, the Syrians were gone. These four men took the great spoils left by the Syrians, but in time, these four men went back to their people to let all know that God had opened the windows in heaven. There were spoils aplenty for all.

I feel somewhat like those four lepers. I am unworthy of God's blessings, but he has opened the windows in heaven on my life, taking me from domestic abuse to divine blessings. Hopefully, my story offers hope for those who seem to have no hope. God can still open the windows in heaven, no matter how dire the circumstances or how bleak the future might appear. Just do right and live to please the mighty Savior, Jesus Christ. Below are the lyrics to a song God gave me about the windows in heaven.

The Windows in Heaven

Verse 1:
Could this be Israel's end – So great was the famine
Hunger raged in every man – Would they ever be full again
The enemy camped about – No hope within or without
They needed God to open – The windows in heaven

Verse 2:
Four men go to surrender – The enemy's camp they enter
They can't believe their eyes – What a glorious surprise
There was food set aplenty – No trace of the enemy
God had swung wide open – The windows in heaven

Chorus:
God opens windows in heaven – Just to pour down a mighty bless'n'
Undeserving and unworthy – Yet he pours down grace and mercy
He opens windows in heaven – Just to take care of his children

Verse 3:
These men did eat and drink – The spoils were for the taking
But they said we do not well – If the others we don't tell
To our brethren we must go – So that everyone may know
God has swung wide open – The windows in heaven

Verse 4:
I thought I'd come to my end – The storm left such destruction
Didn't know if I'd stand again – My world was so broken
God's put it all back together – Now with others I must share
God has swung wide open – The windows in heaven

(Chorus Repeats)

Dee and I both enjoy sitting around the woodstove on a cold winter's day. Age-related poor blood circulation increases the pleasure of heat. It is a great time to reflect on the past. In this winter section of my life, I will mainly discuss some of the more important aspects of life in which I believe God has been gracious to give us some insight.

Just like the four men in the story, I feel I need to share some of the treasures that I've been given by God. Note, the treasures have all come by grace from God.

Join me around the woodstove in the winter season of my life. I know not everything I share will be accepted by every reader. My goal is certainly not to offend anyone with my message in this book. Rather, I hope some lessons we have learned might be a blessing to you, the reader, or at least food for thought. Consider the aspects of life God has led us through with an open mind, and may the Lord make clear to you what he wants you to take from what Dee and I have gleaned from the school of life we have attended in our many years.

May the Lord guide us all to greater wisdom, in his good time.

25

Booze

Allow me to present my case against alcohol. By choosing to abstain completely from alcohol, I know I am in an extremely distinct minority. I also know there are many good folks who drink socially and do not seem to have any major problems with alcohol. In fact, I have many good friends who drink socially. Hopefully, they remain good friends after reading my case against alcohol. However, I believe anyone who drinks alcohol is playing with fire and risks the distinct possibility of getting burned. Additionally, their drinking could lead someone else to suffer woes from alcohol. Just because one person can seemingly handle their liquor does not mean another friend or a family member will do the same. I know also that much of what we consider to be Christendom today fully approves and supports consuming booze. Many would agree that inebriation is wrong. However, I believe the Bible does not support imbibing for God's children. I will share some thoughts on the subject. In fact, this section will be rather lengthy, but I believe this to be a worthy subject.

I have copied below a few verses from the Bible relating to alcohol:

> Wine is a mocker, strong drink is raging: and whosoever is deceived thereby is not wise. (Proverbs 20:1)

Hear thou, my son, and be wise, and guide thine heart in the way.
Be not among winebibbers; among riotous eaters of flesh:
For the drunkard and the glutton shall come to poverty: and
drowsiness shall clothe a man with rags.
Who hath woe? who hath sorrow? who hath contentions? who
hath babbling? who hath wounds without cause? who hath redness
of eyes?
They that tarry long at the wine; they that go to seek mixed wine.
Look not thou upon the wine when it is red, when it giveth his
colour in the cup, when it moveth itself aright.
At the last it biteth like a serpent, and stingeth like an adder.
(Proverbs 23:19–21, 29–32)

Woe unto him that giveth his neighbour drink, that puttest thy
bottle to him, and makest him drunken also, that thou mayest
look on their nakedness! (Habakkuk 2:15)

But they also have erred through wine, and through strong drink
are out of the way; the priest and the prophet have erred through
strong drink, they are swallowed up of wine, they are out of the
way through strong drink; they err in vision, they stumble in
judgment. (Isaiah 28:7)

And be not drunk with wine, wherein is excess; but be filled with
the Spirit. (Ephesians 5:18)

Be sober, be vigilant; because your adversary the devil, as a roaring
lion, walketh about, seeking whom he may devour. (1 Peter 5:8)

And the Lord spake unto Aaron, saying, Do not drink wine nor
strong drink, thou, nor thy sons with thee, when ye go into the
tabernacle of the congregation, lest ye die: it shall be a statute for
ever throughout your generations: (Leviticus 10:8–9)

If so be ye have tasted that the Lord is gracious. To whom
coming, *as unto* a living stone, disallowed indeed of men, but
chosen of God, *and* precious, Ye also, as lively stones, are built up

a spiritual house, an holy priesthood, to offer up spiritual sacrifices, acceptable to God by Jesus Christ. (1 Peter 2:3-5)

I have experienced surprise over the years when talking about alcohol with someone who has limited exposure to church or knowledge of the Bible. My surprise lies in the fact those same people know the Bible states we can drink wine for our stomach's sake and that Jesus turned the water into wine. Such is the argument of many for drinking alcohol. Hopefully, I will make a logical conclusion from the Scriptures why I believe God's children should not drink any liquid which is intoxicating.

The Bible does not contradict itself. I believe the verses copied above give a simple statement that God does not approve of consuming intoxicating wine or alcohol. How can some verses endorse or bless wine consumption when God forbids even looking at wine when it moves or ferments? God also declares that wine is a mocker. He does not say excessive wine. Rather, the verse simply states that wine or alcohol is a mocker. I believe there is a logical explanation.

I will not list all the verses in the Bible which warn against intoxicating alcohol. However, there are many verses which are overwhelmingly clear that God is against intoxicating drink. Yet, in some verses, there seems to be some wiggle room that gives one the right to imbibe in alcohol with God's blessing, as long as one does not become drunk. The Bible uses the word "wine" to refer to both fresh grape juice and fermented alcoholic beverages, which explains the disparity. We cannot consider God confused or illogical. Negative references or curses towards wine in the Bible pertain to alcohol. Verses in which God approves or blesses wine are referring to fresh grape-juice wine. Pastor George Hendricks, in an article titled "Was Wine in the Bible Alcoholic? An Analysis of Biblical Texts," explains that:

The Bible uses various terms to refer to wine, and each term carries its own nuances and connotations. Understanding the different terminologies is vital to gaining a comprehensive understanding of the nature and usage of wine in biblical times ... The presence of distinct terms for different types of beverages suggests that the ancient Israelites were aware of the various levels of intoxication and differentiating between them. This supports the idea that not all wine consumed in biblical times was necessarily alcoholic.[3]

Furthermore, an article on Bibleinfo.com explains, "Ancient civilizations had several ways of preventing fruit and fruit juices from fermentation, and thus were able to have non-alcoholic wine (grape juice) throughout the year."[4]

Dee has some stomach issues and daily drinks Welch's grape juice. The juice seems to be beneficial to her. There is obviously nothing wrong with drinking fresh grape-juice wine. I believe Jesus turned the water into fresh grape-juice wine. I do not believe Jesus would have miraculously made intoxicating drink to enable a drunken feast when God is clearly against such. However, I believe the fresh grape juice Jesus made would have been even tastier than Welch's grape juice, which is very good. By the way, I have never heard of recommendations for consuming alcohol for stomach problems.

God would be inconsistent if some Bible verses approve of alcohol consumption while others do not. God is definitely not inconsistent. If the argument is still that one should simply not become intoxicated, then how does one know what that limit is? Governments have passed laws defining what the legal limits

---

[3] Jane Danes, "Was Wine in the Bible Alcoholic or Just Pure Grape Juice?," Godsverse, July 23, 2023, https://godsverse.org/was-wine-in-the-bible-alcoholic-an-analysis-of-biblical-texts/.

[4] "What are the facts about fermented drinks in the Bible?," Bibleinfo, https://www.bibleinfo.com/en/questions/what-are-historical-and-scriptural-facts-about-fermented-drinks-bible.

of blood alcohol levels are. However, even a minute amount of alcohol has a physiological impact on a person. Governments primarily focus on driving impairment when passing laws about alcohol. Long before someone is impaired to the point that it is illegal for them to drive, their judgment has become impaired. Alcoholic impairment contributes to many unfortunate outcomes.

Does a small amount of alcohol, even just one beer or cup of wine, truly have an impact on the human body? There is research available that says that it does. I believe the following article from the World Health Organization (WHO-Europe) bolsters my argument:

> Alcohol … has been classified as a Group 1 carcinogen by the International Agency for Research on Cancer …
>
> The risk of developing cancer increases substantially the more alcohol is consumed. However, latest available data indicate that half of all alcohol-attributable cancers in the WHO European Region are caused by "light" and "moderate" alcohol consumption …
> "We cannot talk about a so-called safe level of alcohol use. It doesn't matter how much you drink – the risk to the drinker's health starts from the first drop of any alcoholic beverage."[5]

The rest of the article is well-worth reading, and I believe it does a good job of supporting my argument for zero alcoholic consumption.

The above article mentions just one physiological danger of consuming alcohol: an increasing likelihood of cancer. Research

---

[5] "No level of alcohol consumption is safe for our health," World Health Organization, January 4, 2023, https://www.who.int/europe/news/item/04-01-2023-no-level-of-alcohol-consumption-is-safe-for-our-health.

also shows, however, that alcohol can have negative effects on the human brain:

> Any amount of alcohol can negatively affect brain health. Whether you drink occasionally or you engage in consistent heavy drinking, alcohol has the potential to interrupt essential brain functions and damage brain cells.[6]

I recommend reading the rest of the article (see footnote), as it goes into detail explaining the effects of alcohol on various parts of the brain. Of course, alcohol is well known to have negative effects on many other parts of the body, such as the liver.

I certainly do not support cigarette smoking, as it is definitely harmful to our bodies. However, I would rather smoke cigarettes than drink alcohol. Heavy smokers primarily endanger themselves. Heavy drinkers are a danger to themselves due to the ill effects of alcohol and to society due to the ill behavior induced by alcohol. These articles present scientific evidence that even light drinking is hazardous to the human body.

People like alcohol because of the buzz, but we should look to God for satisfaction. How many of the famous or rich lose it all to booze or drugs? Play with fire and one will probably get burned.

My dad seemingly should have had the world by the tail. He was heavily involved in aviation in its early stages. He could have had a degree from a prominent college. Even though my dad inherited quite a bit of money, he played with the fire of alcohol and suffered great loss.

---

[6] Kent S. Hoffman, "Alcohol's Effects on the Brain," AddictionHelp.com, last updated June 4, 2024, https://www.addictionhelp.com/alcohol/effects/brain/.

A few years after moving to central Missouri, we met a family who lived fairly close to us. They had four young children. The husband drank some. When coming home one night while inebriated, he rolled his car and did not survive.

Grandpa Luther had a cousin who came home drunk one bitter, cold winter night. Failing to enter his house, he sat down and propped himself against the front door. The next morning, they found him frozen to death.

Obviously, I could tell a multitude of stories about problems with alcohol. For every unfortunate alcohol story I could tell, I could also point out that if there had been no alcohol involved, the sad story would not exist. The real problem with social drinking is the fact that anyone who drinks alcohol never knows when they will cross over the line from what is called social drinking to being totally under the influence of alcohol. I once worked with a guy who had a drinking problem. He had been through some withdrawal sessions in Jefferson City. He would undergo being locked up in a hospital ward to dry out where he and others like him had no access to alcohol. The patients' families could visit them and could bring personal items they might need. He told me one of many tricks was to have someone bring them liquid shoe polish so they could polish their shoes. You may have guessed it. They would chugalug it down to get some alcohol in their body.

I do not drink alcohol as I do not know how to identify the moment I might go from thinking I control my alcohol to having alcohol control me.

I would mention again that God declares intoxicating wine is a mocker. In this paragraph, I am using *wine* to refer to any intoxicating alcoholic drink. Wine mocks or makes fun of those who consume wine through the many ill effects of alcohol. Wine takes away inhibitions and opens the door for poor decision making. Wine seems to make merry, but wine is really a depressant and will leave the consumer depressed physiologically and spiritually. Note, wine mocks by convincing the depressed person to believe their need is for more wine. Wine ridicules a user when they do or say something inappropriate. Wine has brought many to poverty or to the gutter with great shame as well. Wine dulls a person's senses so they cannot see the culprit is the wine which is controlling them. Wine has brought a multitude of woes into the lives of many a victim and has even hastened an untimely death for many.

I write as someone who has been on the receiving end of both my dad's and my stepdad's actions when they were physically out of control due to alcohol. As a child, an enraged drunk beat me multiple times. Likewise, many times I witnessed firsthand the bruises on my mother inflicted by a man in a drunken rage.

My friend, if you drink alcohol, how do you know when you might cross the line from just social drinking to being totally under the control of alcohol? Note once again, any alcohol will have some physiological impact. The risk is too great for the temporal reward of a buzz. My choice is to live alcohol-free and to know I will never be under the influence of booze. My plan is to not have a self-inflicted alcohol-intoxication burn.

One can do just a little research to verify that alcohol is a gateway drug. Many a hardcore drug addict began their journey of destruction via the liquor bottle. I have chosen to avoid any potential perils from booze, including the gateway to other drug addictions. My prayer for all my descendants is that they will do likewise.

On September 11, 2001, terrorists killed nearly three thousand people on American soil. I personally supported our military response against those who perpetrated such a heinous act of violence. However, according to our own Centers for Disease Control in 2020–2021, "about 178,000 Americans die from excessive drinking each year."[7] No pun intended, but the economic costs are staggering as well. Can you imagine our national response to an adversary who would kill 178,000 souls on our soil? Well, just look at the liquor industry. I find outrage over that loss. Statistics can't capture or measure the heartache of abuse or neglect from a drunken family member. I would be quite surprised if you, the reader of this story, have absolutely no knowledge of anyone in your family or sphere of friends who has not been harmed by alcohol. Likely, most of us know lives, marriages, relationships, etc., which have been destroyed from alcohol abuse. And yet, most will still partake of booze with the fallacious logic that they will be an exception to the statistics. And yet, most see no great danger or great concern about the perils of alcohol. I believe I am accurate in stating that the majority agree that tobacco smoking is bad due to negative health effects. Alcohol, in my opinion, lies in the same boat, but too many love their booze too much to take the same stand against alcohol that they take against tobacco.

I would like to present another aspect of alcohol consumption, which I believe should be a serious concern. I have asked those who quiz me about my teetotaler position this question: "Businesses which sell alcohol are often called 'liquor and' *what* or 'wine and' *what*?" The answer, of course, is "liquor and spirits" or "wine and spirits."

While calling an alcoholic drink a *spirit* may indicate the amount of alcohol in the drink, alcohol is alcohol, no matter

---

[7] "Facts About U.S. Deaths from Excessive Alcohol Use," CDC, U.S. Centers for Disease Control and Prevention, August 6, 2024, https://www.cdc.gov/alcohol/facts-stats/index.html#:~:text=About%20178%2C000%20people%20die%20from,%20to%20prevent%20excessive%20alcohol%20use.

what the drink may be. I do not know for sure how the name *spirits* came to be related to alcohol, but I believe it is not just a coincidence that alcohol is associated with spirits. I copied the verse earlier in which God commands his children to be sober, as the devil seeks to destroy them. Lack of sobriety creates an opportunity for evil spirits to harm an individual. We do not associate water, fruit juice, soda pop, or tea with spirits, but we do associate alcohol with them. I propose that those who drink alcohol are opening themselves up to the distinct possibility of getting more than just a buzz physically. I believe alcoholic users are opening themselves up to evil spirits.

So that is another reason I do not drink any form of alcoholic beverages. I believe much of the evil committed by those under the influence of alcohol is due to evil spiritual forces who are in control of or at least influencing their minds and bodies, and that this influence or control is enabled by alcohol. So drinking alcohol means flirting with evil spirits or forces, which can result in a person not being in control of themselves. The Bible simply states God's children should be sober or not be drunk with wine or under the influence of alcohol. Instead, God's children should be under the control of the Holy Spirit of God. In fact, the Greek philosopher Aristotle had the same opinion I do. Nick Hines, in an article about why we call liquor *spirits*, reports:

In the "BarSmarts Advanced" handbook by David Wondrich, Dale DeGroff, and Paul Pacult, the term "spirits" for alcohol is attributed to Aristotle. "Aristotle wrote about this process in 327 B.C., but we have no proof that his fellow Greeks distilled spirits on any significant volume level," the handbook reads. "Nonetheless, he was the one who gave the name of 'spirit' to the product of distillation. He thought drinking a distilled beer or wine put 'spirits' into the body of the drinker."[8]

Note, the author of the article does not necessarily agree with Aristotle, but I agree with Aristotle.

I listed verses from Leviticus in which the Lord instructs Aaron that the priesthood should never drink wine or strong drink when they go into the tabernacle of the congregation or when doing the work of a priest (Leviticus 10:8–9). If they did such, they would die. Likewise, the reference I gave in Isaiah tells how priests err through strong drink, are swallowed up of wine, are out of the way through strong drink, err in vision, and stumble in judgment. Of course, that was the Old Testament (Isaiah 28:7). I also listed 1 Peter 2:5, which declares that anyone who is a child of God or a believer is part of a holy priesthood, and their purpose is to offer up sacrifices to God by Jesus Christ. God instructed the Old Testament priesthood to never do the labors of the priesthood, such as making sacrifices, under the influence of alcohol. Likewise, in the New Testament, all believers should be about the business of the priesthood and, I believe, should be sober, as God is clear that is required of the priesthood. Of course, not all believers have the official vocation of a priest or a pastor, but spiritually speaking, all believers are priests. All believers have access to the very throne of grace.

I have tried to present an argument as to why life is better without alcohol. However, I doubt my rationale will convince many to join the teetotaler bandwagon. If it does, praise the Lord and welcome on board. The teetotaler wagon is a great ride. From my experience, life just goes better without booze, and I think Scripture supports that. Of course, many do not

---

[8] Nick Hines, "Why Is Liquor Called 'Spirits'?," VinePair, March 7, 2017, https://vinepair.com/articles/why-liquor-called-spirits/.

even believe the Bible. My arguments thus far may be to no avail. I will make one more appeal from a different angle.

What I can argue with absolute certainty is the fact that I have never suffered from any of these ill effects due to me being under the influence of alcohol: I have never woken up hungover, I have never beaten my wife and children, I have never been beaten up because I made myself vulnerable by getting drunk, I have never killed another person by driving under the influence or going into a drunken rage, I have never raped a woman, I have never missed work because of being drunk, I have never lost family and friends by being drunk, I have never had a child of mine drink alcohol because their old dad does, I have never been out of control from the ill effects of alcohol, I have lost no wealth from drinking alcohol, I have no health problems from alcohol, etc., etc., etc. All this, because *I do not drink booze, period.* Therefore, alcohol has no influence on my body, mind, or spirit. If I lose a loved one, I do not have to be concerned that in my grief I will cross over the line from just social drinking to becoming an alcoholic, because I do not drink alcohol. If I lose what wealth I have tomorrow, I will not become an alcoholic, because I do not drink alcohol. If I lose my health soon, I will not become an alcoholic, because I do not drink alcohol. I trust you are getting my train of thought. There are a multitude of lives around the world that are being controlled by the liquor bottle. The best way I know to not be in that group, or not even *possibly* be in that group, is simply to abstain from all alcohol. To ensure no alcoholic stains on my life, I simply abstain from alcohol.

Alcohol can easily become a weight or a trap or a snare that can hinder us from running the race of life. I choose to not be entangled with booze. Have you ever heard of anyone who never drinks alcohol becoming an alcoholic? Old age has slowed me down quite a bit in running the race of life. I do not need any additional weights. I will run the rest of my life's race without the weight of alcohol.

If we personified alcohol, we'd find that many perceive Mr. Alcohol to be a fun-loving guy. The world certainly portrays that perception. He can seemingly help a person loosen up—you know, help folks to enjoy life. Have some fun. Help a person forget the problems and struggles of life. In reality, Mr. Alcohol wants to become the obsession of your life. He wants to have total control over your life. He is not really a friend. I suppose the majority of folks who engage with Mr. Alcohol do not allow that to happen to the full extent—perhaps they do not give him total control. Unfortunately, many do. My dad was one of those. Worldwide, millions upon millions of souls live their lives totally dominated by Mr. Alcohol. As for me and my family, we prefer to have no association with him at all. His reward is not worth the risk.

I rest my case.

26

---∞---

A Really Big Deal

The last chapter was about the dangers of alcohol. In other words, it was about preventing harm. Now I want to switch to a happier subject. Instead of talking about *preventing harm*, I want to talk about *actively doing good*. In particular, I want to talk about some things I've learned about forming and maintaining good households—households where people are loved, cared for, and provided for. I'm going to share some thoughts about raising children, about marrying well, and about being financially wise.

People talk about tough love, and I don't want to deny that tough love is a real thing. The phrase does make me think back to my childhood, though, and to the way Leonard ran his household. Leonard did not use tough love. He was just tough without love. Maybe that is better than easy love, as life needs to be tough to make hardened men and women, yet I think that what is right is to have both toughness *and* love. The greatest commandments God has given us both involve love. Love is necessary.

Love is also sturdy. Love is tough. Love helps build *people* who are sturdy. Love necessitates learning discipline, as the Bible is clear that if we love God, we will strive to obey him or be disciplined to his will.

I propose that work is an absolute minimum of tough love. Parents need to teach their children to work as no work makes no building. Grace is important, but when it comes to building, obedience is important too. Muscles have to be exercised to grow. This world will not coddle our children.

When you work, let your children do some of it. Lead by example, but let them get their hands dirty. Often work is easier to do by yourself, but children have to learn, so get them involved. Children should contribute to the family unit by working, even at a reasonably young age. God's Word instructs us to consider the ant (an industrious worker). Music, art, sports, studying, etc. are all good, but children need plain old work as well. With our large family, everyone had to contribute some to the cooking, dishwashing, cleaning, laundry, mowing, milking, gardening, chores, etc. Work makes a person feel of value. There is nothing dishonorable about work. Our children had chores. Dee and I expected them to contribute to the family's needs. Of course, we had a farm, which affords a great opportunity for working, but whatever the child's environment is, they need to work.

While I am 100 percent for raising children who know how to work, I would pass on a concern about children working outside of the home. While our children were still young, we had friends older than us who shared how their children had worked in fast food restaurants, Walmart, etc. Their children wound up running with the wrong crowd. The warning was to be careful about where you allow your children to work. So we heeded their counsel. We had some men in our church who owned construction businesses. They provided Aaron, while he was a teenager, with his first job. These were men we trusted, and he learned valuable skills in construction. As teenagers, our girls all worked at housecleaning or assisting older ladies for work outside the home. Lydia also worked some at a childcare facility. The last three boys, while still at home, worked at a nearby small engine repair shop, where they learned valuable mechanic skills for their first jobs outside the home. None of these environments were risky in the sense of getting yoked up with the bad apple that can spoil the whole barrel. I would guess some might consider our work arrangements to be overly protective. I agree with "an ounce of prevention is worth a pound of cure."

The bottom line is that children need to learn to work. I am not talking about abuse but rather good, hard work!

A Corvette Marriage

A few years ago, Dee and I attended a couple's retreat. The key speaker was from the vicinity of Kentucky, where Corvette cars are manufactured. The theme of the retreat was "The Master's Design" for marriage, with a specific focus on the union of one man and one woman. Drawing a comparison between marriage and the assembly of a Corvette car, the speaker made an interesting point. In his analogy, the man would be the engine, drivetrain, gears, pistons, grease, oil, gas, etc. You know, guy stuff. The woman is the covering for the engine and drivetrain. The woman provides beauty, such as the luxurious interior and attractive exterior of what would otherwise be just mechanical. In the Corvette plant, they manufacture one body for one drivetrain. Kind of like God's ideal for marriage. When the body is complete and likewise the engine/drivetrain, they mate the two together. Interestingly enough, the manufacturers call this the process of the body being *married* to the drivetrain.

I have always wanted to own a Corvette, but practicality and financial resources never allowed that to happen. A car like that probably would not have been the best transportation for a family of nine. However, after attending the retreat, I realized I have had a Corvette marriage all these years and just did not know it. I was so excited about my Corvette marriage, God gave me a song about it:

A Corvette Marriage

Verse 1:
In my youth I could have been – A Corvette V8 racing engine
Seems there was horsepower aplenty – There is no speed like when you're twenty
And this engine was made complete – When I married that curved body so sweet
We've run together oh so fine – All thanks to the Master's design

Chorus:
Oh the last time I checked – Honey we're a-livin' at the same address
At the corner of love and respect – In the state of oneness
We only take one parkin' spot – We're built and blessed by God
What therefore God hath joined together – Let not man put asunder

Verse 2:
Now the years have come and gone – Now antique but we're still rollin' on
This old engine has lost some power – Zero to sixty seems like an hour
The body has some wear and rust – And the paint could use some polishin' up
But our ride has been oh so fine – All thanks to the Master's design

(Chorus Repeats)

Before moving on from the subject of marriage, I would like to reference Mark 10:7–9: "For this cause shall a man leave his father and mother, and cleave to his wife; And they twain shall be one flesh: so then they are no more twain, but one flesh. What therefore God hath joined together, let not man put asunder."

While my mom and dad were married, they stayed quite a bit of that time with his parents. I have mentioned that I believe

Grandma Kissock did my dad no favors by always trying to justify his drinking problems. I believe my dad did not heed the counsel in Mark about leaving father and mother. All of my children are married; I have told some of them that if I saw they were about to step in front of a Mack truck barreling down the road, I would try to warn them, but other than that I am not over them in terms of authority. In other words, Dee and I try to stay out of our children's married lives, short of giving a warning about stepping in front of a truck. Likewise, Mark instructs the husband to leave mother and father and then cleave to his wife.

Having seen so many divorces in my lifetime, I cannot emphasize enough the importance of a marriage commitment. God declares he makes a husband and a wife one entity that by the Master's design is not supposed to be put asunder by man or divided. Hence, the importance of making sure one's marriage is in the will of God and both parties seek God's blessings. Of course, the plans of us mortal beings often go awry. By God's grace we can still be used for his honor and glory. Yet, marriage failure often comes at a great cost. How much better to do all that is possible to ensure compatibility before tying the knot? Once married, husbands and wives should never lose sight of the importance of their union. Always labor for a Corvette marriage!

A Dodge Omni

Now to move from the luxury of a Corvette to the austerity of an old beater. I have mentioned how we lived frugally to get out of debt when we bought our first house. We had also taken one small loan on a car. Based upon God's Word, we decided our marriage and life would be better if we simply did not get into debt again. God had answered our prayers and here we were, debt free.

I was in Jefferson City one day and saw a used Dodge Omni for sale. Although I wasn't familiar with the Dodge Omni, Dodge usually made quality cars at that time. The Omni was supposed to get great gas mileage, about thirty mpg. I did not have quite enough money in my checking account to pay for the car. The dealer said he would set up a very small loan. I could pay it off as soon as possible.

I had a fair commute to work and did quite a bit of running around. The children we had at the time would even fit in the car. I thought I would save enough gas money to justify the small debt.

The Omni was my worst vehicle because the Omni was one pitiful excuse for an automobile, but it made a magnificent piece of junk. I spent a small fortune trying to keep the vehicle on the road, but I finally had to cut my losses and get rid of it.

The Omni was my best vehicle, though, because I believe God taught me a valuable lesson with that vehicle. We had done all we could to get out of debt and God had blessed us to be debt free. What did I do? Immediately, I went into debt again. I did not have to have that vehicle. I had no good excuse for going into debt for that vehicle. I did, however, learn my lesson because of that vehicle, and by God's grace, Dee and I have remained debt free ever since the Omni. That lesson was certainly expensive, but it was a lesson I consider to be invaluable.

Raising children is expensive, and the more children you have, the more the expenses. We chose to have a large family and homeschool, which necessitated a single-earner income. Fortunately, I've always had a decent salary, but with just a single income and a large family, we never had a lot of extra money. The times we live in are not financially conducive to a single income. Thus, throughout our marriage, Dee and I have used the saying, "We've done so much with so little for so long, we think we can do anything with nothing in no time at all." By adjusting our lifestyle to what we could afford and by being frugal, we never got ourselves in debt again.

I can't say financial debt is a sin, but unnecessary debt is unwise. God has supplied all our needs. Much of the problem with unwise debt is simply not being content with what God has provided. Debt in the Scriptures is typically associated with bondage, which is not a good image for the children of the King of Kings. Going into debt on a house is often better than paying rent, as equity should build up in a house whereas there is no financial gain from paying rent. However, so many get themselves overextended financially by incurring too much debt. I like financial advisor Dave Ramsey's favorite motto: "If you will live like no one else, later you can live like no one else."

I just mentioned the importance of being content. The song God gave me below echoes the Apostle Paul's counsel, "Not that I speak in respect of want: for I have learned in whatsoever state I am, therewith to be content" (Philippians 4:11).

Be Content

Verse 1:
From a cold and dark dungeon – Even midst persecution
In life every circumstance – Paul knew was more than chance
For Paul God was sufficient – He had learned to be content

Chorus:
Be content – In whatsoever state you're in be content
God's school of life is meant – To teach his children to be content
Whatever God has sent – Learn to be content
Whether abased or abound – Contentment can be found
God's children – In Christ be content

Verse 2:
Godliness with contentment – God declares is great gain
Fall not into temptation – Drowning men in destruction
But having food and raiment – Let us therewith be content

(Chorus Repeats)

I would clarify that frugal living should not correlate with frugal giving. Be generous. Scripture states that those entrusted with much are expected to give much. In fact, being frugal and avoiding debt enables a person to help others in need as God leads. Politically, I do not support today's liberalism, which supports socialism where the government takes our money in order to redistribute it to others, but the money often ends up being absorbed by the ruling elite. However, I support the biblical definition of being liberal, as in being willing to give generously or to help others. I agree with Will Rogers in one of his many famous quotes: "I remember when being liberal meant being generous with your own money."

Following is a song God gave me about a widow in the Bible who faced starvation but was willing to give her last morsel of food, literally. Because she was willing to give, God met all of her needs.

Willingness to Give

Verse 1:
In the land of Zarephath – A widow woman gathered sticks
You see times were so bad – That she was preparing to fix
The handful of meal she had – With her little oil she would mix
And make a morsel of bread to be their last – She saw no way they
could live

Verse 2:
God had a different plan – It had to seem so strange to her
God sent a preacher man – Who asked her to do more than share
Bring all the bread in your hand – And assured her to have no fear
For there was just no way she could understand – Yet in faith she
did offer

Chorus:
You see from this woman – We can all learn a lesson
Circumstances matter not – When you're dealing with God
Her barrel of meal would not waste – Neither her cruse of oil fail
For her willingness to give – This woman and her son would live
There's just no need to be afraid – When we obey God in faith

Verse 3:
This woman heard her son – Mama, where did this food come from
Son, just like yesterday – This is another day of grace
Son, you see it matters not – If you've a little or a lot
But rather all that really matters is what – You have will be used for
God

(Chorus Repeats)

27

---∞---

A BSA

Instead of a PSA, I would like to share a Bible Service Announcement: *Love thy neighbor as thyself*, the second of the two great commandments given by Jesus. (Of course, to *love the Lord thy God* completely is the first commandment.) The Bible commands God's children to be good neighbors. If at all possible, God's children should get to know their neighbors and be a godly witness to them.

In this chapter I'm going to talk about things that fall under that second commandment: about loving our neighbors and, in the bigger picture, loving our country.

I have mentioned that when our children were young, we would often sing for elderly neighbors. Unbeknownst to us at the time, this simple effort would lead to the purchase of our second farm. Everywhere we have lived, we made lifelong friends with neighbors. Of course, we have always lived out in the country, which might make that easier, but we would try to do the same even in town or in a city.

Our reward for trying to love our neighbors was all the neat people we met. Many of the older folks we have met have been quite the characters. In Tebbetts, we often visited with an older couple, Thurman and Velma. They were quite a hoot to visit with. Elijah was about three years old when he acquired a colorful plaid sport coat. Thurman and Velma always called him a used-car salesman, as he looked pretty slick in that coat.

Invest in others and it will pay great dividends in blessings. If you do something nice, my experience is that something nice will come back to you. It's not particularly profound, but we often say, "Well, that's the way it goes," and we picked up that saying from an elderly man who lived near our first house. Our small investment in Mr. Redman has enriched our life. He had never married and lived in his parent's farmhouse by himself. He would share life stories, concluding each with, "Well, that's the way it goes." We gave him a little food at times and visited with him. In return, throughout the years we have had many times of stating, "Well, that's the way it goes."

I believe the Bible does not restrict neighbors to being just those who live reasonably close but to all we encounter on our earthly journey.

Of course, in life's journey, we may cross paths with some who may seem somewhat unlovable. Such was the case with the story Jesus tells of the Good Samaritan. Jews and Samaritans were basically foes. Yet, when a certain man, presumably a Jew, was attacked and left to die, the religious crowd wanted nothing to do with the man. Of course, the story shows how a Samaritan was moved with compassion and stopped his journey to help a soul in need, even though the world would consider them natural enemies. This old world needs more Good Samaritans. Additionally, this old world affords an abundance of opportunities to help another soul in need. The question is, will we be like the religious crowd that passed by or like the Good Samaritan? The following song that God gave me poses the same question.

Don't Pass By on the Other Side

Verse 1:

He came from Jerusalem – Fell among thieves who wounded him
A priest and a Levite passed by – On the other side
But the Good Samaritan – He was moved with compassion
He went to him and bound his wounds – Stopping his journey was not opportune
But he stopped for a soul in need – This Good Samaritan showed mercy

Chorus

Don't live life passing by – On the other side
Do all you can – Lend a helping hand
In the name of Jesus – For God be a witness
Use your life to touch a soul – That our God they might know
Don't pass by – On the other side

Verse 2:

As I walked down the street – There sat a drunk on the concrete
My first thought was to pass by – On the other side
From the Lord I knew I heard – Give him a tract, it won't hurt
I thought of that priest and Levite – How they passed by on the other side
As this world perishes in sin – Who will be a Good Samaritan

(Chorus Repeats)

Closure

Loving our neighbors also matters when it comes to the end of someone's earthly journey. I mentioned earlier in this writing about the importance of closure after losing a loved one. I would guess over thirty years ago, a local funeral home director in our area gave a seminar to the public about funeral options in the state of Missouri. Dee and I attended the meeting, and it was quite informative. The director had a lifelong career in the funeral business and was quite experienced.

He spoke about cremation, which was not very common at that time. However, cremation has become much more common today, likely because of the quite expensive costs of traditional funerals. The funeral director said that if the deceased had no one left for whom experiencing closure would be an issue, then he was quite supportive of cremation. His issue with cremation pertained to situations where someone might struggle with closure. I believe the director's words used were, "You can mark it down, any person who does not have closure regarding the loss of a loved one will mentally and emotionally struggle the rest of their lives."

The director's words definitely caught my attention. I clearly recognized that I had struggled with closure with the passing of Grandpa Luther. Fortunately for me, he had a traditional funeral, and I was able to experience closure eventually with his death. Without that funeral, I can honestly say I might not have mentally or emotionally handled the loss.

I agree with the funeral director in relation to cremation. If no one will have closure issues, then I can't say cremation is wrong. If anyone might struggle with closure, then I believe a funeral service would still be a good idea before the cremation, if possible, or even after the cremation.

Dee and I plan on having traditional funerals when the time comes. With a traditional funeral/burial service, family and friends can hopefully hear the gospel. Those attending can encourage the surviving family. A funeral service makes all attending face the reality of death and hopefully will be an encouragement to make preparations for eternity. Thus, a funeral helps to bring closure for the loss of a loved one, even for cremation.

My goal is not to criticize those who have used cremation. Rather, it's to offer some food for thought about the importance of providing a means of closure for the loss of a loved one.

Authority: Good or Tyranny?

In our deaths, we belong to the Lord, just like we do in our lives. In life, however, the Lord has put certain authorities over us, and the question of how to think about authority is something all of us must face. Authorities can help neighbors live in peace. Authorities can also cause great harm; authorities can become tyrants. Following is a definition of a tyrant as defined by *Merriam-Webster* dictionary: "an absolute ruler unrestrained by law or constitution; a usurper of sovereignty; a ruler who exercises absolute power oppressively or brutally; one resembling an oppressive ruler in the harsh use of authority or power."

I know something about the ugly face of tyranny from my childhood days with Leonard. He ruled unconstrained by law. His rule was often brutal and harsh. Perhaps my childhood has made me more conscious of the reality of tyranny than others are. Fortunately, I grew up in a nation formed on the concept of trying to prevent tyranny. Unfortunately, tyranny has survived and is still alive and well. My heart breaks for a wife and children who live under the tyranny of an abusive husband and father. Tyranny spans a territory far greater than the home.

Governments, businesses, churches, and all forms of authority can suffer the putrid effects of tyranny.

Lord Acton, a British historian, wrote "that the same moral standards should be applied to all men, political and religious leaders included, especially since 'Power tends to corrupt and absolute power corrupts absolutely.'"[9]

Authority by design is not a bad thing, as God ordains it. Of course, God is the ultimate and only perfect authority. However, I agree with Lord Acton that authority or power tends to lead to corruption. The greater the power, the greater the likelihood of corruption. Our founding fathers understood tyranny. In fact, they risked their lives and fortunes to form a nation free from a tyrannical government. How does one go about trying to minimize the corruption of power that Lord Acton talked about? John Farmer had this take on it:

> It seems that the three branches of government found in our Constitution are the result of a scripture. "For the LORD is our judge (Supreme Court), the LORD is our lawgiver (Congress), the LORD is our king (Presidency); He will save us" (Isaiah 33:22; parenthesis inclusions are mine).
>
> It seems that the verse inspired James Madison to separate the powers while attending the Constitutional Convention of 1787. Many forget that our founders were deeply religious men who drew the inspiration for our Declaration of Independence and Rights from the Bible and Christianity.[10]

---

[9] "Quotes," OLL, The Online Library of Liberty, https://oll.libertyfund.org/quotes/lord-acton-writes-to-bishop-creighton-that-the-same-moral-standards-should-be-applied-to-all-men-political-and-religious-leaders-included-especially-since-power-tends-to-corrupt-and-absolute-power-corrupts-absolutely-1887.

[10] John Farmer, "Isaiah 33:22 – Our Form Of Government," VoteSmart Facts for All, June 30, 2006, https://justfacts.votesmart.org/public-statement/191389/isaiah-3322-our-form-of-government.

In my opinion, the best mechanism to prevent the abuse of power is a system of checks and balances, just like our founding fathers believed and implemented. I cannot fully explain it, but God has revealed himself in three persons, Father, Son, and Holy Ghost, even though God is just one God. I am not suggesting God needs checks and balances, but perhaps there is a lesson to be learned from the triune Godhead. We have one federal government but three major branches of that government. We have only one God, in three persons: Father, Son, and Holy Ghost.

The definition of a tyrant which began this section includes "unrestrained by law or constitution." Our founding fathers intended our Constitution to be the supreme law of the land. Thus, our Constitution should be a major check on the powers of government. Likewise in a church, the Bible should be the constitution or supreme law of the church. Of course, tyrants will do their best to rule unrestrained by laws, a constitution, or the Bible.

In our government today, judicial supremacy often attempts to escape checks and balances by trying to make laws as opposed to just enforcing the laws as legislated by Congress and by our Constitution. Congress has the means to abuse power by financially enriching their own selves via corruption. The executive branch can also bypass checks and balances via excessive executive orders. However, our system has worked for about 250 years. I am uncertain how much longer our system of checks and balances will work, as power has reached an enormous magnitude of corruption.

I believe every power structure should have some checks and balances. Without such, power will likely become corrupt and lead to tyranny. Anyone who is too high and mighty to submit to some form of counsel or subjection or consideration of another point of view is simply too high and mighty. If a pastor does not allow any form of checks and balances, they are a tyrant or headed that way. The same is true for a husband who leads without input from his wife or children: he is a tyrant or is at least headed in that direction.

God's Word instructs us to obey those who have power over us. However, if that power does not align with God's Word, God instructs his children that it is better to obey God than to obey man. The apostle Paul declared in 1 Corinthians 11:1, "Be ye followers of me, even as I also am of Christ." I believe this verse implies that if a spiritual leader is clearly following Christ, then we should follow that leader. If a spiritual leader is clearly not following Christ, then do not follow that leader. God's Word is the determining factor as to whether a leader is following Christ or is not following Christ.

Of course, no authority short of God is going to be perfect, so grace is always appropriate. God's children should obey and follow authority up to the point where leadership is not in line with God's Word. Likewise, I believe all who are in a position of authority should take great effort and concern to not abuse their power in order to avoid becoming a tyrant. Hence the need for some form of subjection or checks and balances. Due diligence is required by those with authority to not fulfill Lord Acton's prediction that absolute power will corrupt absolutely.

Proverbs 29:2 declares, "When the righteous are in authority, the people rejoice: but when the wicked beareth rule, the people mourn." Thus, whether in the home, a church, or a nation, the need is for those with authority to use that power in a manner pleasing to God.

Country Before Country Was Cool

I've spoken about the government that oversees our country. I realize my experience of being an American might not match your experience of living here—or your experience of living in your own homeland, if you're not an American. All of us, though, have something to add to the story of life in our country (or countries). The specifics are what make life interesting.

In reviewing my text, I may not have conveyed how hillbilly country we were at the time of my childhood in southern Missouri. As the song says, we were country before country was cool. My sister Glenda met her husband to be, Jim, shortly before Grandpa Luther passed away. This was the only time Jim and Grandpa would meet. Being a country soul, Grandpa asked Glenda's Jim if he squirrel hunted. Jim acknowledged he did, so Grandpa asked him where he would shoot a squirrel's body to kill it for eating. Jim was unsure why Grandpa was asking such but stated he would shoot a squirrel in the head so as to not damage the rest of the body for eating. Grandpa quickly corrected Jim, "Oh no, not the head; that's the best part of the squirrel"—the brains!

I suppose one could be country and have not eaten squirrel brains. However, being a connoisseur of squirrel brains definitely lends credibility to being real country. Squirrel brains are quite tasty, but still not as good as frog legs (in my opinion). I rest my case that we were country!

We definitely lived in a different era at that time in southern Missouri. I don't remember any of our houses ever having locks, let alone locking the house or cars. Before my teenage years, I don't believe anyone had much, if any kind, of insurance. No one was looking to sue anyone. Medical bills were not huge. Country life involved hard work but was simpler and more relaxing than today's rat race. Amid all the farm work, there were lots of fun times, like making homemade ice cream, hayrides, or making hard candy via a taffy pull.

My experience of my country is very *country*. If your experience is different, well, that's part of what makes a great nation great—many different people coming together to work together and to love their neighbors well.

One Nation Under God

Hopefully, I have conveyed my love for our country and the fact that America has been a land of opportunity. I would like to share a letter from a friend of Dee's, Edith, who attended church with Dee during Dee's childhood. For a college project, Dee requested Edith to write about her childhood immigration to America. I feel comfortable stating that Edith's story is the story of millions of other immigrants in that era. I have copied her handwritten letter below, which was written around 1970.

Born June 2, 1900, in Lycksele, Sweden, near the Arctic Circle in the land of the midnight sun, where the sun never sets for two months of the summer and shows slightly at the horizon two months of the year in winter. Reared in central Sweden, where I attended school in Gothenburg and other cities. In Sweden I met my Lord and Savior and I became a child of God, through the shed blood of Christ and the Spirit gives witness to this transaction yet today, Praise His Name.

We left Sweden on the 2nd of October 1912, crossed the North Sea to Hull, England, and then by railroad to Liverpool, and by horse-drawn carriage to our place of the dock where the ocean liner Corona was waiting for us. First stop was Dublin, Ireland, where more passengers were picked up. The trip across the Atlantic was stormy and caused the ship to pitch and we all became seasick.

Arriving in New York, we were taken to Ellis Island, where we went through the customs and also eye examination and rough check-up was made. Since our father could not meet us, we were ushered into a cage until someone would claim us. There Rev. Samuelson of the rescue mission came to pick us up. This was a real treat, and he took us with him, after a night's rest, on to Chicago, where Dad had a home waiting for us.

Going to school was not a pleasant experience. "Greenhorn" was a word we often heard, while my braids were pulled till my head was sore. My brother, with the sanction of the school principal, fought our way out of this torment. Not knowing one word of the language, and the alphabet different, as well as coming from being used to the metric system and having to learn oz. and pounds caused quite a problem. With the help of a schoolmate and his tutoring during study periods, we made progress and with the help of a kind teacher and tutor, we (brother and I) were able to graduate two years later with the class.

How about church? Many of the young folks spake some Swedish and accepted us kindly and we enjoyed church. Can you feature living in a land where you couldn't understand a word? It's not easy. What do I think of our beloved U.S.A.? To me, it's a land of opportunity where anyone who really wants to can accomplish something. One brother became an ordained minister, the other brother became Chief Electrical Engineer for Delta Star, Chicago, IL, and two girls married farmers and "lived happily ever after."

When I became a naturalized citizen, I promised, by the help of God, to break a relationship with King Gustaf of Sweden and all he stood for. I am a loyal American and proud to say we've never gone hungry, never suffered want, we worked for what we got and never looked for a handout. I praise God for leading us to the U.S.A. and the many blessings we've received. After all, if we submit our lives to Him, everything is for our best.

My prayer is that our beloved U.S.A. will come back to the "old paths" and make our motto on our coin, "In God We Trust," true and that we may remain "One Nation Under God."

I trust Edith's letter about her becoming an American is as touching to you, the reader, as it has always been to me. Edith tells the story of so many who came to this country for nothing more than for the freedom to worship God Almighty and to take advantage of this land of opportunity. In my opinion,

Edith's story embodies the spirit of what being a great American is all about. Note, Edith came to America to be an American. Socialism/Communism/dictatorships are the antithesis of freedom and opportunity. I wholeheartedly join with Edith's prayer for the USA. I know well the blessings of living in a country which has allowed a kid with nothing to grow up and have something. God bless America!

I too join with Edith's prayer for our country in the song below, which God gave me about my beloved country, America.

America, My Country

Verse 1:
America, my country – You've been so good to me
I've never taken lightly – Your freedoms and liberty
Now how it breaks my heart to say – I see those freedoms slipping away
As America turns from – The God who's blessed this nation
Freedom's flame will only burn – If to God America will return

Chorus:
God's people, won't you please – Join with me on bended knees
And humbly pray as we seek God's face – And turn from our wicked ways
Then our God will hear from heaven – And forgive our sin
And his mighty hand – Will heal our land
Only God's blessings will make – America great

(Chorus Repeats)

28

———∞———

Life Is Precious

In the last few chapters, we've talked about life in the household, and life lived among our neighbors. Now I want to move to a bigger topic: life itself. God is the author of life, and I believe that has implications for how we think about each human being—how we think about births, about population, and even how we think about the simple wonder that we are here in this universe at all.

I would like to share some thoughts on another subject which I believe is of great importance. I have already mentioned that I am pro-life. As a Christian, I believe God is the giver of life and only he can create life. I have already mentioned that mankind can prevent life via birth control. Dee and I eventually used no birth control, as that is what we believed God wanted for our lives. I am opposed to surgical abortion, as it ends life after conception. The new life conceived within a woman's womb is not just an extension of the mother's body but rather the body of a new person with unique DNA and unique blood created by God Almighty.

If birth control never allows conception to take place, then life is simply being prevented but not ended. However, I would like to discuss the kind of birth control which causes the end of a new life, that is, abortifacient birth control. Many in the medical world will argue that modern birth control is not abortifacient. However, some disagree and believe strongly that some forms of birth control can end life after conception. If Dee and I could roll our biological clocks back forty-some years, we would use no birth control at all. However, if we used birth control, I would not use a birth control in which there is any possibility of ending new life after conception. I trust you, the reader of this section, will take the challenge to do the same if you are using or plan to use birth control.

If you simply google to see if birth control methods (such as birth control pills) are abortifacient, most responses will declare they are not abortifacient. This is likely because the medical world redefined the beginning of life to be when a fertilized egg successfully implants within the mother's womb rather than when an egg is fertilized and becomes a human being.

Below, I've copied a small excerpt from the Wisconsin Pro-Life website. I think their presentation is very concise. Their website has much more information on this subject. I recommend studying this subject in more detail on their website. While most birth control's primary objective is to prevent conception, the issue lies with the fact that no birth control is 100 percent effective. Occasionally, birth control allows conception and may then subsequently, by design, prevent implantation, which ends a life. Without implantation, the new life is not viable.

> In fact, many forms of hormonal birth control can be abortifacient (cause early chemical abortions) by obstructing the implantation of the newly formed human embryo in his or her mother's womb.[11]

---

[11] "Contraception. Know the Facts." ProLife WI, Pro-Life Wisconsin, **Reprinted with permission from Pro-Life Wisconsin. ©2024, Pro-Life Wisconsin, Education Task Force. All rights reserved. Accessed on 2/1/2025.** https://www.prolifewi.org/contraception.

I believe everyone who is using or plans on using birth control, and especially Christians, should study this issue out to make certain they are not taking part in abortion by preventing implantation of a fertilized egg. I am not sharing this to be controversial or holier-than-thou, but rather my goal is just to be informative. Dee and I did not know of this concern for many years. I am guessing there are others in the same boat of ignorance we were in. At a bare minimum, this topic is worthy of study given the potentially serious outcome.

Earlier in my writing, I briefly mentioned a pro-life song God gave me. I would like to share that song now. I am thankful my mom "let me grow" while I was in her womb. I trust you are thankful for your experience of that with your mom as well.

Let Me Grow

Verse 1:
Kick'n' around in here – Just wait'n' until I appear
Daily I'm chang'n' so much – Sure you've noticed my hiccups
Every now and then – I can't help but smile when
I think of all you have been through – Mama, I am count'n' on you to

Chorus:
Let me grow – Only God knows
How my life will unfold
If you let me grow – This one thing I know
Mama, so much to you I'll owe – If you will let me grow

Verse 2:
Liv'n' inside of here – You know it's not easy to hear
I just can't believe my ears – My heart is now filled with fear
I guess I have no rights – These my God-given eyes
May never see the light of day – If I could talk, Mama, I would say

(Chorus Repeats)

Was I Wrong?

Having just talked about being sure that we don't end life in the womb—that we welcome the children God sees fit to give us—it makes sense to move to the topic of overpopulation. Overpopulation is portrayed as a bleak consequence for the future of mankind. The liberals of this world believe that global warming, which scientists renamed to *climate change* due to a lot of cold weather, will bring destruction to this planet and end life on earth. Liberals claim that overpopulation contributes to climate change. Certainly a former boss of mine thought I was wrong to have a large family. We have encountered others along the way, including some even in churches, who thought we were wrong for having a large family. I had a preacher once tell me that God never intended for one family to populate the entire planet. Yet, I am still advocating for good, godly homes to raise as many good, godly children as God allows.

An article from *Israel365News* supports the idea that overpopulation is not our primary worry. Below, I am copying an excerpt about Elon Musk's position on overpopulation. I do not personally know Elon Musk. However, he and I share the same sentiments about the population of mankind on this planet:

> "There are not enough people. I can't emphasize this enough. There are not enough people. I think one of the biggest risks to civilization is the low birth rate and the rapidly declining birthrate," Musk said at the Wall Street Journal's annual CEO Council. "And yet, so many people, including smart people, think that there are too many people in the world and think that the population is growing out of control. It's completely the opposite.

Please look at the numbers. If people don't have more children, civilization is going to crumble, mark my words." [12]

The article goes on to state that "the numbers support Musk's assertion. The global growth rate in absolute numbers accelerated to a peak of 92.9 million in 1988 but has declined to 81.3 million in 2020. Long-term projections indicate that the growth rate of the human population of this planet will continue to decline and that by the end of the 21st century, it will reach zero." It further states that "the main driver of this trend is a decreasing fertility rate."

This article was written in 2021 and states the birthrate in the United States was 1.6. A birth rate of 2.1 is required for any nation to maintain a stable population.

The article clearly shows the reality that for any nation or population group to survive, there must be a high enough fertility rate to sustain that group. Our country and many other countries are on a population trajectory that does not allow national sustainability, due to low birth rates. I have heard the phrase "figures don't lie, but liars do figure." Such is the case with overpopulation claims. Not to mention the always-present depopulation dangers of war, famine, disease, and dictatorial governments, as we have seen from Communism.

Unfortunately, the deadly effects of socialism/Communism are still flourishing. Our country seems headed down that death spiral as well. Thus, I believe God's children should do as God states in the first chapter of the first book in the Bible: "Be fruitful, and multiply, and replenish the earth" (Genesis 1:28). As I said earlier, we can block life, but only God can give life. I

---

[12] Adam Eliyahu Berkowitz, "Elon Musk declares greatest danger to mankind: anti-Bible zero population growth," Israel365News, December 12, 2021, https://israel365news.com/350267/elon-musk-declares-greatest-danger-to-mankind-anti-bible-zero-population-growth/.

trust God knows all about the creation, the climate, and the population.

Obviously, multitudes have lived in great difficulty due to poverty and repressive forms of government. Hence the beauty and glory of freedom and liberty. I wonder what nation has tried that. Oh, I almost forgot, *my* nation!

Unfortunately, my nation is under attack for affording freedom. Freedom which allows a kid born into a dysfunctional family to prosper. Freedom that allows everyone to make some change, whether big or small, to make this world a better place. God bless the USA with lots of babies!

He Numbers the Stars

Just as God knows how many people he has put into the world, he knows how many stars he has put into the universe. Contemplating the vastness of that knowledge and creative energy can lead us to marvel at his greatness!

In the late '90s, I attended a computer class in Chicago when the world population was about six billion and Bill Gates was the wealthiest person in the world (worth about fifty billion dollars). Dee, Ben, David, and I visited the Chicago Planetarium. The planetarium had a display about the number of known galaxies and the number of stars in a galaxy, which caught my attention. I did some additional research and wrote a paper on that very subject. The Bible declares God made all the stars, numbers them, and has even given them a name. I am not updating this write-up but rather just copying it as I wrote it several years ago. My hope is we might gain just a little better awe of Almighty God.

And God made two great lights; the greater light to rule the day, and the lesser light to rule the night: he made the stars also. (Genesis 1:16)

He telleth the number of the stars; he calleth them all by their names. (Psalm 147:4)

The above verses declare God made the stars, has them all numbered, and even has them named. It's reasonable to assume that God, being God, knows and names all the stars he made. However, I fear we often do not fully recognize the wonder and glory of God Almighty. Following are some statistics which I hope will increase our wonder of the Creator God of the universe. Note, I will use statistics from the labors of mortal man. I will use mortal man's statistics, though they are likely small compared to God's actual numbers.

So just how many stars are there? Well, we don't know. How about a whole bunch of them? The fact of the matter is that we don't know how big the universe is. There is light traveling towards our planet that has not reached us yet. Thus, modern technology has no way of counting that light source. There are many estimates as to the number of stars. Following is an excerpt from the European Space Agency website:

For the Universe, the galaxies are our small representative volumes, and there are something like 10^{11} to 10^{12} stars in our galaxy, and there are perhaps something like 10^{11} or 10^{12} galaxies. With this simple calculation, you get something like 10^{22} to 10^{24} stars in the Universe. [13]

To restate, we have about one trillion stars per galaxy and about one trillion galaxies. I will use the 10^{24} (or

---

[13] "How many stars are there in the Universe?," ESA, The European Space Agency, http://www.esa.int/esaSC/SEM75BS1VED_index_2.html.

1,000,000,000,000,000,000,000,000) number of stars for a nice round number of one septillion stars. Of course, this is not an exact number as no man knows and, as I said earlier, it is likely only a fraction of the real number of stars. Now to make some sense of a number like one septillion stars. First, let's make a comparison. Contemplate the number of sand grains on all of Earth's beaches and deserts. Following is one calculation[14] for an estimated total of grains of sand on planet Earth:

> Let's assume that all the grains of sand are spherical and of equal size. If so, they will 'pack together' with maximal compaction, such that the spheres themselves fill 68% of the total volume. If the diameter of the grains is on average 1 mm, this would give 1.30×10^9 (1,300 million) grains in one cubic meter of sand.
>
> For the sake of argument, say that all the sand in the world forms an even layer, 10 cm thick, over the entire surface of the earth, which covers 510 million km^2 (200 million square miles). Then the volume of the sand will be 5.10×10^{13} cubic meters and the number of grains, thus
> $$5.10 \times 10^{13} \times 1.30 \times 10^9 = 6.63 \times 10^{22}$$

So, the estimated number of stars (1×10^{24}) is even greater than the estimated number of grains of sand (6.63×10^{22}).

Note, in the following verses, God declares the descendants of Abraham to be innumerable. Isn't it interesting that God used the number of grains of sand upon the seashore and the number of stars of the heaven to illustrate God's blessing upon Abraham? We certainly cannot physically count the grains of sand or the stars.

---

[14] Sigurður Steinþórsson, "Question: How many grains of sand are there in the world?," The Icelandic Web of Science, May 3, 2005, https://www.why.is/svar.php?id=4803.

> That in blessing I will bless thee, and in multiplying I will multiply thy seed as the stars of the heaven, and as the sand which is upon the sea shore; and thy seed shall possess the gate of his enemies. (Genesis 22:17)

> Therefore sprang there even of one, and him as good as dead, so many as the stars of the sky in multitude, and as the sand which is by the sea shore innumerable. (Hebrews 11:12)

Of course, the telescope did not exist in Bible times. Without such an aid, human eyes can only observe a few thousand stars in the night sky. The Holy Spirit inspired men to record that the number of stars is actually comparable to the number of the grains of sand on our planet.

Imagine each of one of our septillion stars to be one second of time. Next, imagine stringing together each of these septillion-second intervals into a single timeline. The allocation would exceed 31 trillion millennia of years. Compared to the vastness of eternity, our timeline is brief; however, it's longer than your average DMV visit to license a vehicle.

For another illustration of one septillion, suppose you were offered the net value of one penny for each of the one septillion stars, or you could have the equivalent wealth of Bill Gates (about fifty billion dollars). Hopefully, you took the penny deal. If you did, you would have two hundred billion times the wealth of Bill Gates. (Note, that amount would be pretax, so don't start spending just yet).

Let's suppose every star represented one home. If we could distribute the homes to every person on earth, we would have just solved the homeless problem. In fact, every man, woman, and child would have 166 trillion homes each. Talk about a lot of cleaning! And you will need the penny deal we spoke of earlier to pay those real estate taxes.

Now let's suppose that every star represents a problem or a prayer request or a heartache or a burden or a need or a trial or a care or a challenge or a hardship or a persecution, etc. Just like the homes, these needs would translate to 166 trillion per man, woman, and child on our planet. Now most of us have fewer problems than that. However, God can keep track of our needs as effortlessly as the stars in heaven.

> Are not two sparrows sold for a farthing? and one of them shall not fall on the ground without your Father. But the very hairs of your head are all numbered. Fear ye not therefore, ye are of more value than many sparrows. (Matthew 10:29-31)

Our God knows when a sparrow falls to the ground. He knows the very number of hairs on your head. (Note, at about 100,000-150,000 hairs per head for about six billion heads, we will use the lower number for about six hundred trillion hairs that God keeps track of.) I propose to you that God Almighty knows all about you. He knows your problems. He knows your needs. God knows you better than anyone else. Men, women, boys, and girls are far more valuable to God than sparrows, hairs, and stars. He takes care of the universe, but he also takes care of each of us.

We serve a great and mighty God. Don't lose faith in him. He knows us, cares for us, and is more than able to meet any need we have or deliver us from any danger.

> He telleth the number of the stars; he calleth them all by their names. (Psalm 147:4)

> For as the heavens are higher than the earth, so are my ways higher than your ways, and my thoughts than your thoughts. (Isaiah 55:9)

Not long after completing my write-up on stars and hairs, God gave me a song about those very subjects as well.

The God Who Knows

Verse 1:
Well, if you stop and think about it – All the hairs on every head on this planet
Most women fuss a lot about them – Men just hope they got 'em
On six billion heads or so – That's a lot of hair can grow
But my God numbers every one – Those growin', those that are gone

Chorus:
God's ways are so much higher than – You or I can understand
He's bigger than the universe – Yet he came to this old earth
Where he died on Calvary's tree – So his children we can be
Whosoever in faith shall call – He is able to save all
The God who knows your every hair – Is the God who knows your every care
Whatever your need today – He's only a prayer away

Verse 2:
Now look into the sky at night – If you could count every twinkling light
After a trillion times a trillion – You'd still be a countin'
God knows every star by name – He knows you just the same
The God who numbers every star – That same God knows who you are

(Chorus Repeats)

29

No Self-Made Man Here

Some may consider themselves to be self-made. I can say with absolute certainty that I am not a self-made man. God has given me every breath I have breathed for over seventy-plus years. If not for our fallen soldiers' graves, I would have likely never experienced the freedom to pursue my life's dreams. Without so many friends and so many in my family who have helped me along life's way, where would I be today? If not for those who prayed for my soul and for those laboring in the ministry for my soul, where would my soul be today? Last, and most importantly, where would I be without a loving God who paid so much to offer me so great salvation? I owe so much to so many. There is no way I can lay claim to being a self-made man. Frank Sinatra sang the famous song "My Way," but in reality, genuine success only comes from doing life God's way. Living life God's way, according to God's Word, brought good to my life. I am not self-made but God-made, and God has used so many to get me to where I am today. I thank God for the many people he has used in my life to be a blessing, and I offer praise to my mighty Savior, Jesus Christ.

Following is a song of tribute to those who have served our country, my loved ones, my friends, and those who have been a spiritual blessing in my life.

I Thank You

Verse 1:
I stand before you today – Because of our fallen soldiers' graves
War protestors have their rights – Thanks to those who've given their lives
Our flag can even be burned – Because of freedoms others have earned
This tribute I pay – Is to all who have fought for the USA

Chorus:
I just want to say – Thank you on this day
Where would I be – Without all you've done for me
Words cannot express – All my thankfulness
The least that I can do – Is to say, I thank you

Verse 2:
Throughout the many years – They have shared my joys and my tears
They have always been there – When it seemed no one else cared
I could always count on them – The love of my family and friends
This tribute I pay – Is to those who have helped me along life's way

(Chorus Repeats)

Verse 3:
While as a child I did grow – Others were praying for my soul
Preachers preachin' faithfully – Teachers that taught me of Calvary
A loving God in heaven – Who gave me so great salvation
This tribute I pay – Is to God and those who've shown me Calvary's way

(Chorus Repeats)

A Few Hopes

I certainly have a few hopes regarding what will come from sharing my life story. I hope to encourage you, the reader of this story, to surrender your life to God's will. If you do not know Jesus as Savior, then I hope that by faith in the gospel you will call upon him today and receive so great salvation.

I hope some young gals who read this book will have a heart's desire to be godly wives, and moms to children someday, if that is God's will for their lives. Also, I hope some young guys will use their youth to prepare to be godly husbands and fathers someday, if that is God's will for their lives.

If married, commit to making your marriage work. If committed to your marriage, infidelity should not be an issue. God's perfect will is to let no man put asunder what God hath joined together. If married, seek children as a blessing but be content with what God gives. There is enough oxygen to go around. If you have children, be diligent in making those little arrows as straight as possible. No work and no discipline is not good parenting. Family should be fun. While dad and mom are in charge, family should still be a team.

I would encourage financial responsibility rather than a life of bondage to being indebted.

Be content.

Be generous.

Be a good neighbor.

Keep yourself and your family in a good Bible-preaching church. Church is to the Christian like the steering wheel is to a car. A car's direction has to be corrected constantly via the steering wheel to handle the curves on the road ahead. A good church will use God's Word and other Christians to help a Christian navigate the curves on the road of life. We need constant correction to stay on the King's highway throughout our journey here below. A good church will support the values of your family and reinforce those values. For example, I would not regularly attend a church where the pastoral staff drinks alcohol. Doing such would undermine the message I am passing on to my descendants. Attending church regularly was a value we instilled in our children, as we never missed a service unless there were slippery roads or sickness. At church, our children learned about giving, helping others, bearing one another's burdens, etc. Our experience has been that finding a good church is not always an easy feat and, just because a church is good today, does not mean it will stay that way.

God's Word is our instruction book of life. Don't forget to read the instructions. Also, the author of the book, God, appreciates feedback from the reader. That feedback is called prayer.

If you're bitter, let it go to begin the healing process. God desires those harmed by someone else to forgive the offender. No matter how great the offense, God desires his children to forgive. Once the healing process begins, be willing to encourage others from your healing. For those who have suffered great loss or misfortune through no fault of their own, keep trusting God, as he numbers the stars and knows what is going on. The purity of gold increases with each round of refinement. My hope is those with painful wounds will be healed by God, and that your wounds will become painless scars by which your healing might encourage others.

I hope the reader of my story will seek to be guided and blessed by the Holy Spirit of God rather than the buzz of booze or drugs.

I hope all in a position of authority will seek some form of checks and balances or some degree of subjection to avoid becoming a tyrant.

I hope the American readers of my story will pray, vote, and labor to make America great again.

I hope my story has been a blessing to you, the reader, and glorifying to God.

After I'm gone, I hope to leave a legacy of God-fearing descendants, my songs, and my story.

Hopefully, my children and their children will carry on the mantle of gospel music or use whatever talents they might have for the glory of God. The song below attempts to show why God's children should labor to show and to share the glory of God.

A New Song

Verse 1:
This song that I sing – Is a new song for the King
Like thousands of songs before – You might ask why one more
The need for this song you see – Is the riches of God's glory
The half has yet to be told – Of the Father Son and Holy Ghost

Chorus:
The singers could never sing enough – To tell all of God's love
The poets could never express – All the wonders of Jesus
The writers could never pen – All about God omnipotent
The artists could never draw – The full glory of God
Oh the half has yet to be told – Of the Father Son and Holy Ghost

Verse 2:
The message I tell – Of my God incomparable
Is a story greater than – The power of any man
To show the glory of God – Who endured that old rugged cross
The half has yet to be told – Of the Father Son and Holy Ghost

(Chorus Repeats)

Your Story

As I reach the end of this book, I have one more additional hope: that my story inspires you, the reader, to share your own story. How has God built your life? What are the stories behind the scars in your life which might help another pilgrim journeying through this old world? What are the lessons you have learned in the school of life that could be a blessing to others? Perhaps you enjoy writing and might help someone else who might need help in writing their story. Note, your story or your friend's story does not have to be a top seller or even be published to be a blessing to future generations. However, it does need to be recorded in a lasting form to withstand the test of time.

I have made little reference to my grandpa Kissock, as he passed away a few months after my birth. Hence, I know very little about him. He left no memoir of his life. I have talked to a few people who knew him, and they told me a couple of things about him. He was a cattle whisperer: he had an unusual talent working with cattle that no one else could do anything with. He was also reported to be a very talented ice-skater. That is about all I know about him. I would love to read some stories about his life and his family, but there are none recorded. How many of us will leave so many stories untold to future generations?

While future generations will likely never know our life story unless recorded, the world will see our life story as we live it. Following is a song God gave me many years ago.

Your Life Story

Verse 1:
How does your life story read – What do others see
Is it just about you – Or does God's glory shine through
Every reader will know – The author will show
What will be – Your life story

Chorus:
Now when this old world takes a look – At your life story book
The story it tells – Is it just about your self
Will it say, I did my way – Or is it a story of God's grace
What will be – Your life story

Verse 2:
My friend, whether rich or poor – All need the Savior
If you have fortune – For God what have you done
If you have nothing – Do you still praise him
What will be – Your life story

(Chorus Repeats)

To God be the Glory

I have tried to convey the message throughout this story that all the good in my life is attributable to God. Dee and I get along pretty well, but at times we have had some intense fellowship over some difference of opinions—which is likely to occur during almost fifty years together. However, I can say with absolute certainty that one thing we have 100 percent harmonious agreement on is the fact that whatever success in life we have had, it is all a blessing from God. The two of us on our own lack anything of character, wisdom, intelligence, strength, etc. to accomplish anything of great value or of eternal worth. God deserves all the glory for every achievement in our lives that has been good.

I believe God made that message clear to me in the song below, which he gave me many years ago. God took me in as a mess and straightened my old neck, cleaned me up, tuned me up, and made me playable when I could have easily wound up in a pile of useless instruments. If each of us were a musical instrument, the music that would resonate from our existence would sound really good if we allowed God to tune us up and play his melody through our lives. Yet, those instruments would not be able to legitimately boast of the beautiful music they made. Rather, we should boast in the glory of the Master Musician. To God be the glory!

The Master Musician

Verse 1:
It was a guitar so old – It was dusty, the neck was bowed
The strings covered with rust- It sure didn't look like much
Marks and scratches, it had some – And sounded oh so bad when it was strummed
Many said, throw it away – Because it will just never play

Verse 2:
But the Master Musician – He looked at that old instrument
It was so imperfect – But he straightened that old neck
Put on strings that looked like gold – And polished it up with a shine that glowed
Now so many are amazed – To hear when the Master plays it

Chorus:
Lord, I am that old guitar – The Master Musician you are
This instrument's not much – Apart from the Master's touch
Make my heart in tune with thee – Through my life you might play your melody
This instrument's not worthy – To the Master goes all the glory

Make my heart in tune with thee – Through my life you might play your melody
This instrument's not worthy – To the Master goes all the glory

In Conclusion

In conclusion, I can say God has been good to me throughout the building process and the seasons of my life. From a troubled childhood, to being born without a dad present because of alcohol, to crying on a wet concrete sidewalk with a busted head, to peeing in my pants out of fear, to hiding in cornfields, to a one-room country school, to peeking in the gate at Disneyland, to mopping milk, to playing hide-and-seek, to finding a car key, to mowing and re-mowing, to dodging flying coffee cups, to standing in a ditch full of weeds covered in road dust, to standing at attention, to seeing stars during the daytime, to no music, to ugly memories, to a heart full of hate, to heartbroken from the loss of a loved one, to milking early in the morning, to fixing flat tires, to receiving a free gift from God, to playing football, to belly crawling in a ditch full of weeds, to leaving home at fourteen, to lots of music, to hauling hay, to making filters, to a state championship, to installing air conditioners, to not getting court-martialed for activating every B-52 bomber in the United States Air Force, to putting the matter of marriage into God's hands, to being smitten, to making a lifetime deal, to saying "I do," to graduating from college, to a heart smitten to forgive, to hearing many times "hope my next delivery is easier," to delighting myself in the Lord and establishing some desires of my heart, to eleven precious gifts of life, to clearly hearing "homeschooling," to a family singing together, to a multitude of precious memories, to amazing real estate deals, to farm livin', to milking again, to trials like a flood, to crossing the Missouri River at the crest in '93, to writing songs, to a lifetime of gardening, to hearing "I'm sorry," to a house full of grandkids, to a career of computer work, to turning gray-haired, to cutting firewood, to an alcohol-free life, to a wife who has put up with me all these years, to a Corvette marriage, to the providential guiding hand of God, to writing this story, to "Well, that's the way it goes," and from domestic abuse to divine blessings, I can say that God has been good to heal the wounds of my childhood and allow me to share some of the stories behind my life's scars.

I pray God's glory shines in my story and in his healing of my life's wounds. There are no wounds so great that the Great Physician cannot heal them. "He healeth the broken in heart, and bindeth up their wounds" (Psalm 147:3). The scars Jesus bore on the Cross of Calvary were visible after his resurrection. They bore witness to his sacrificial death. The goal of every Christian should be to be like Jesus. I trust the scars of life that God's children bear are a witness of a loving God who heals his children's wounds. I will close with the song below about the "Marks of the Crucifixion". Only God knew how to best build my life. He is indeed the Master Builder and makes no mistakes.

The Marks of the Crucifixion

Verse 1:
Sometimes the wounds of life are so small – In time they will leave no
mark at all
But some wounds are so large – They will leave a lifetime of scar
For only God's Son can bind up life's wounds – For a troubled soul
found in ruin
We are blessed by the God of all comfort – The Son of God who can
take away the hurt

Chorus:
The marks of the Crucifixion – Show so great salvation
Oh he could have made them go away – But he chose to let them stay
So that all might see – Redemption's story
The price he paid for our sin – The marks of the crucifixion

Verse 2:
He was wounded for our transgressions – He died to take away all our
sins
How great our blessings are – When Jesus heals a broken heart
But by God's grace the hurt can go away – Til we enter eternity's day
Where wounds and scars won't matter anymore – When we glory in
the marks of our Savior

(Chorus Repeats)

About the Author

Jim Kissock is a retired mainframe system programmer with a bachelor's in computer science. Having been raised on a farm, Jim and his wife Dee acquired an eighty-acre farm in central Missouri to raise their good-sized family on. Jim is a country boy who also enjoys singing with a guitar and gospel songwriting.

Hear Jim's songs mentioned in the book at https://tinyurl.com/JimKissock, and also see some song videos and family pictures. (The Google Drive App may enhance viewing for non-  Android devices.) Special thanks to Joshua Tomlin for allowing me to post my songs that he has performed.

Website: www.jimkissock.com